AF477117

ART ON SILK

ART ON SILK

CORNELIA HESSE–HONEGGER

SCHEIDEGGER & SPIESS

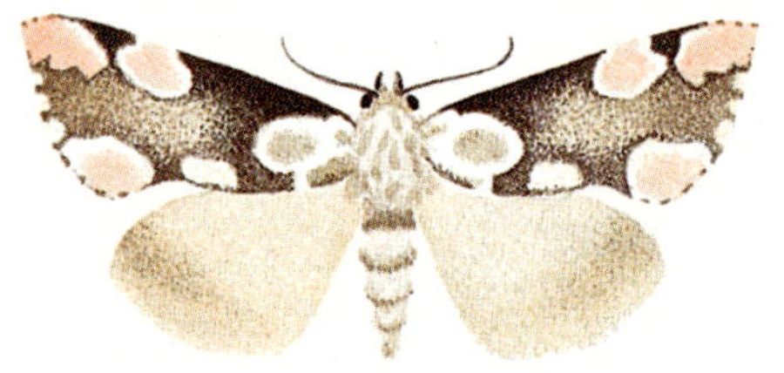

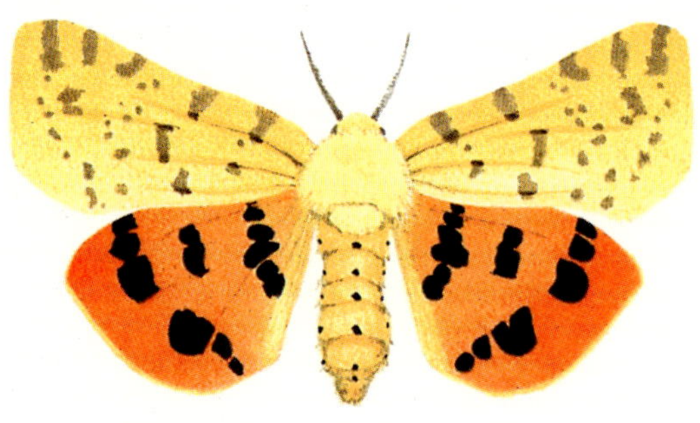

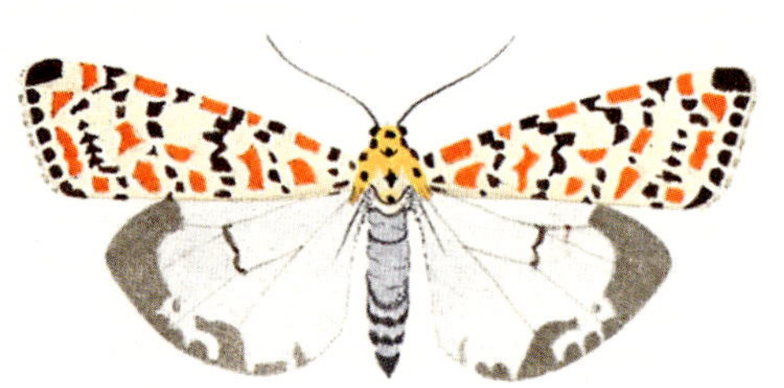

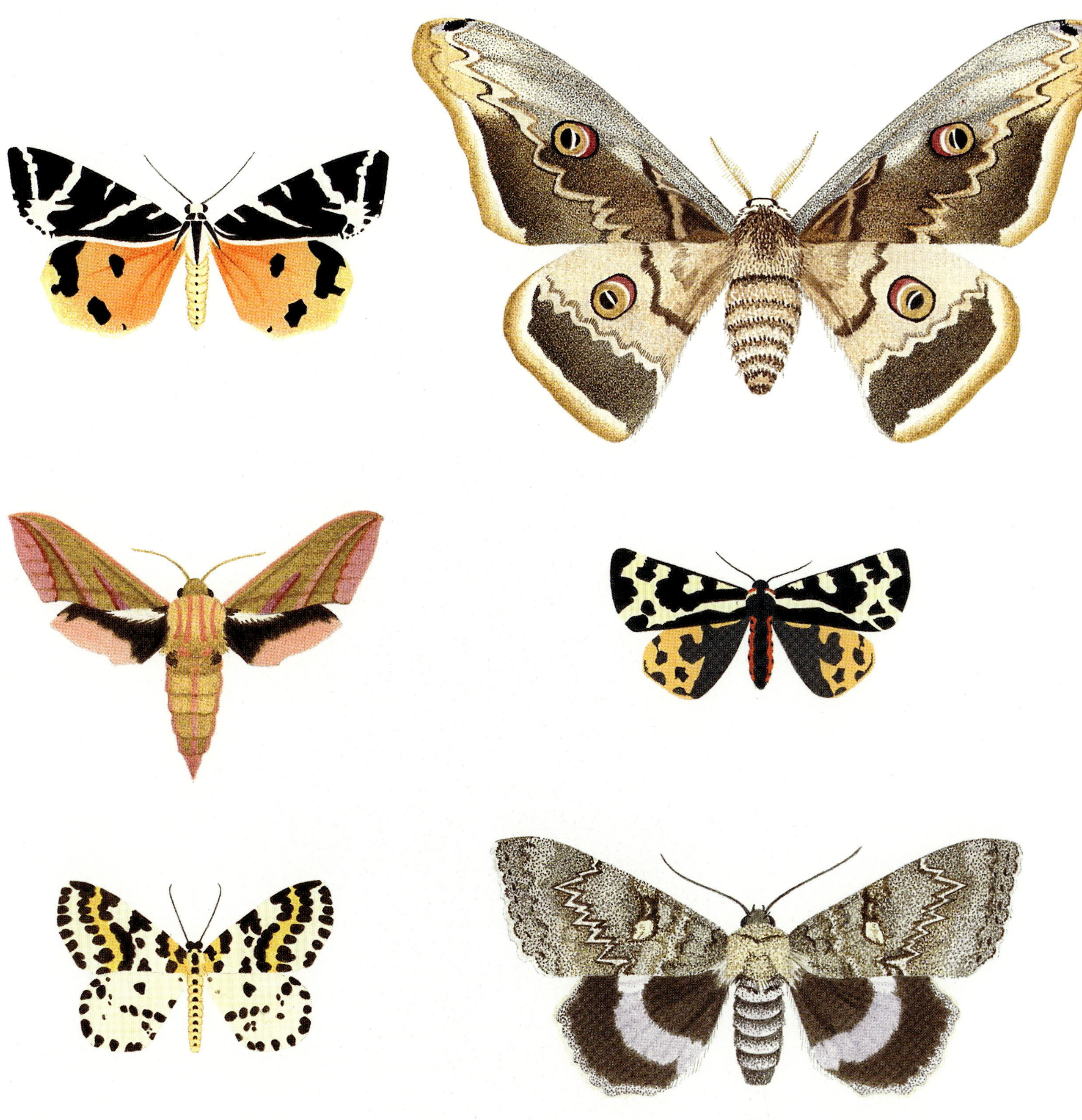

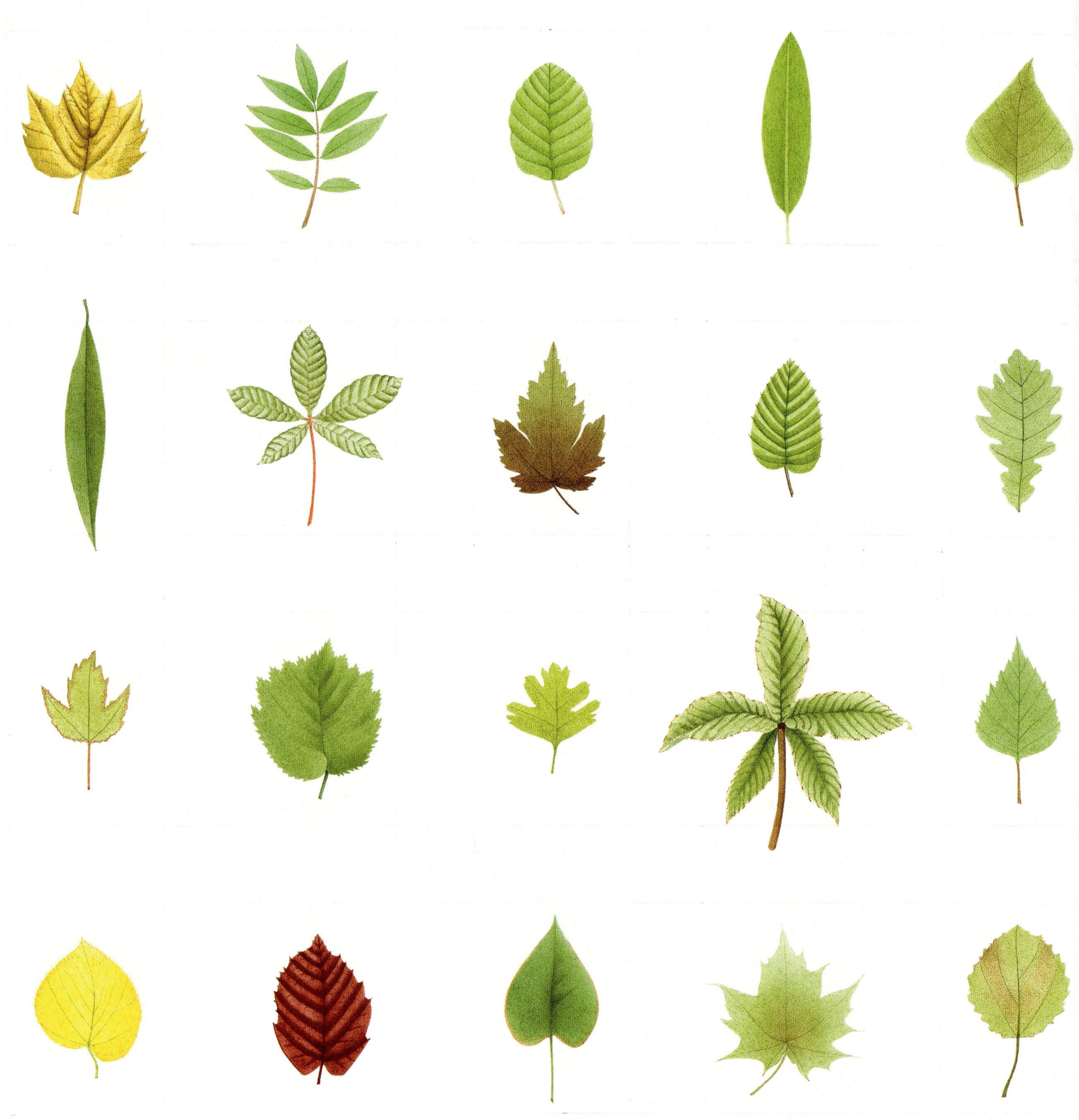

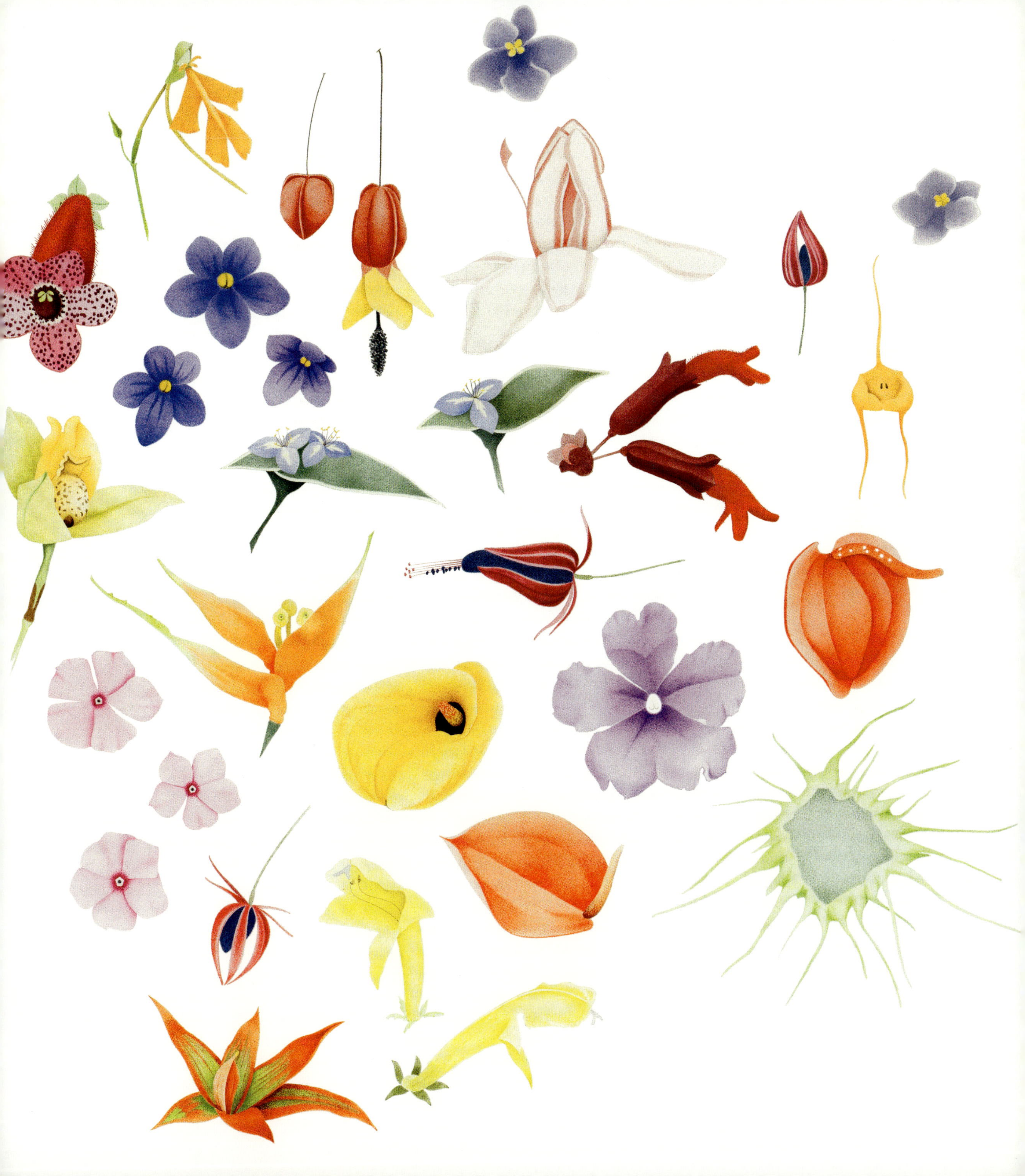

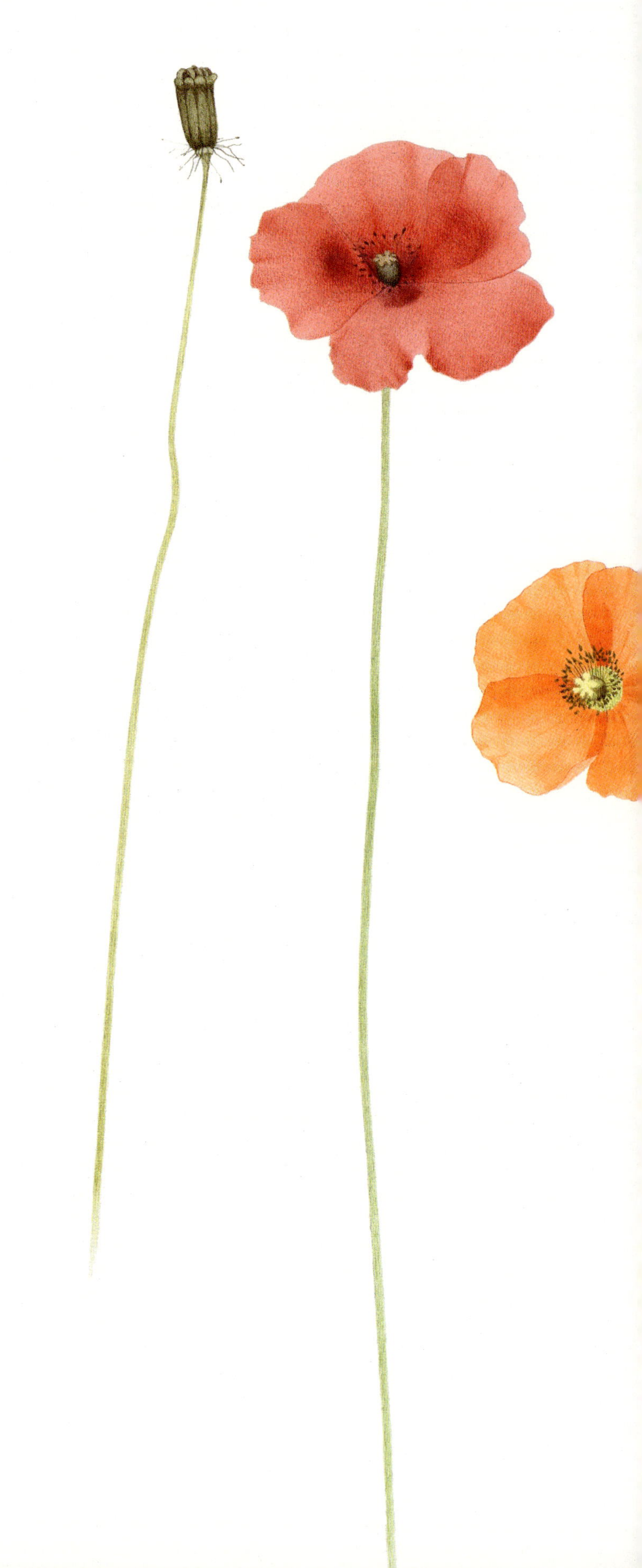

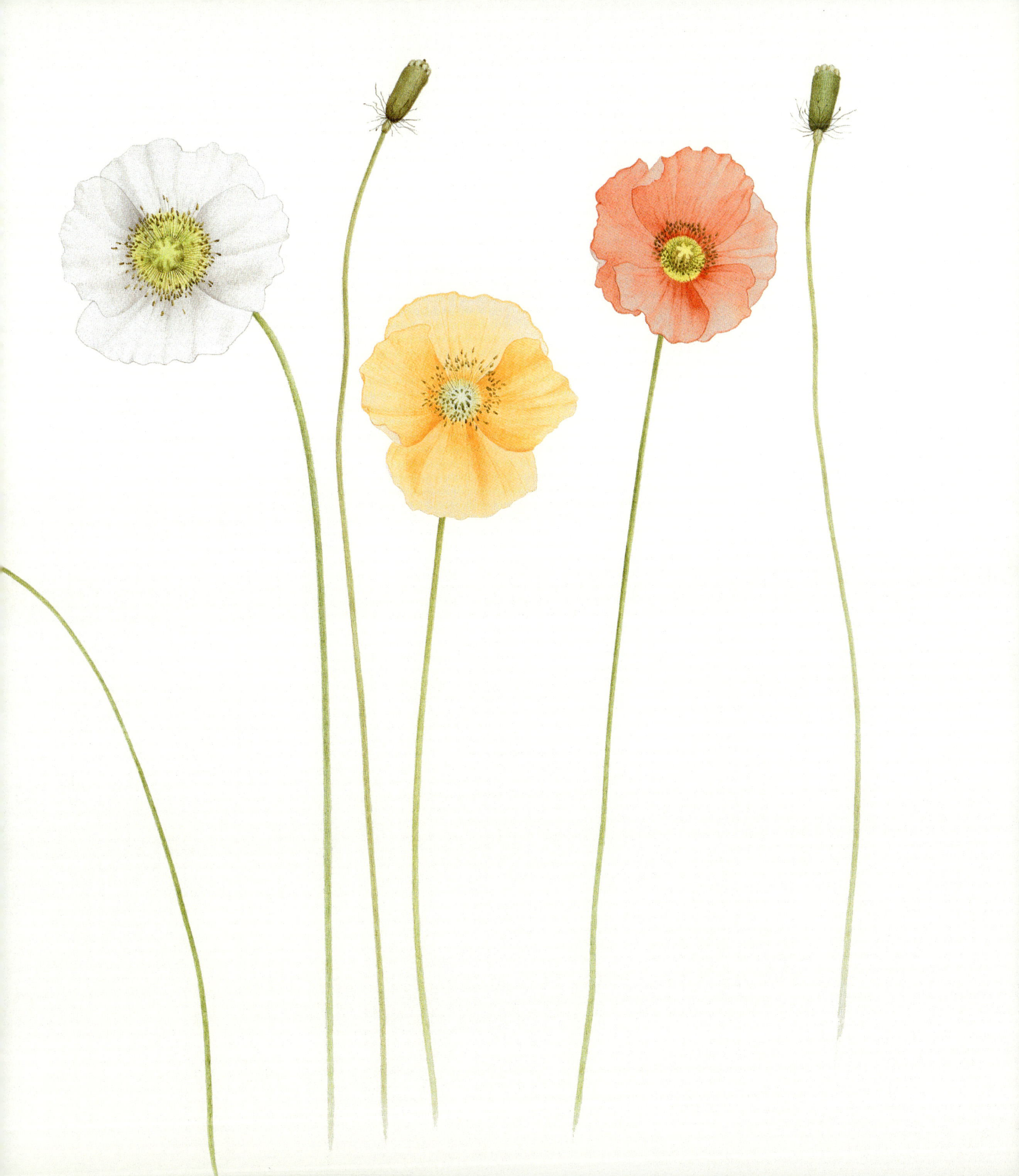

Das Angewandte sollte auch Kunst sein.
The applied should be art too.

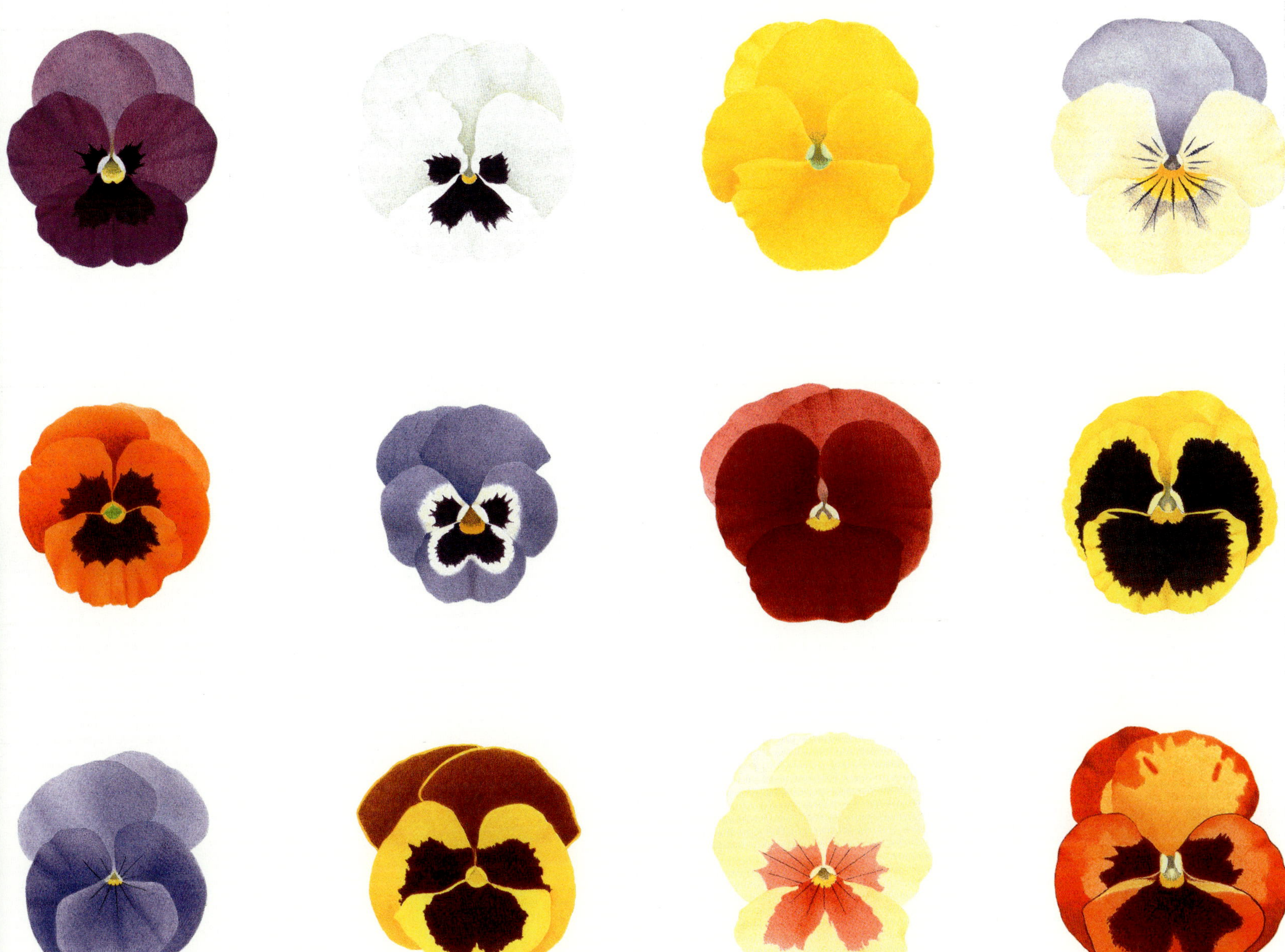

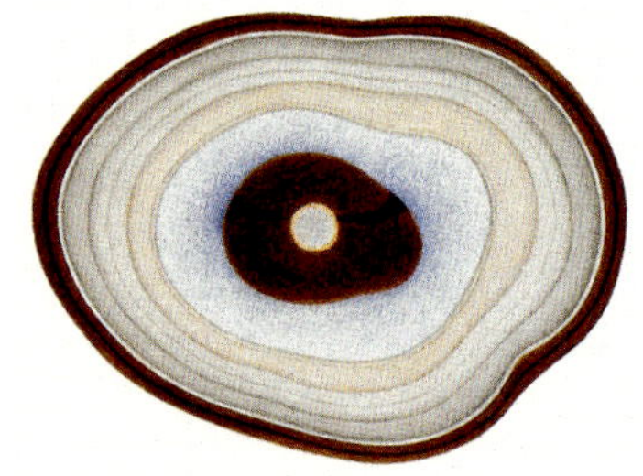
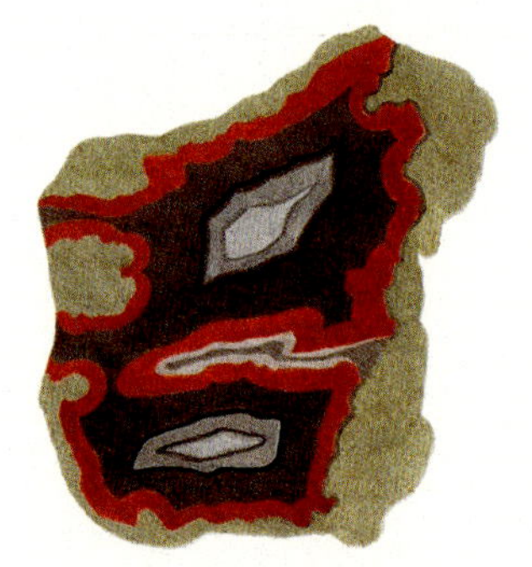
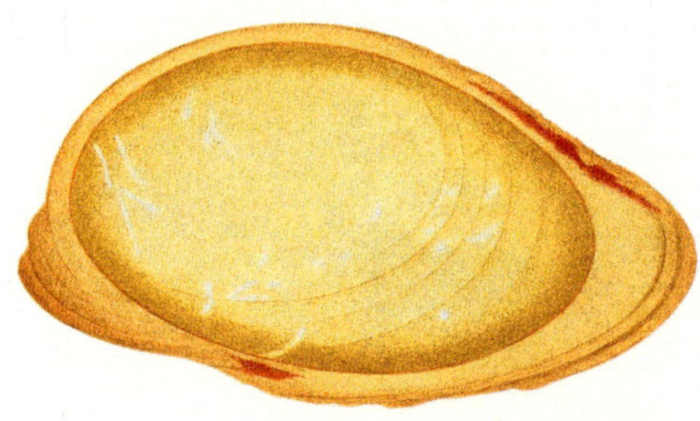
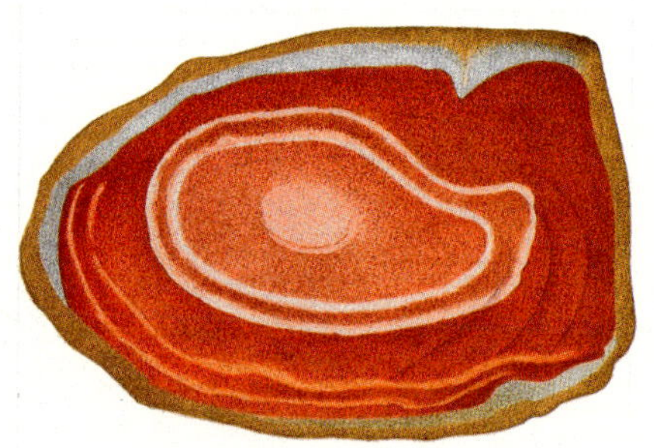
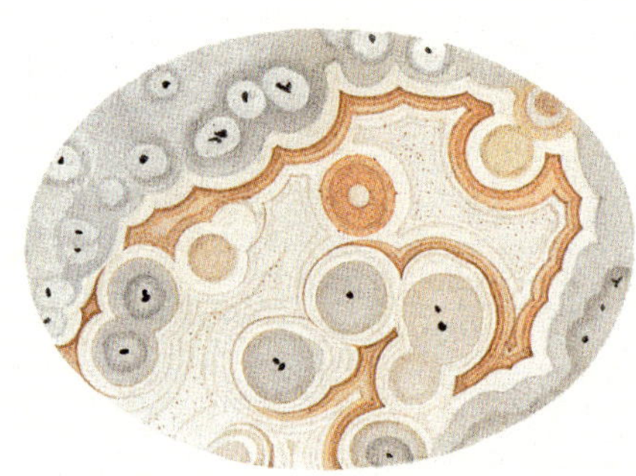
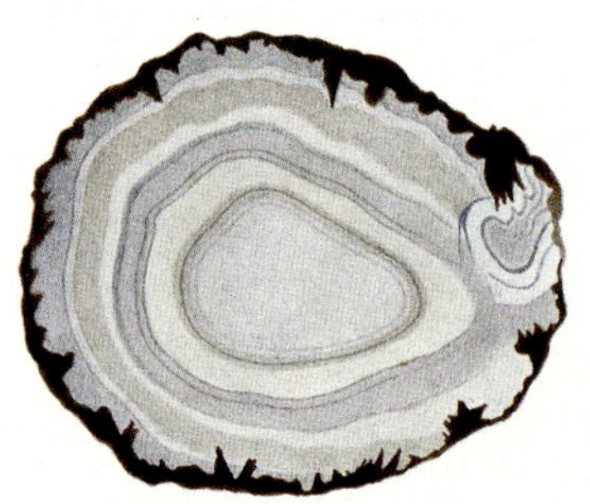
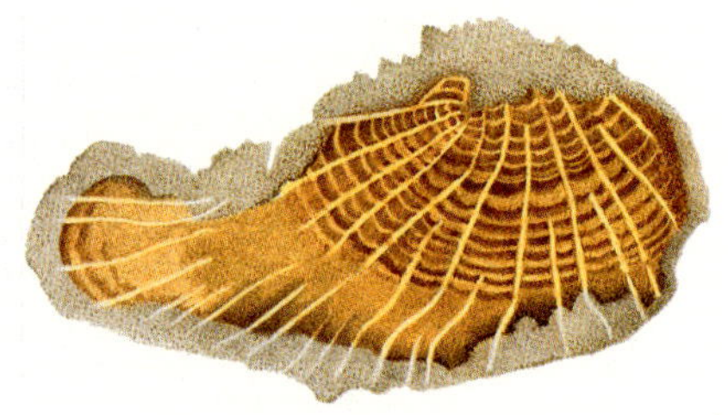
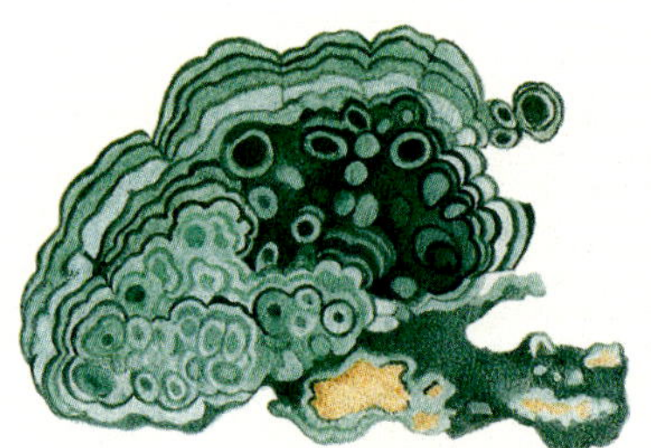
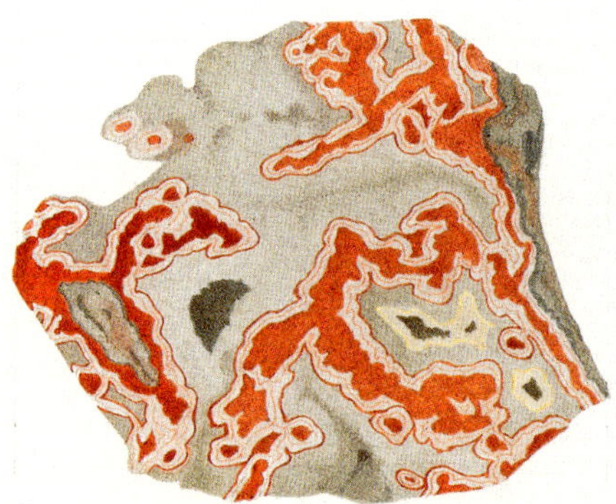

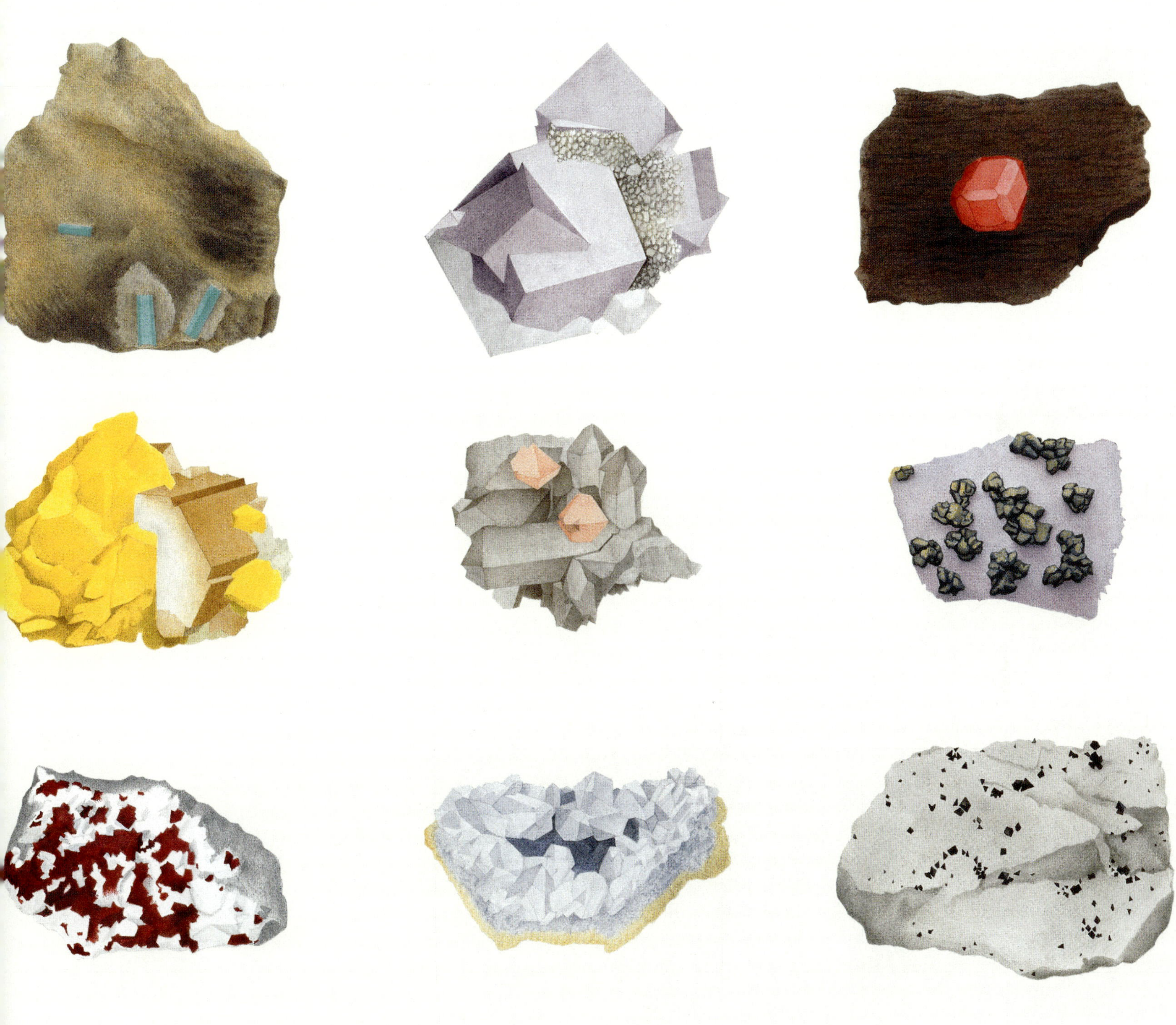

Die Ästhetik ist eine existentielle Notwendigkeit.
The aesthetic is an existential necessity.

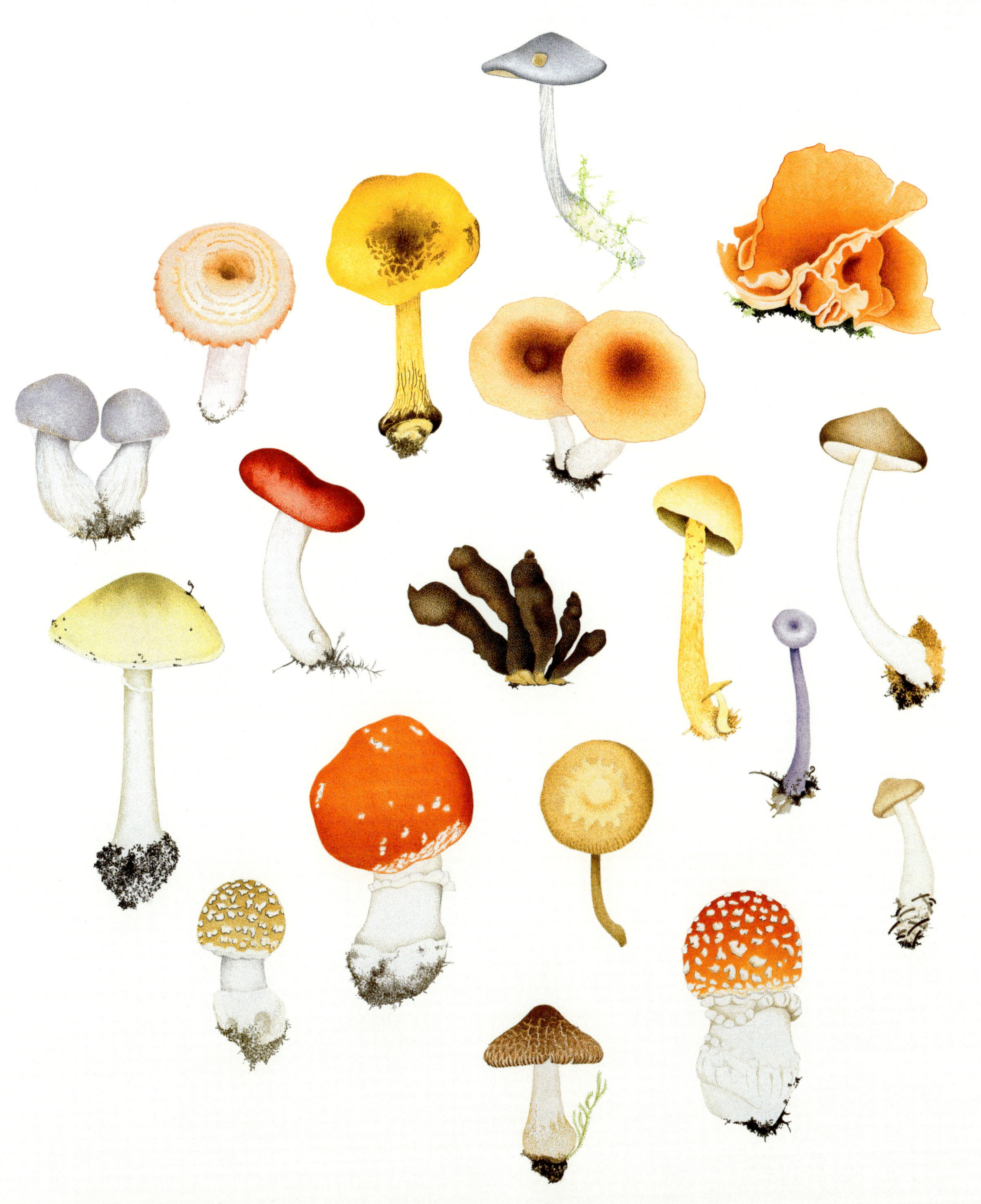

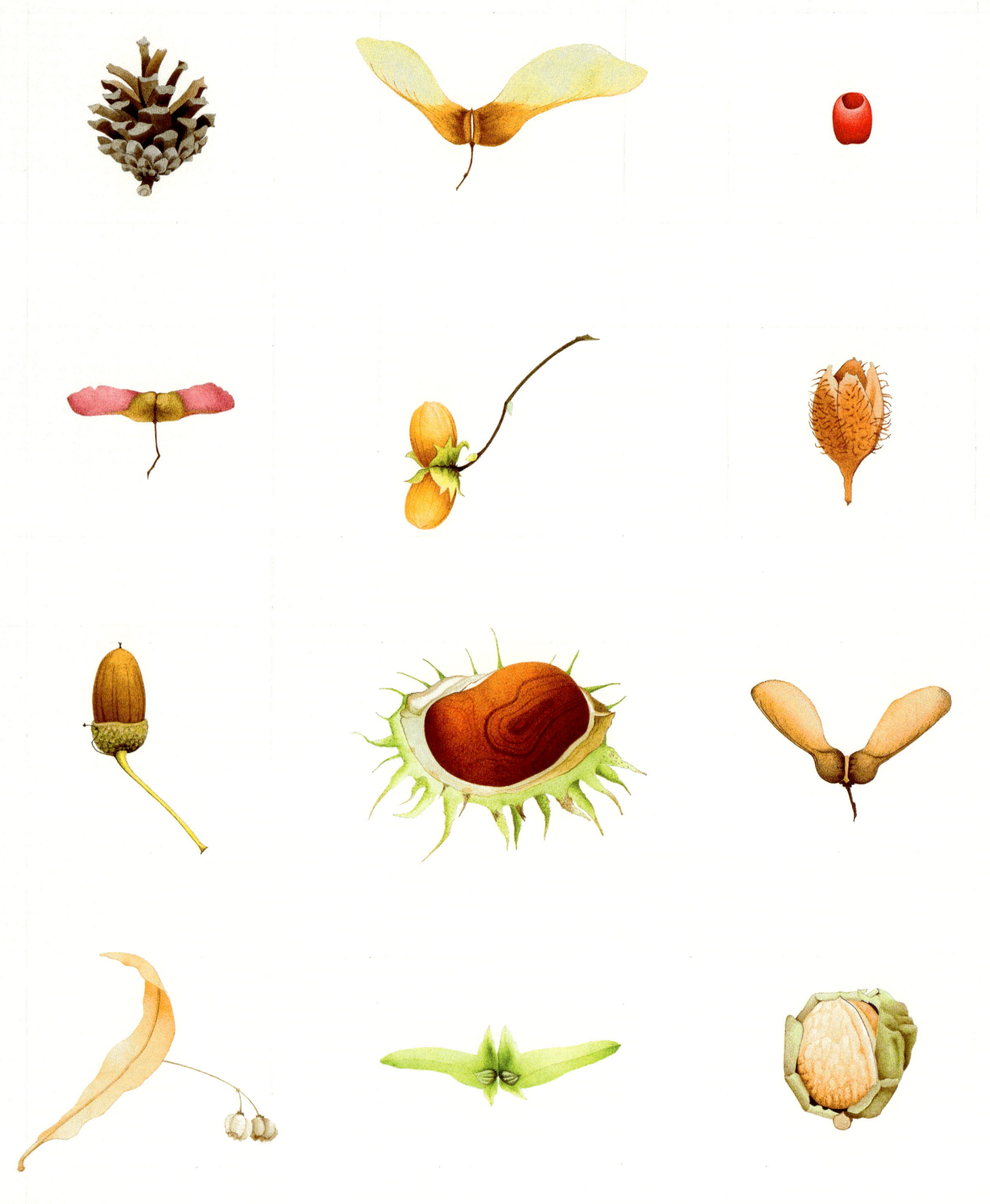
Okt. 1989

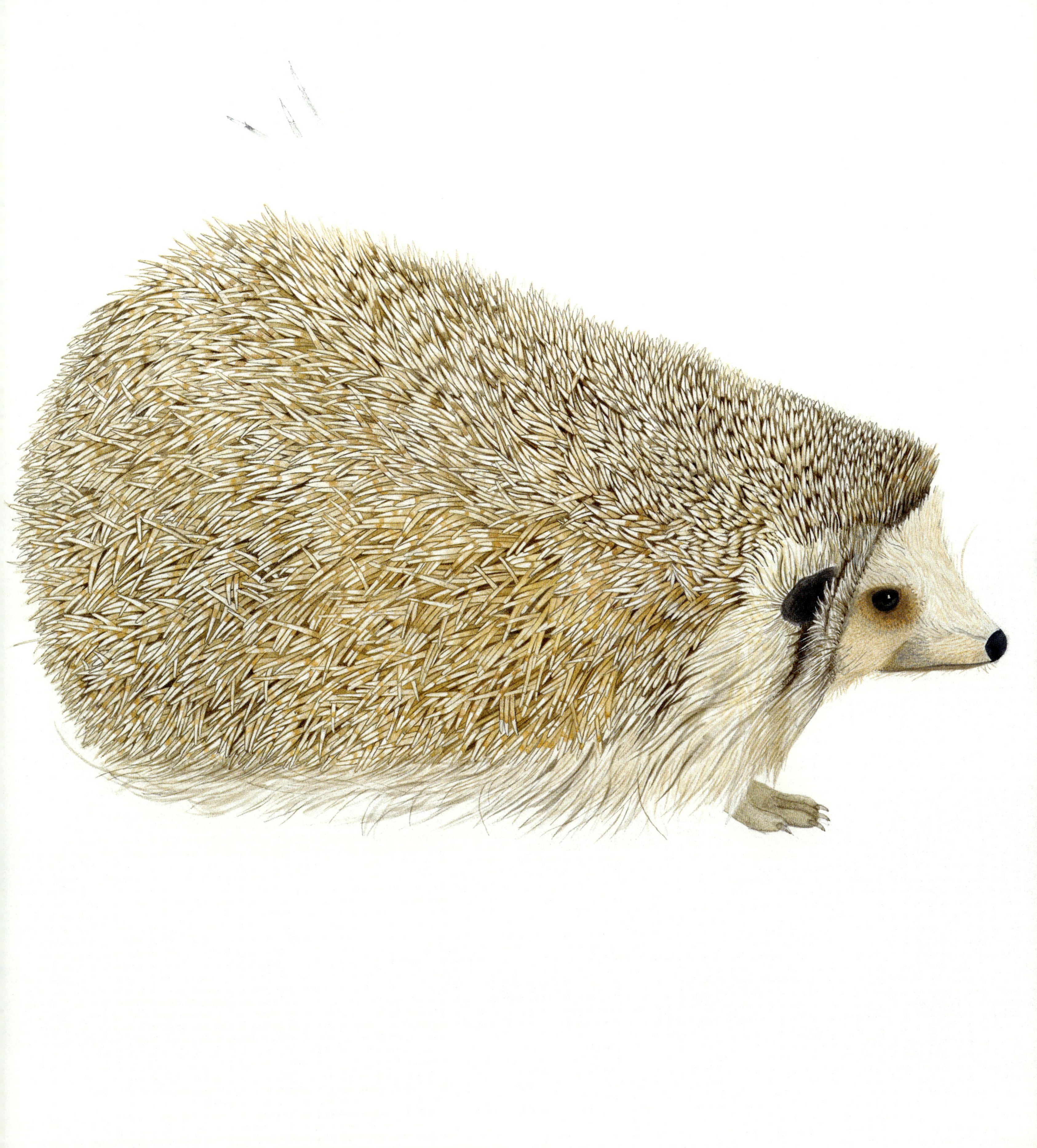

Das Wort «Seide» weckt eine Fülle von Emotionen. Seide hat eine Jahrhunderte alte Geschichte. Man denkt an China und die Seidenstrasse. Der Zauber der Seidenraupe, ihre Metamorphose: die Verwandlung von der Raupe zur Puppe zum Schmetterling. Die Seidenraupe spinnt einen so regelmässigen Kokon, dass man den Faden maschinell abspulen kann. Jeder Kokon liefert ungefähr 400 Meter Seidenfaden. Wunder — alles Wunder.

Die Arbeiten von Cornelia Hesse-Honegger behüten, bewahren das Naturwunder Seide. Sie schafft mit ihren Tüchern eine Symbiose aus Natürlichem und Künstlichem. Auf die Noblesse des Materials Seide reagiert sie mit ihrer Kunst, einer Kunst, die das nur Dekorative, das Modische vermeidet. Ihre Tücher haben etwas Klassisches, wollen mehr sein als blosse Konsumware.

Seit vielen Jahren fühlt sich die Künstlerin mit der Natur verbunden. Zeichnend und malend führt ihre Kunst uns eine wunderliche Welt vor Augen.

Ihre Welt sind die Insekten, Wunder der Miniaturisierung. Eine Welt, die wir ignorieren, die jedoch Träger einer Fülle von Formen und Farben ist. Viele dieser Insektenarten sind vom Aussterben bedroht. Den Atomreaktoren und ihren tödlichen Strahlen hat sie darum ihr Werk gewidmet; sie zeigt uns in ihren Untersuchungen die Gefahr einer Technik, die letztlich uns alle bedroht.

Sie war in Tschernobyl, in Sellafield und in Three Mile Island, an jenen Orten also, die mit atomaren Katastrophen oder Beinah-Katastrophen verbunden sind. Ihre Bilder sind eindrucksvoller Beleg für die reale Not.

Ihre Kunst ist deshalb getragen von Verantwortung. Sie glaubt, dass unsere künstliche Welt — wie die natürliche Welt auch — Schönheit, Wahrheit vermitteln mus. Für sie ist Kunst die höchste Ausdrucksform des menschlichen Geistes. Schönheit als Harmonie, als Wohltat, und dies in einer Zeit, da vieles zu Abfall wird.

Cornelia Hesse-Honegger glaubt, dass die Kunst nicht reserviert ist für gerahmte Bilder über dem Sofa. Kunst darf für sie nicht zum Elite-Objekt, zur Spekulationsware verkommen. Sie glaubt, dass die Kunst eindringen muss in unseren Alltag, wieder Teil unserer täglichen Umwelt werden muss.

Bilder früherer Zeiten zeugen dafür, dass alle Lebensbereiche als Kunst erlebt wurden. So sind auch ihre Tücher ein Beleg dafür, dass dies möglich ist. Form, Material und die handwerkliche Verarbeitung ihrer Tücher haben eine Haltung, werden bestimmt vom Gedanken, dass auch die Mode etwas mit Gesinnung, etwas mit Charakter zu tun hat.

«Kleider machen Leute» — auch Seidentücher sind Teil der Kleidung, spiegeln die Persönlichkeit der Trägerin wider. Das haben Modeschöpfer wie Yves St. Laurent verstanden. Seidentücher von Cornelia Hesse-Honegger wurden zum Begriff, eine begehrte Marke, selbst für die Haute Couture.

Gottfried Honegger

The word "silk" awakens a cornucopia of emotions. Silk has a centuries old history. One thinks of China and the Silk Road. The magic of the silkworm: its metamorphosis from larva to pupa to moth. The silkworm spins such an even, continuous cocoon that the thread can be unwound by machine. Each cocoon provides approximately 400 meters of thread. Astonishing, wondrous.

Cornelia Hesse-Honegger's work protects and preserves the natural wonder of silk. With her foulards she achieves a symbiosis of the natural and artificial. She reacts to the noblesse of the material with her art, an art that avoids the purely decorative or fashionable. Her scarves possess something classical, want to be more than simply consumer goods.

Her world is the insect world, the miracle of miniaturization. A world that we ignore, despite its wealth of form and color. Many insect species are threatened with extinction. Thus she dedicates her work to nuclear reactors and their deadly radiation and through her investigations shows us the danger of a technology that ultimately endangers us all.

For years, the artist has felt connected to nature. Sketched and painted, her art parades a fantastical world before us.

Her art is therefore borne of responsibility. She believes that our artificial world — like the natural world as well — must convey beauty and truth. For her, art is the human spirit's highest form of expression. Beauty as harmony, as beneficence, and this at a time when so much is left to become refuse.

Cornelia Hesse-Honegger believes that art is not exclusively for framed pictures over the sofa. Art should not become objects for the elite, or degenerate into speculative commodities. She believes that art must penetrate our everyday lives, become part of our daily environment once again.

Images of earlier times prove that all spheres of life were once experienced as art. Her foulards are further proof that this is possible. The form, material, and craftsmanship of her scarves have class, are shaped by the idea that fashion too has something to do with disposition, with character.

"Clothes make the person" — silk scarves are also part of our clothing, reflecting the personality of the wearer. Designers like Yves St. Laurent understood that. Cornelia Hesse-Honegger's silk scarves have become well-known, a coveted brand, even in Haute Couture.

Gottfried Honegger

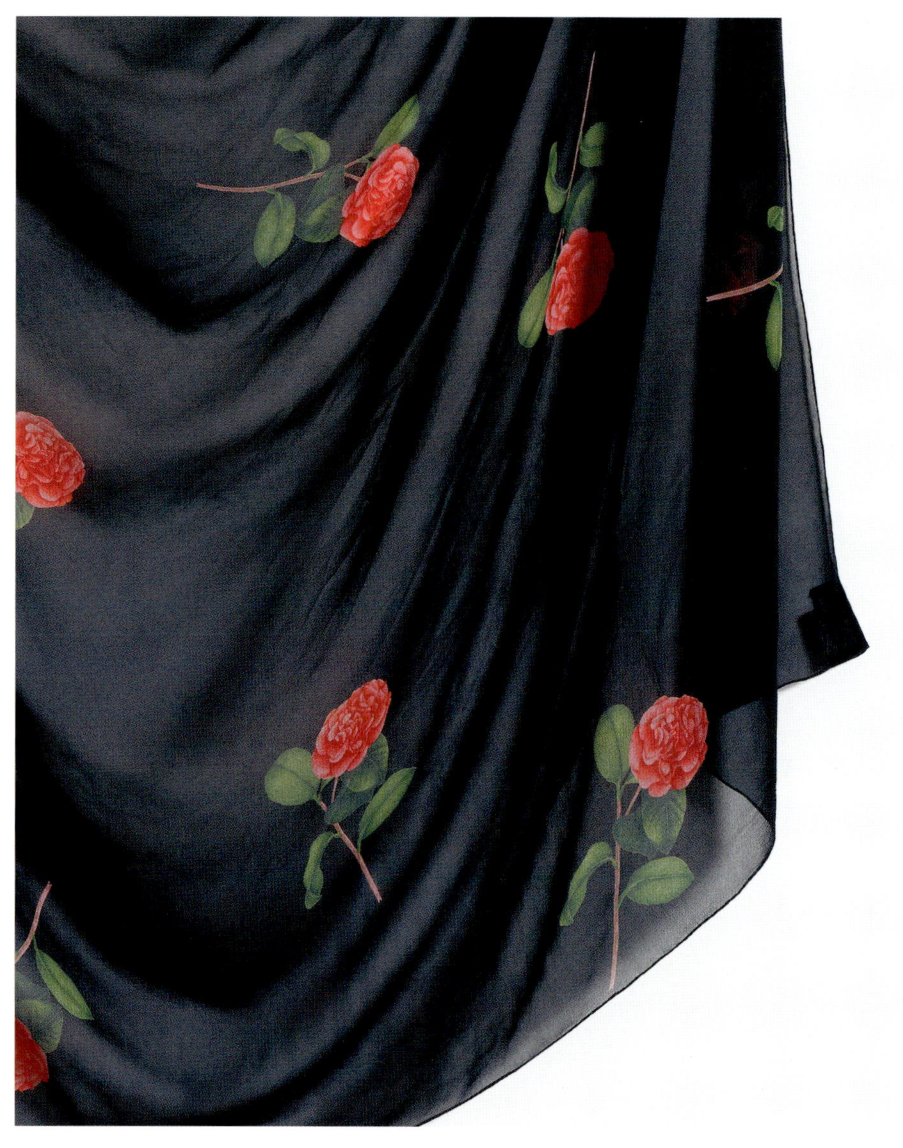

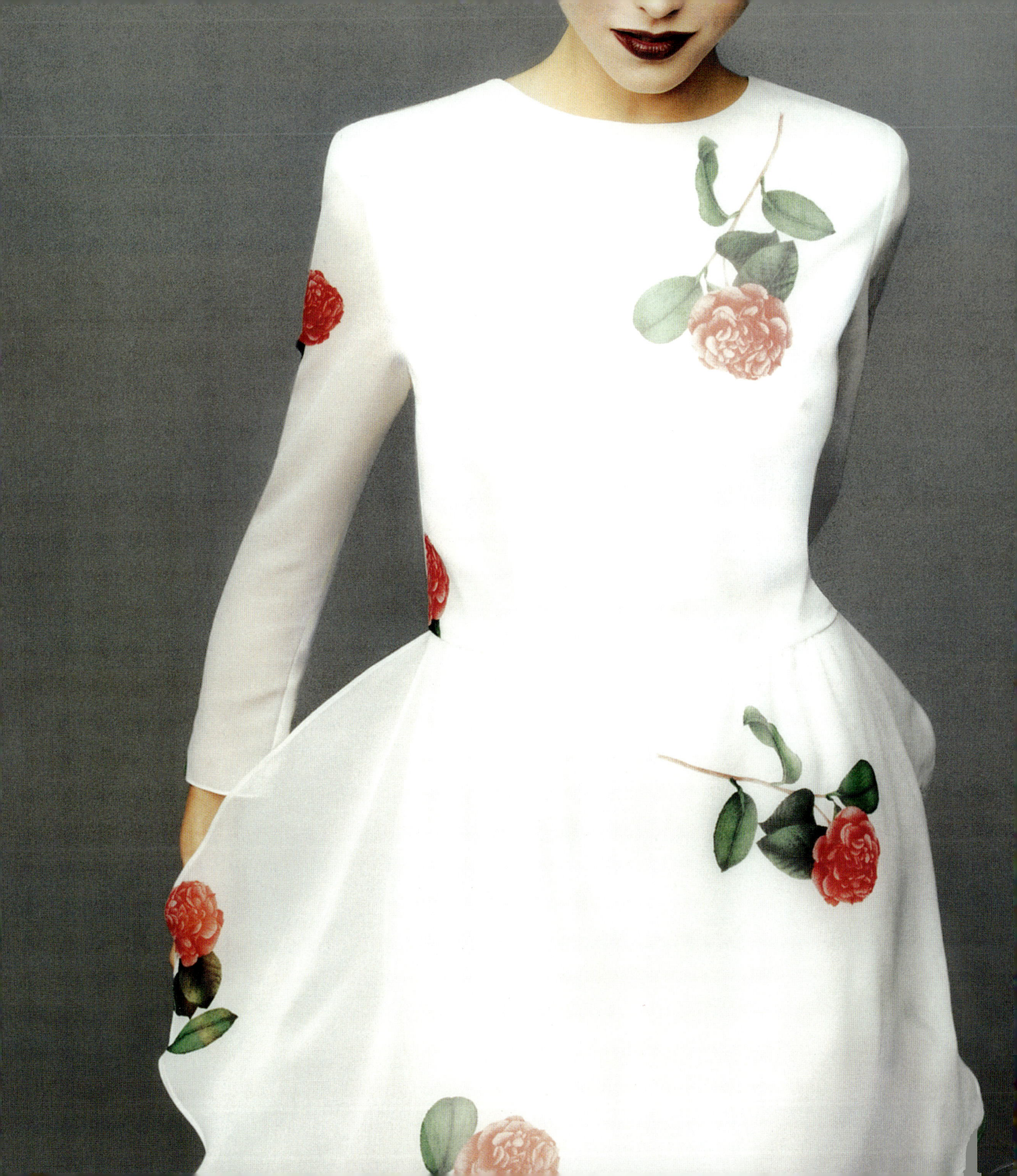

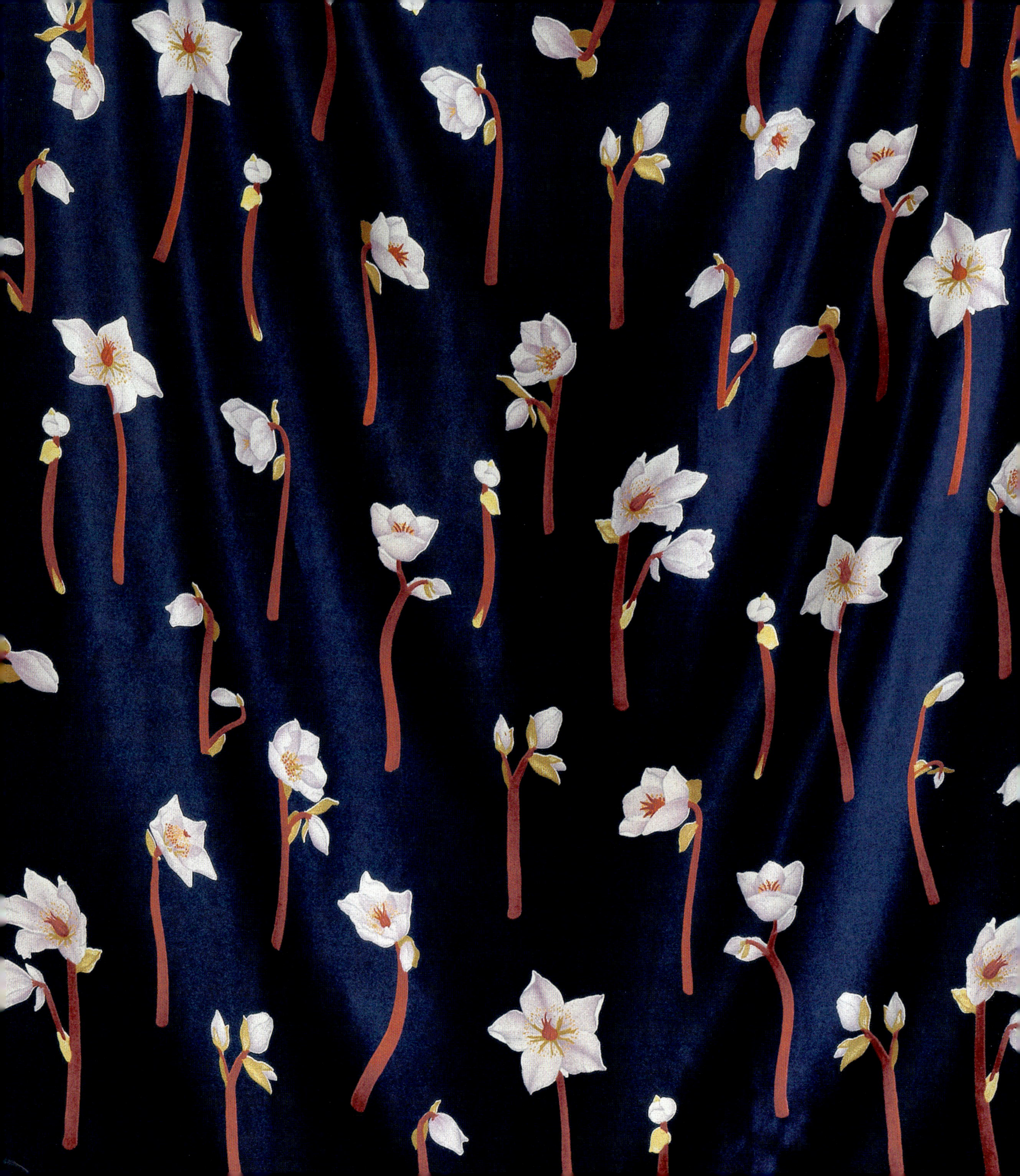

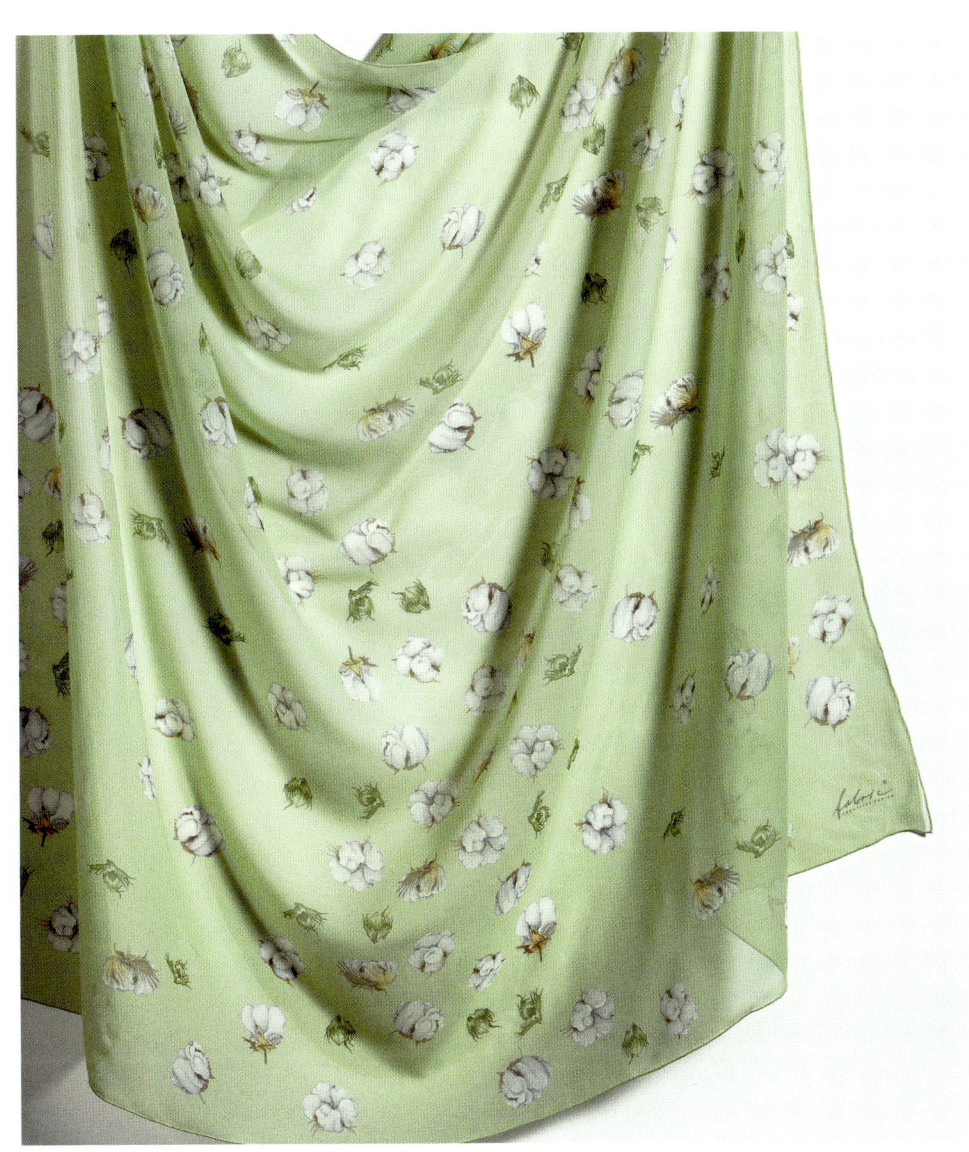

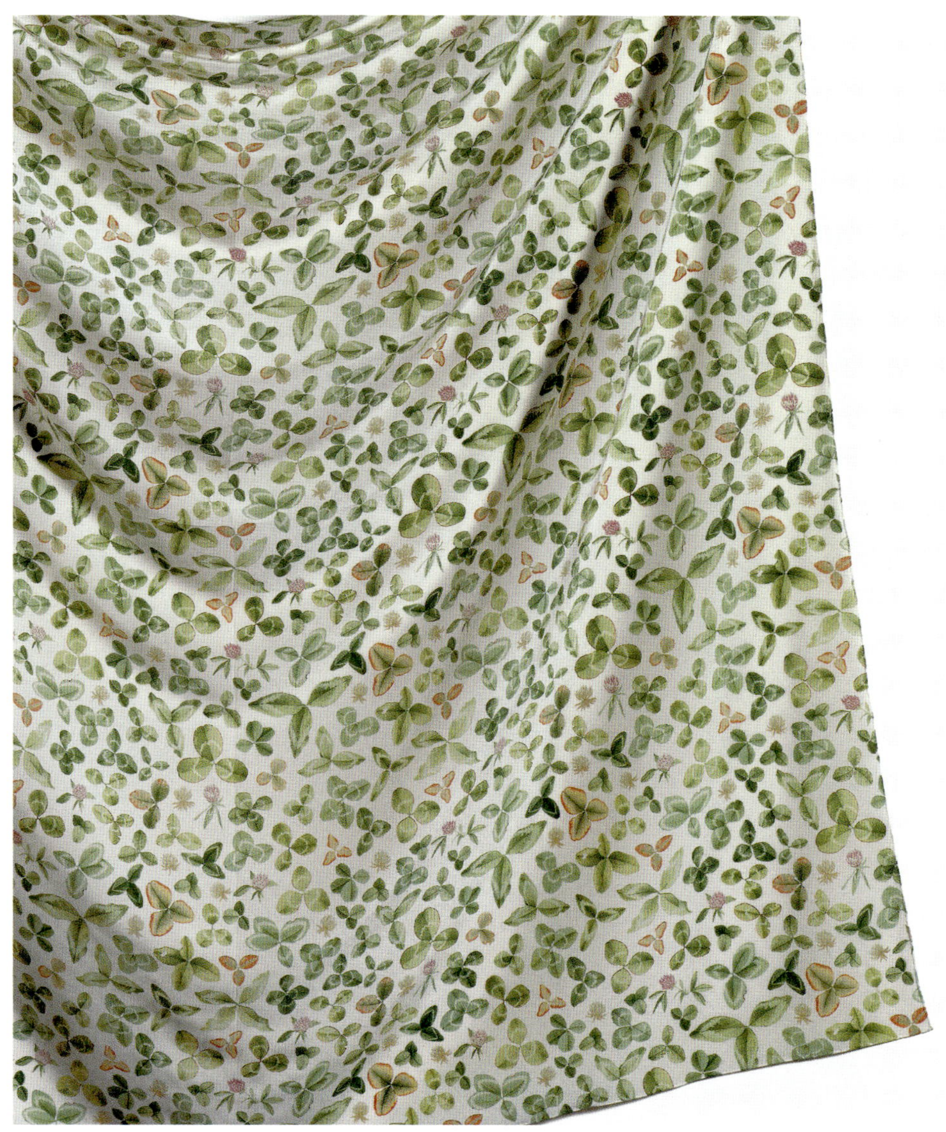

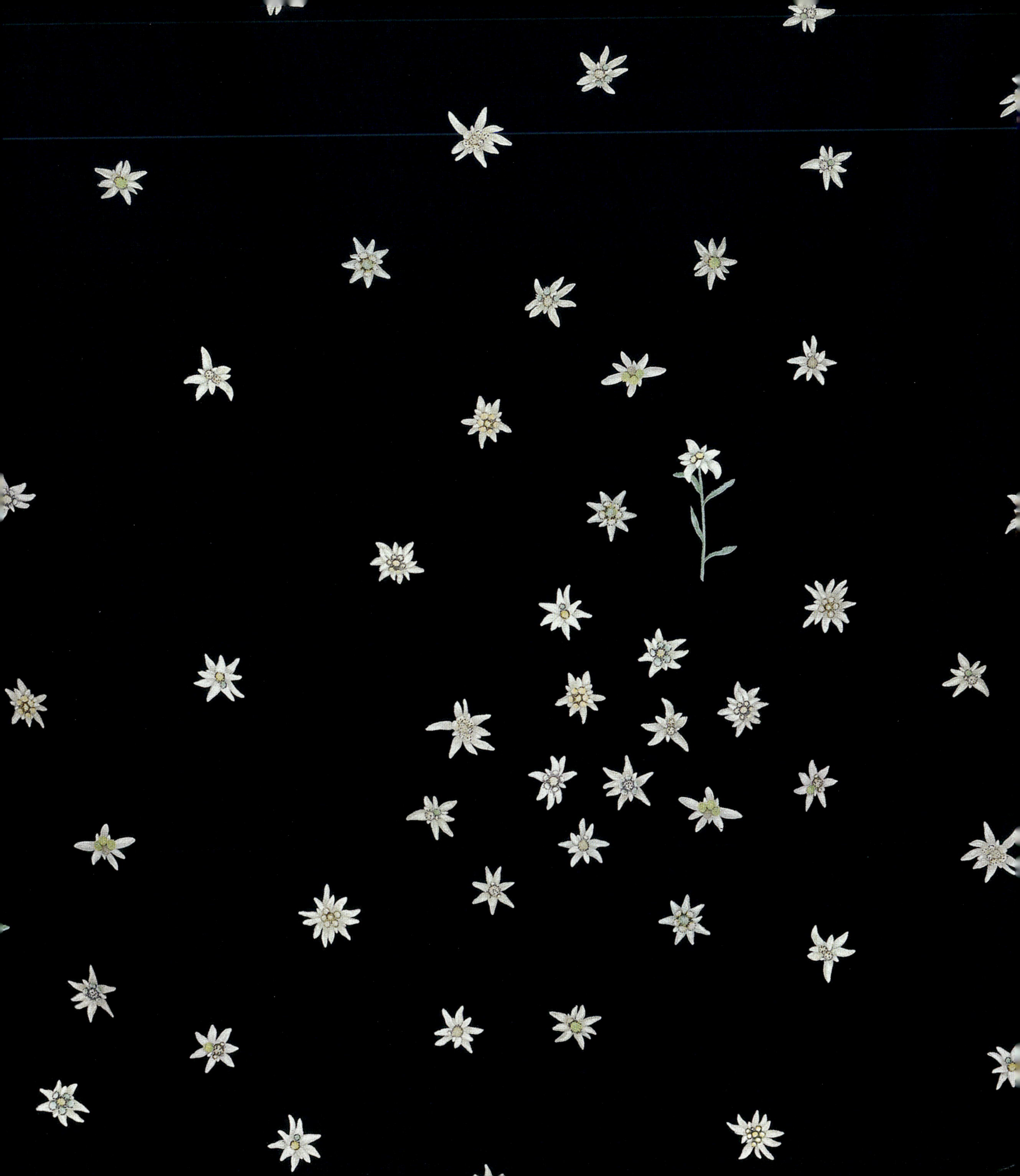

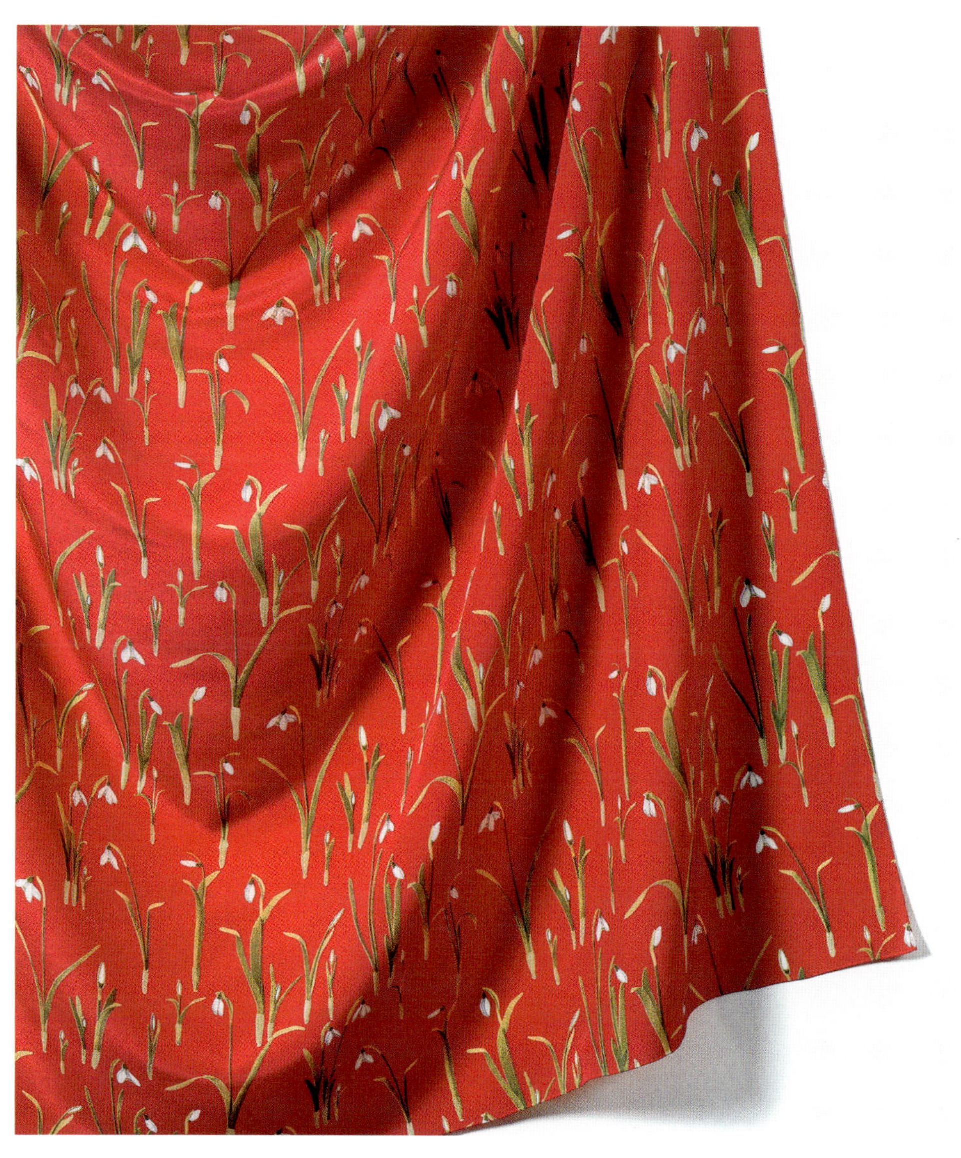

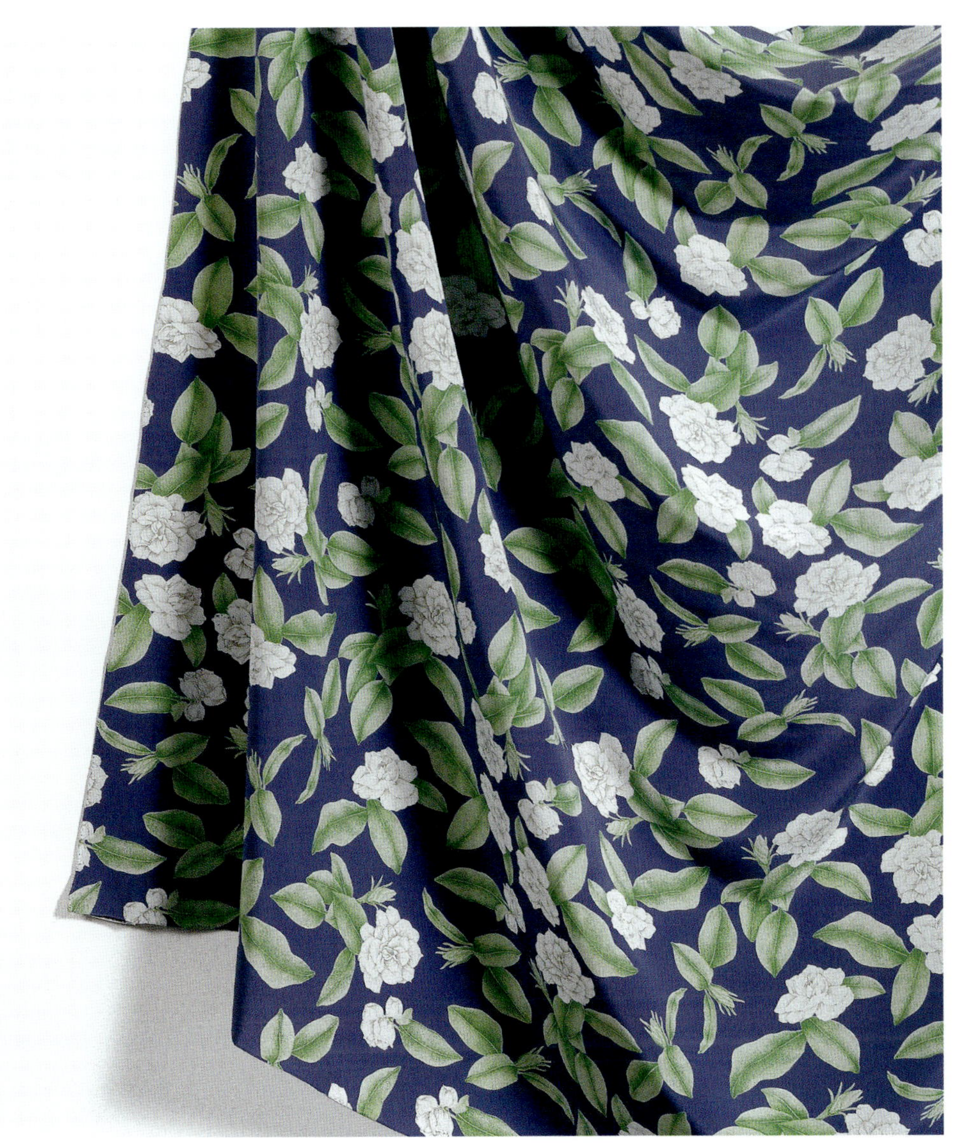

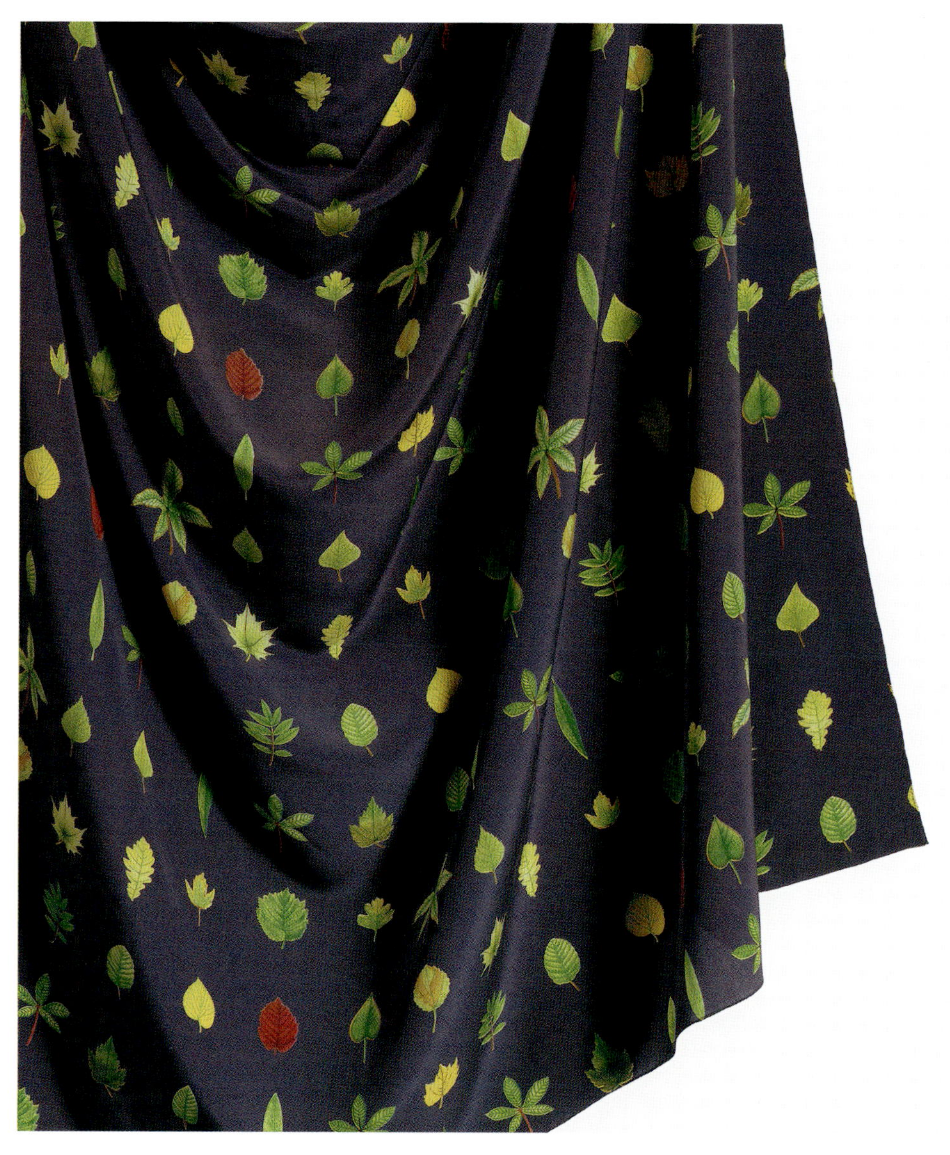

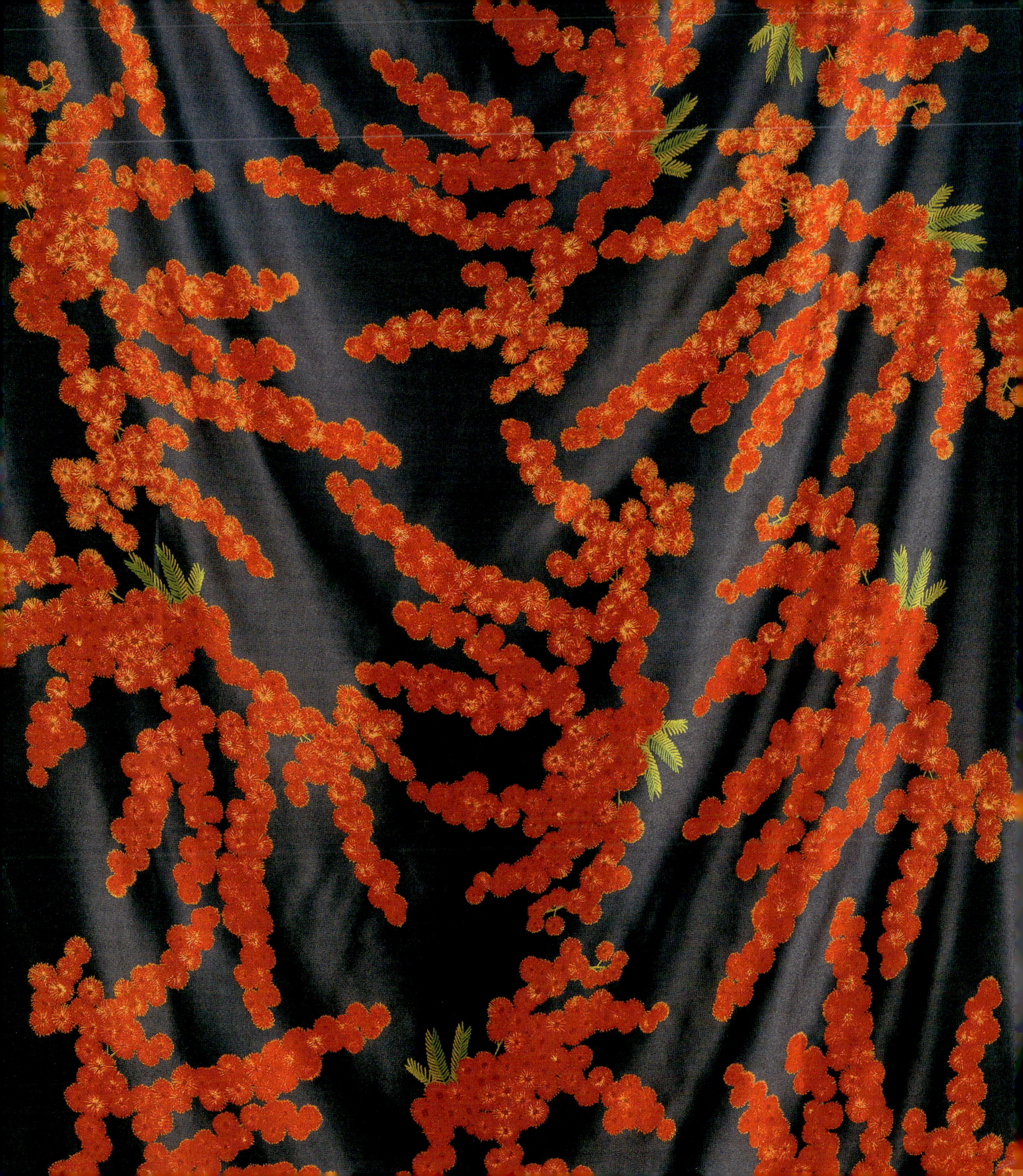

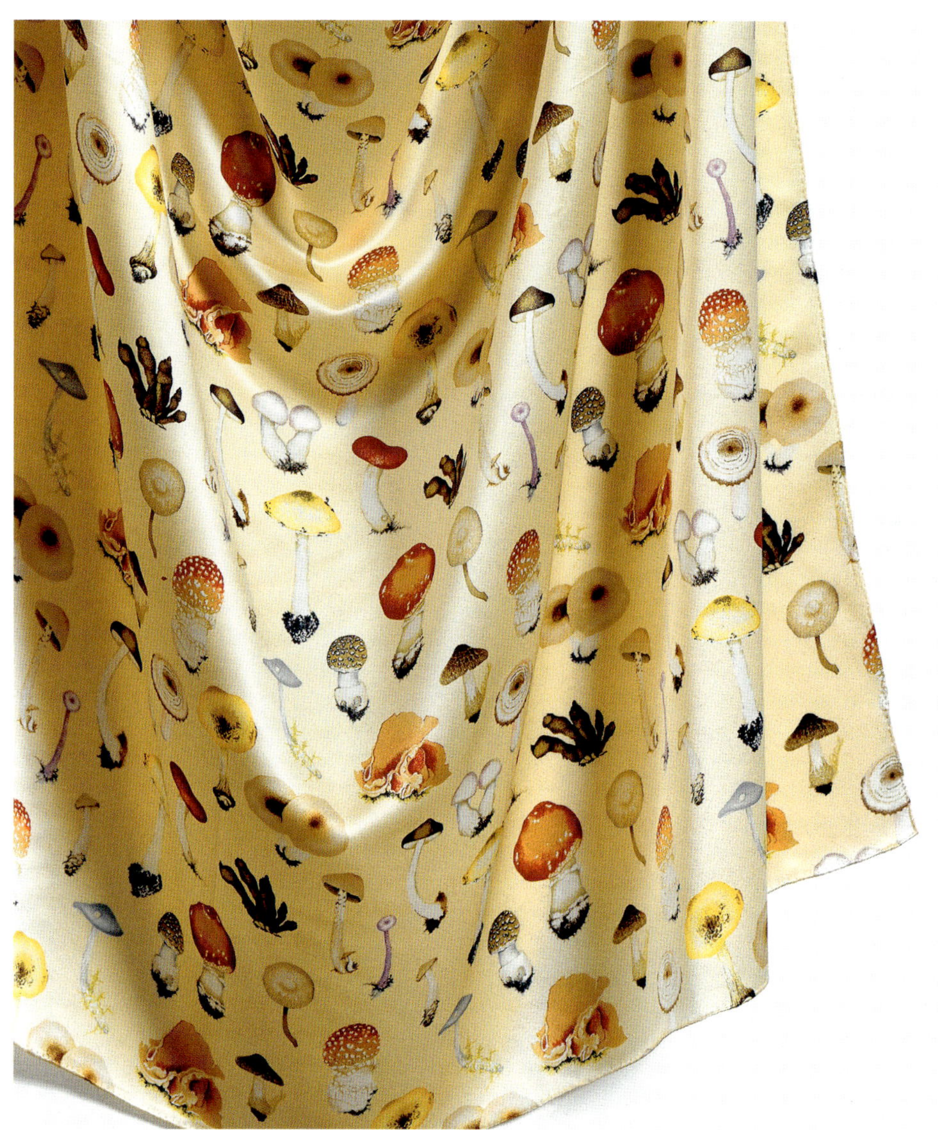

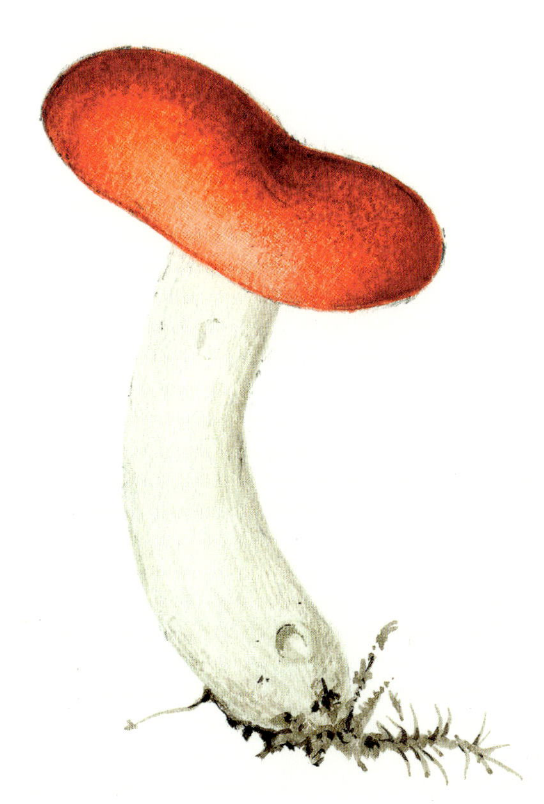

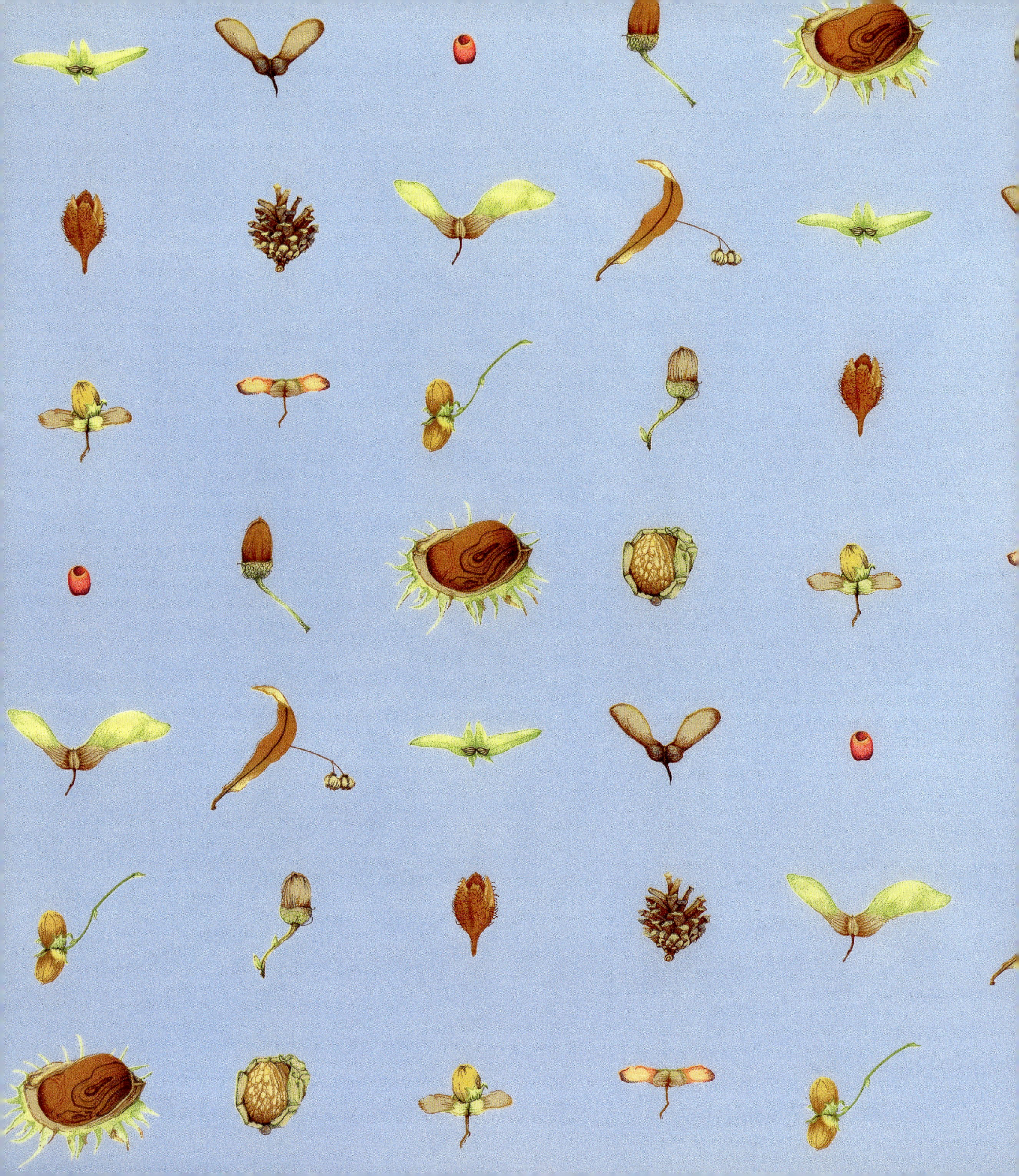

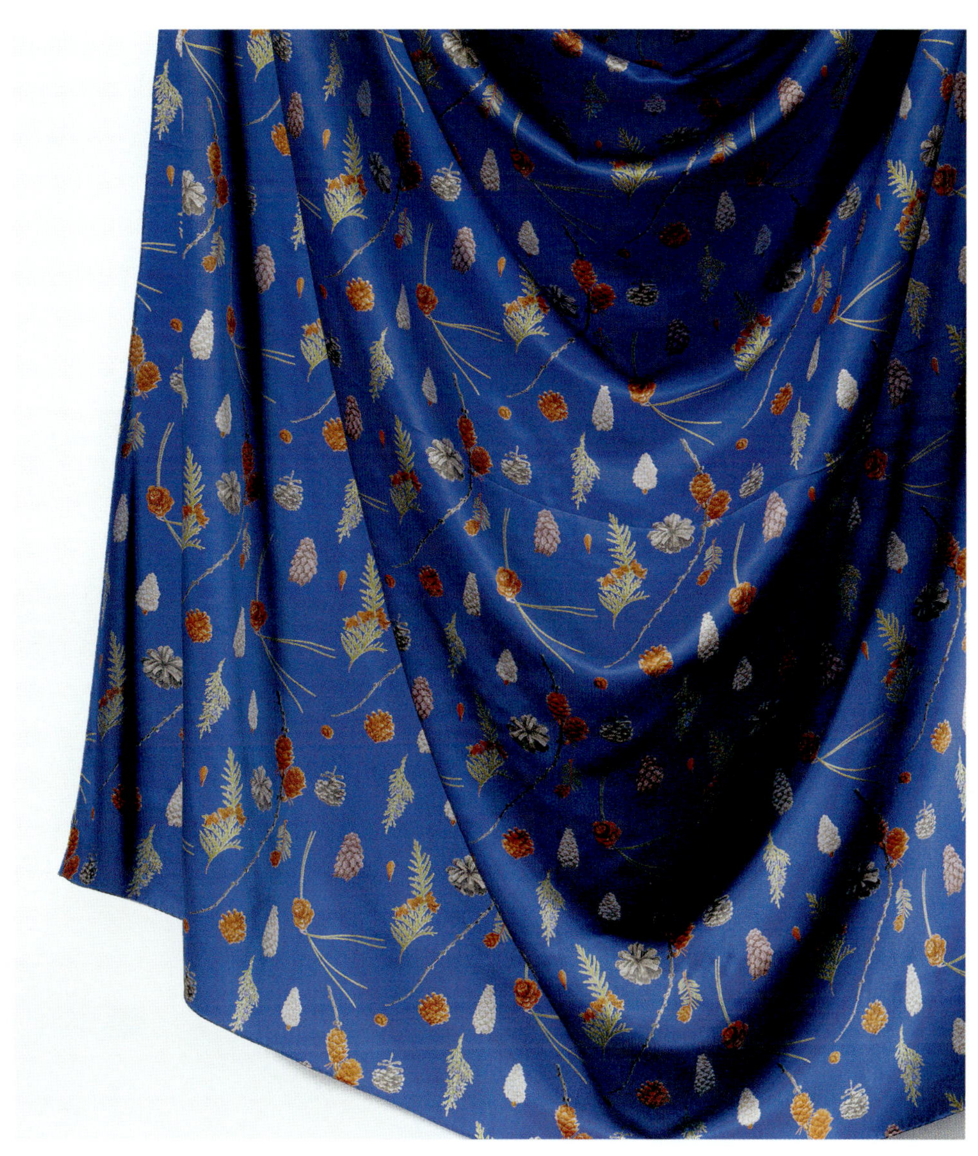

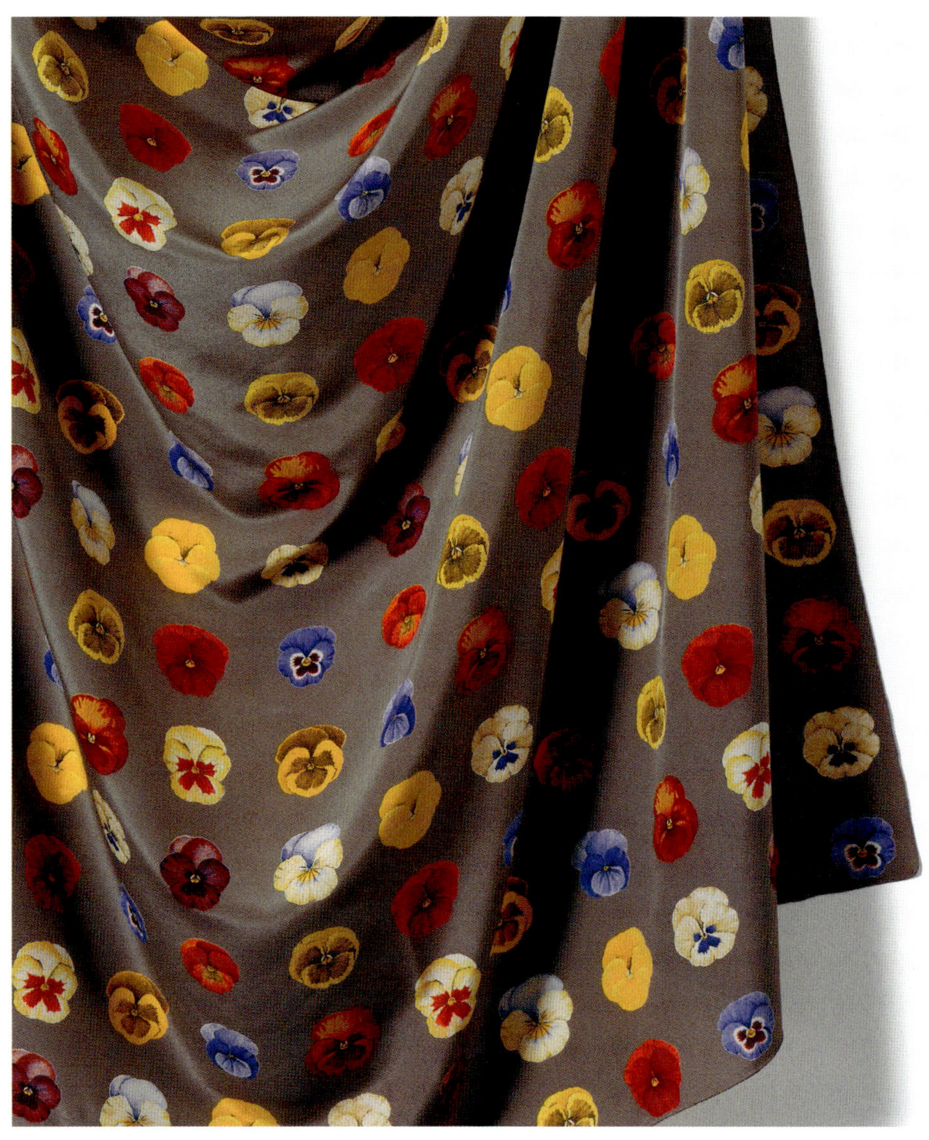

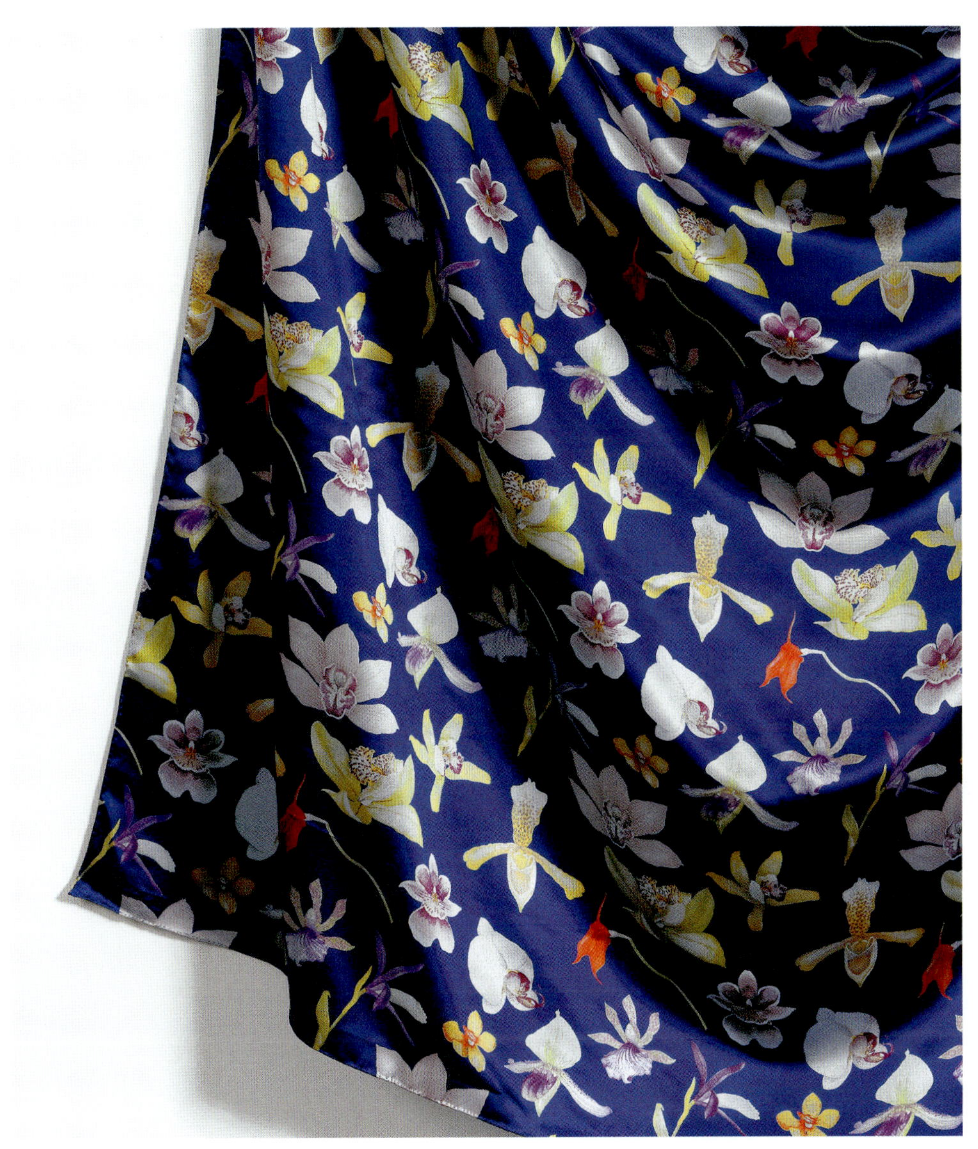

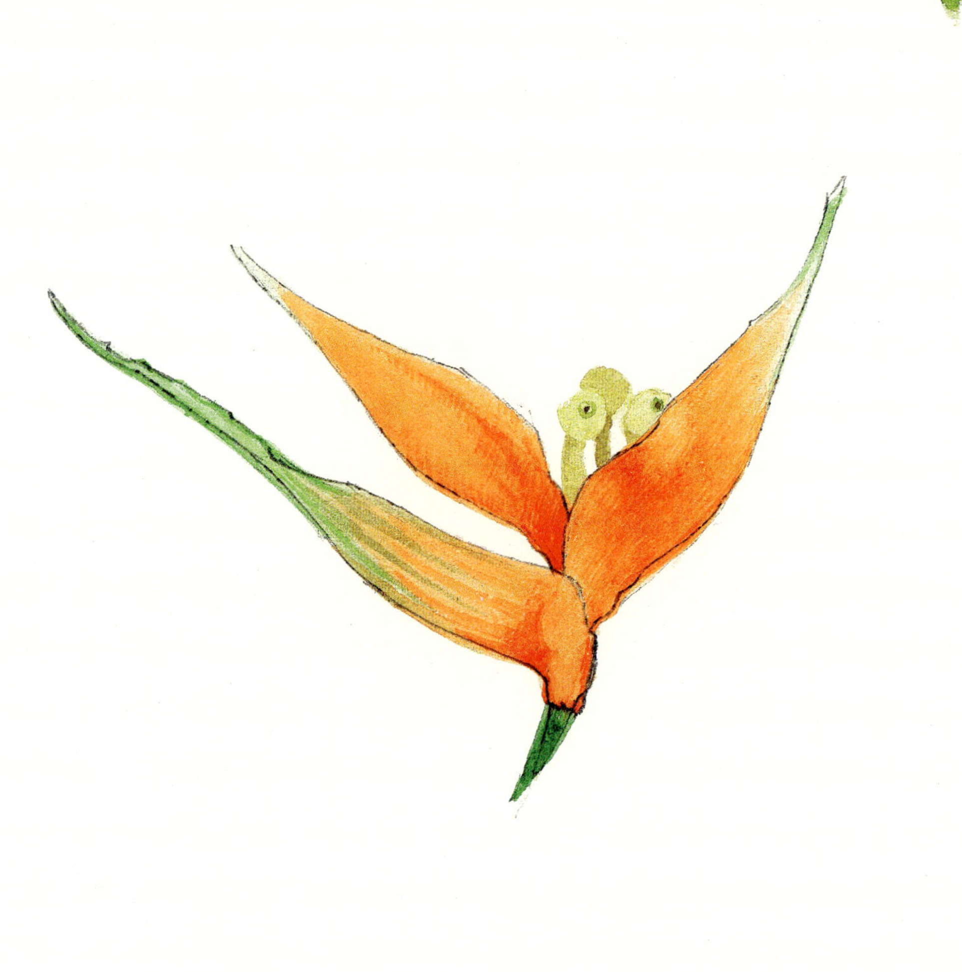

Mexico –
Panama
Heliconia
aurantiaca

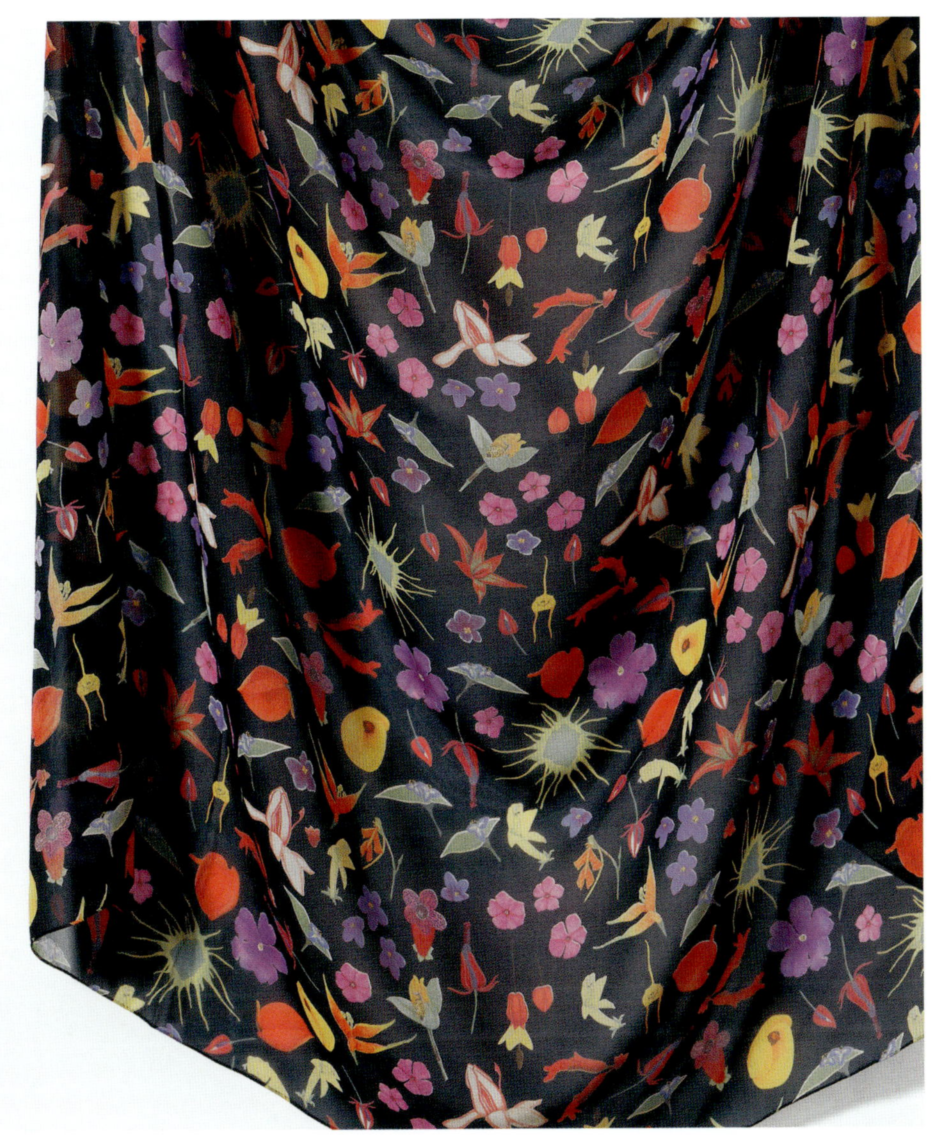

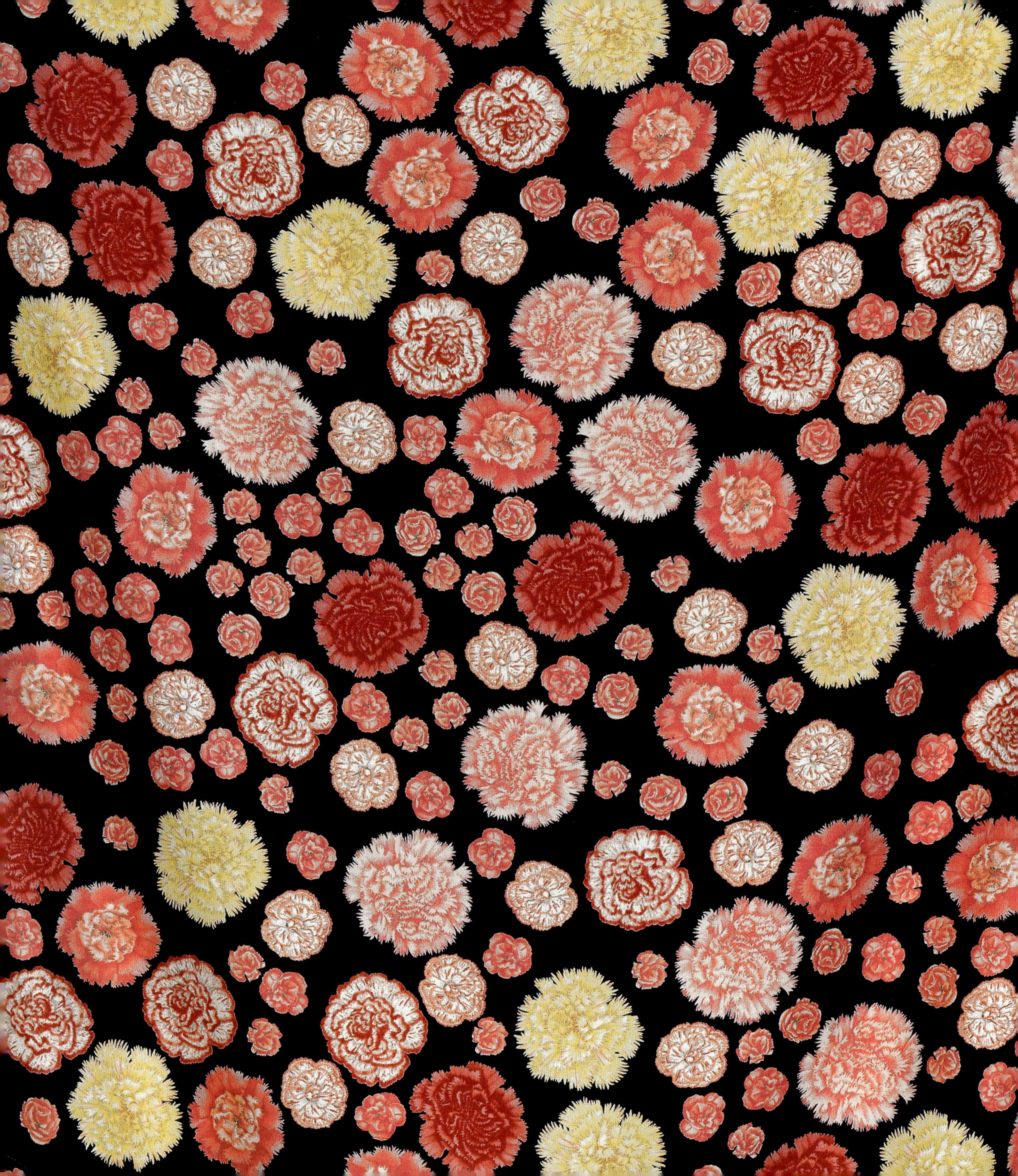

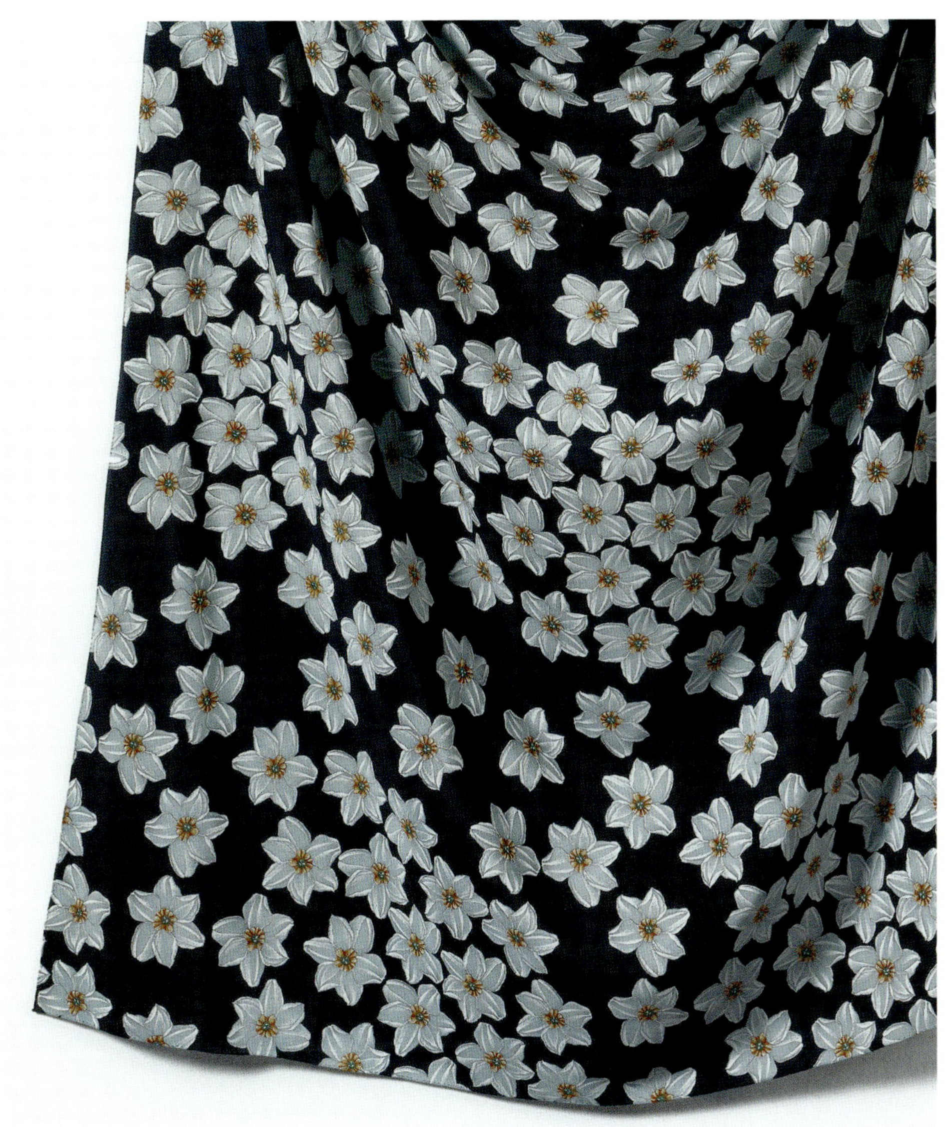

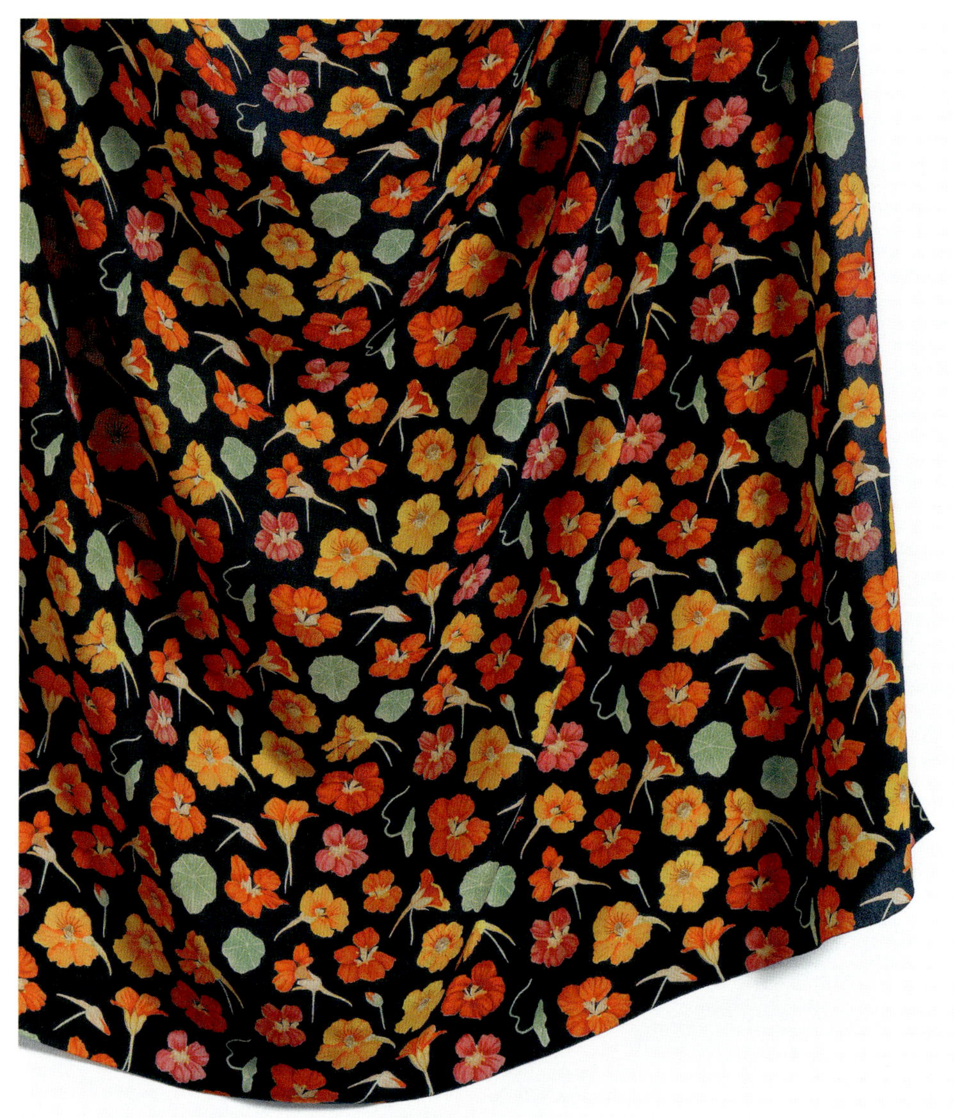

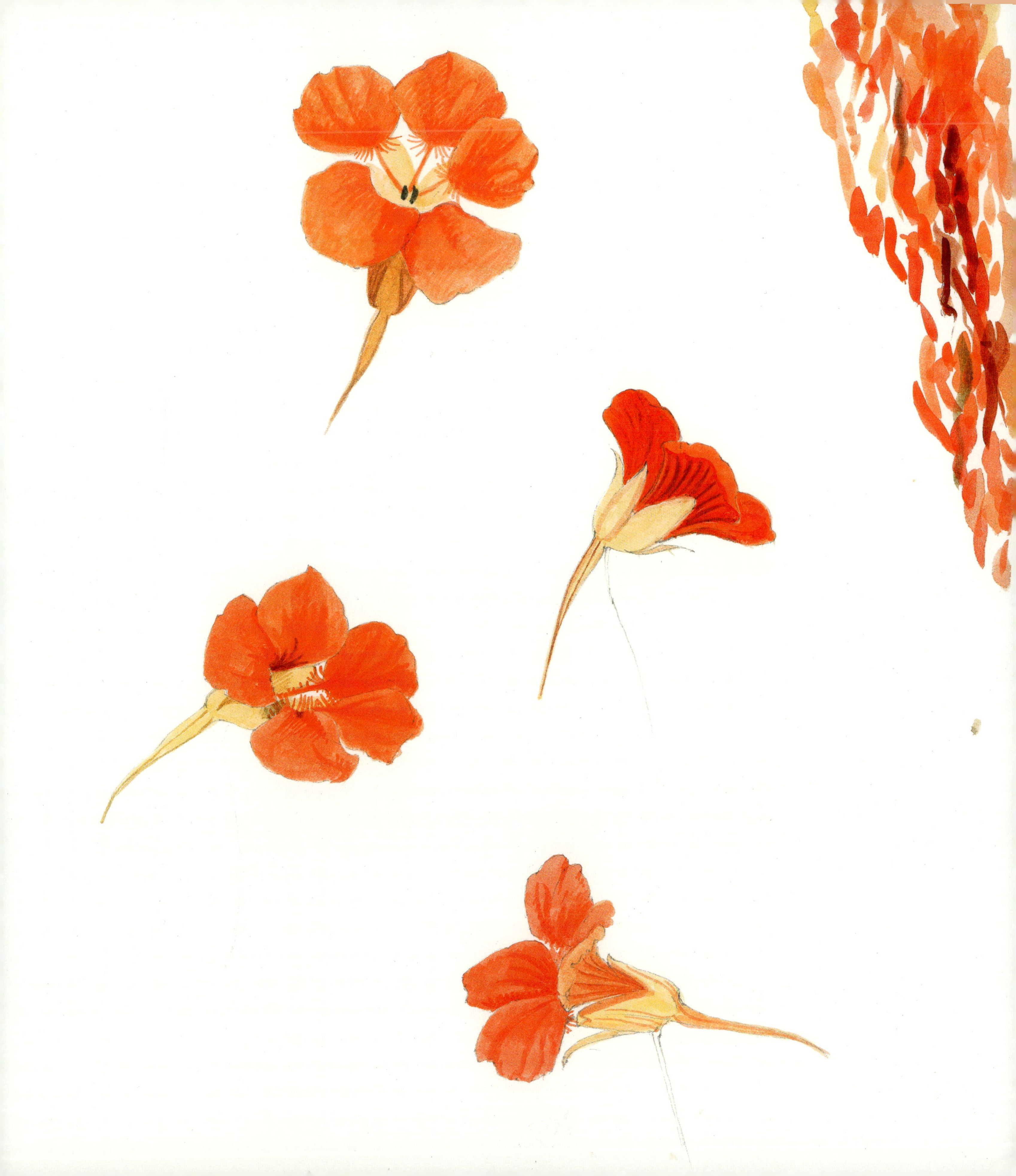

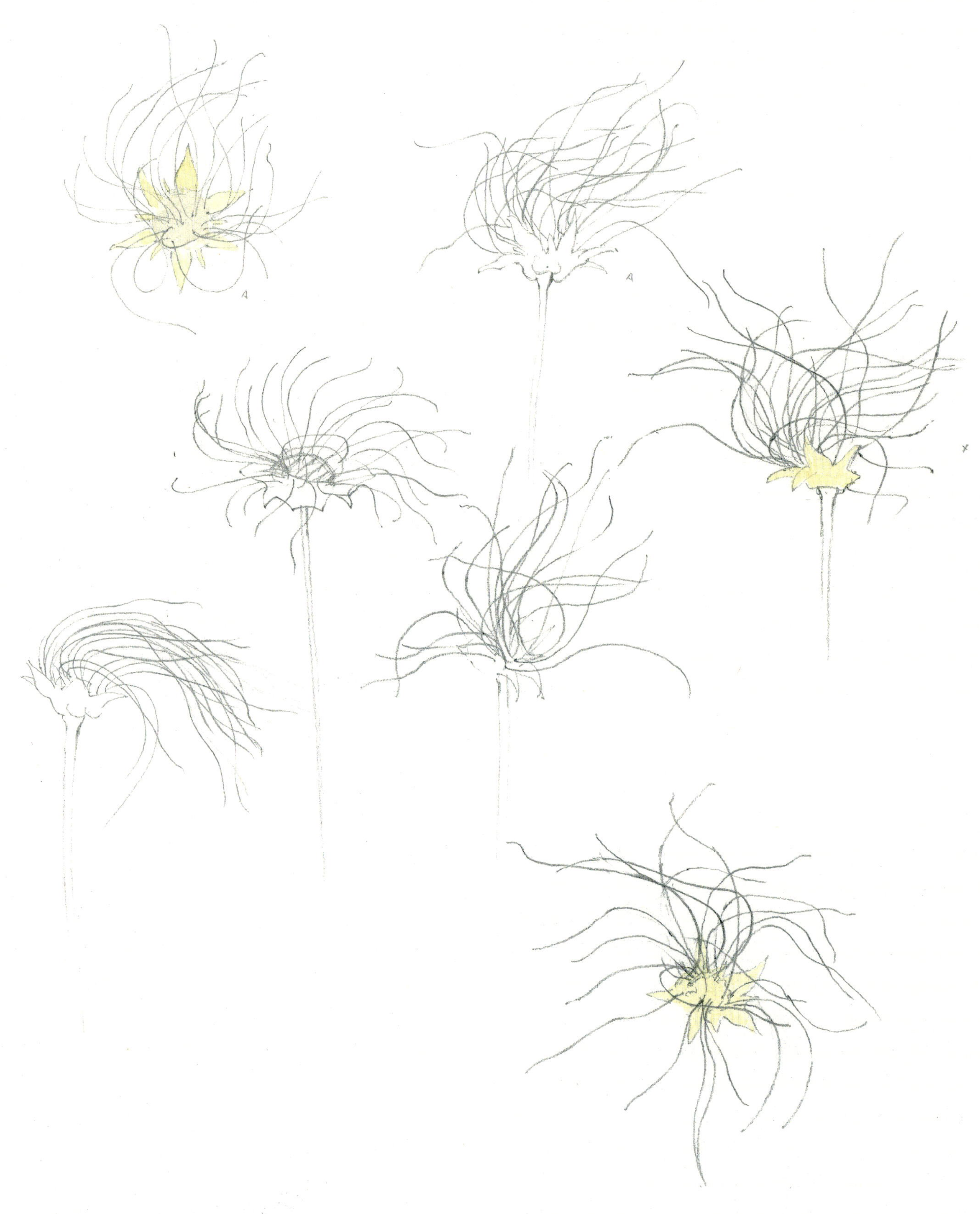

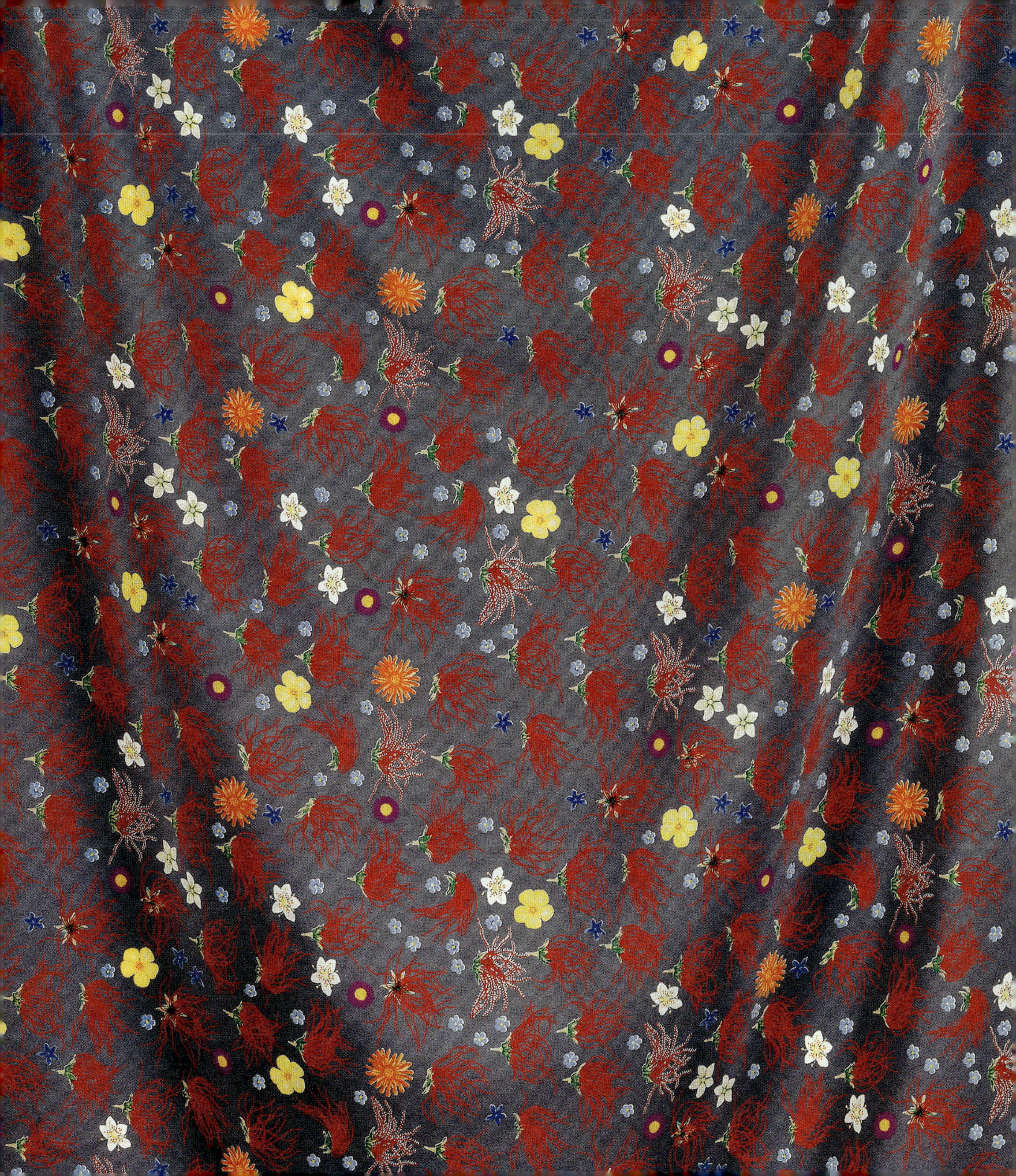

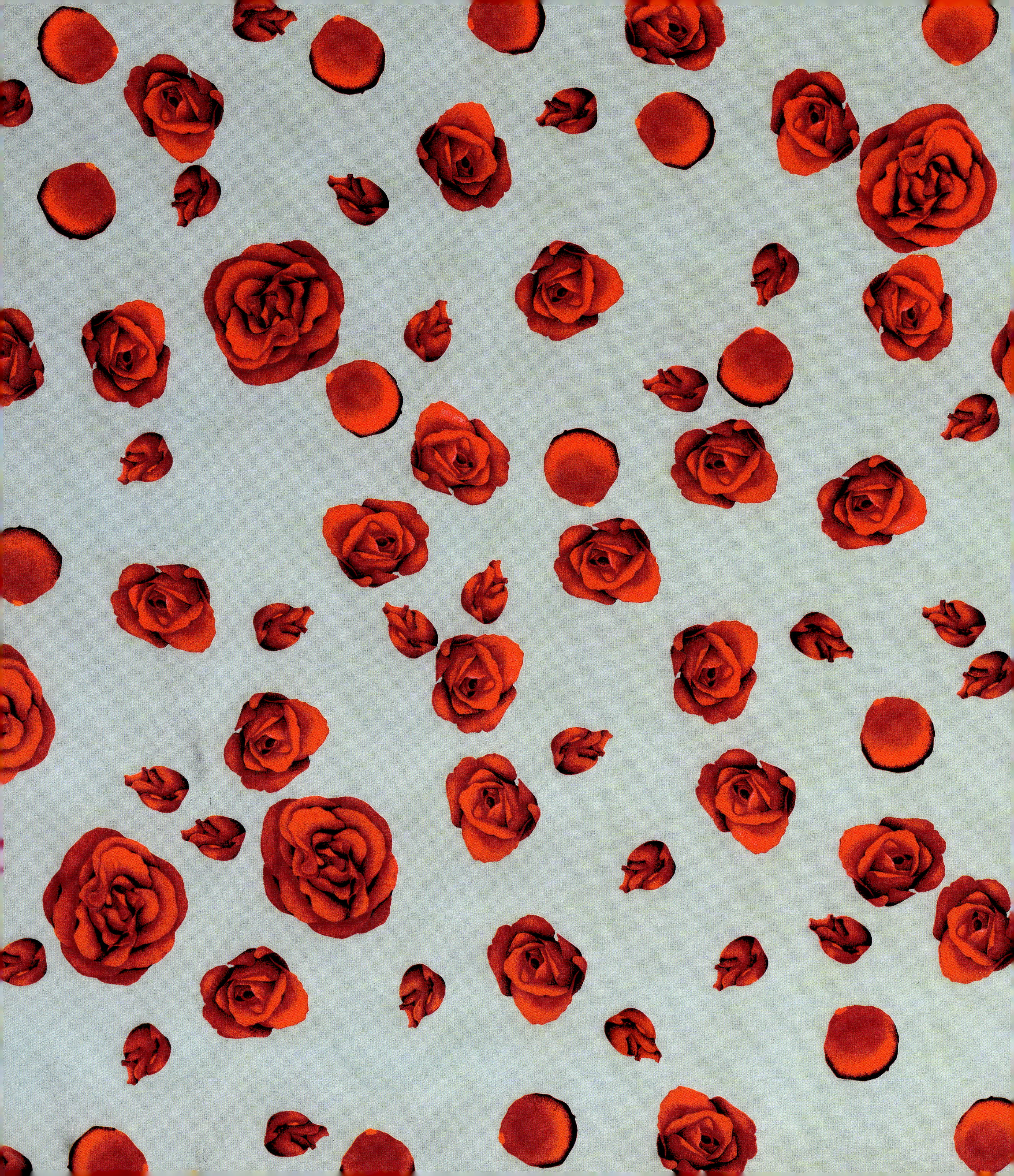

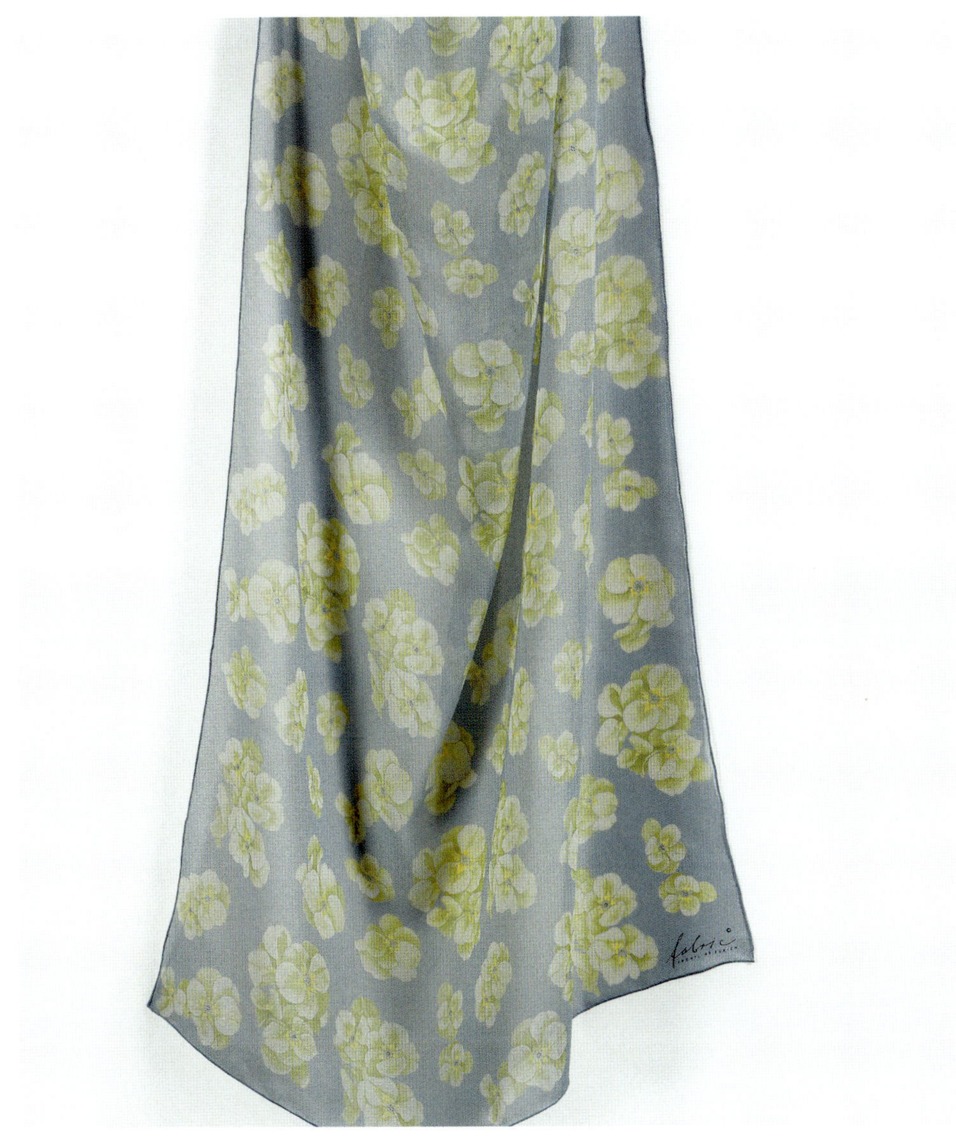

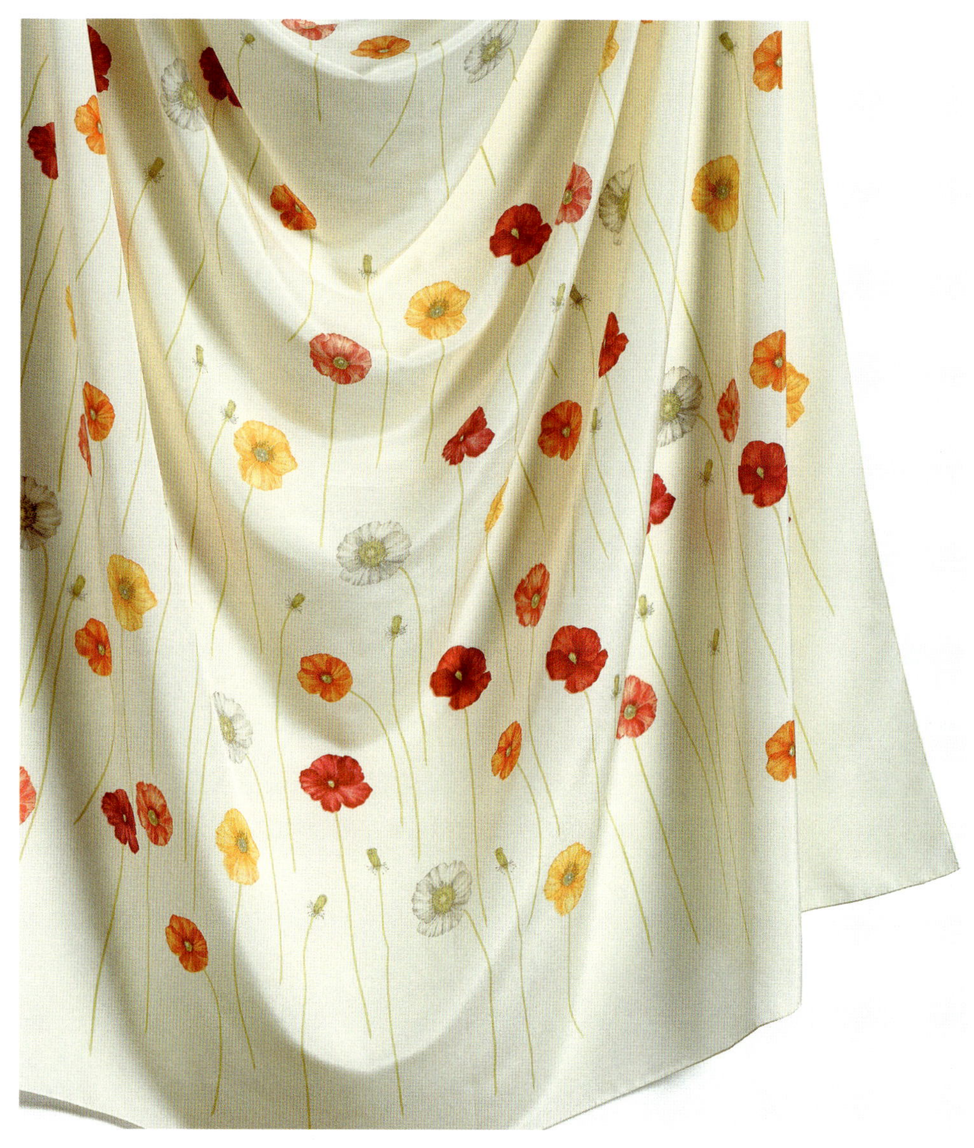

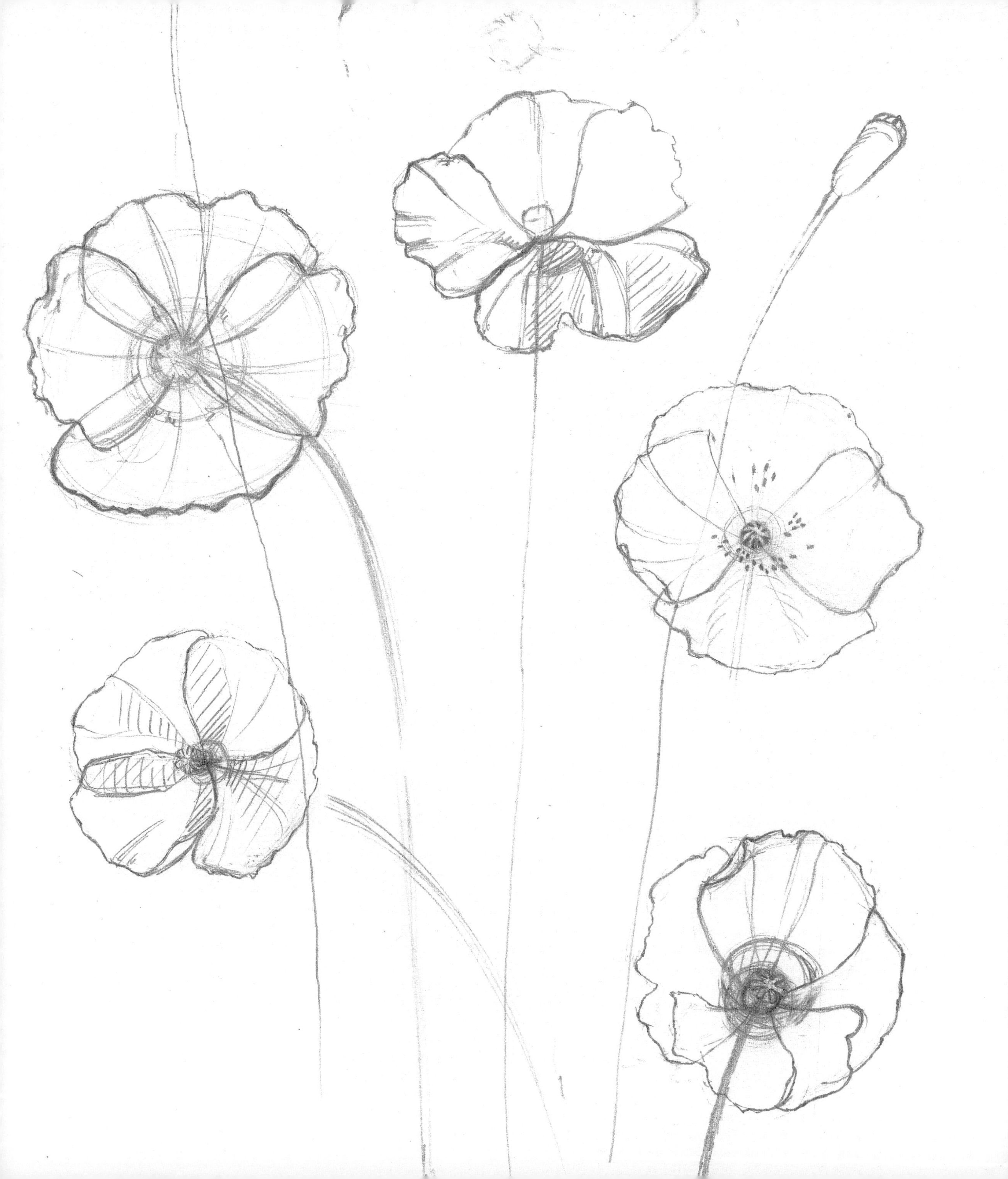

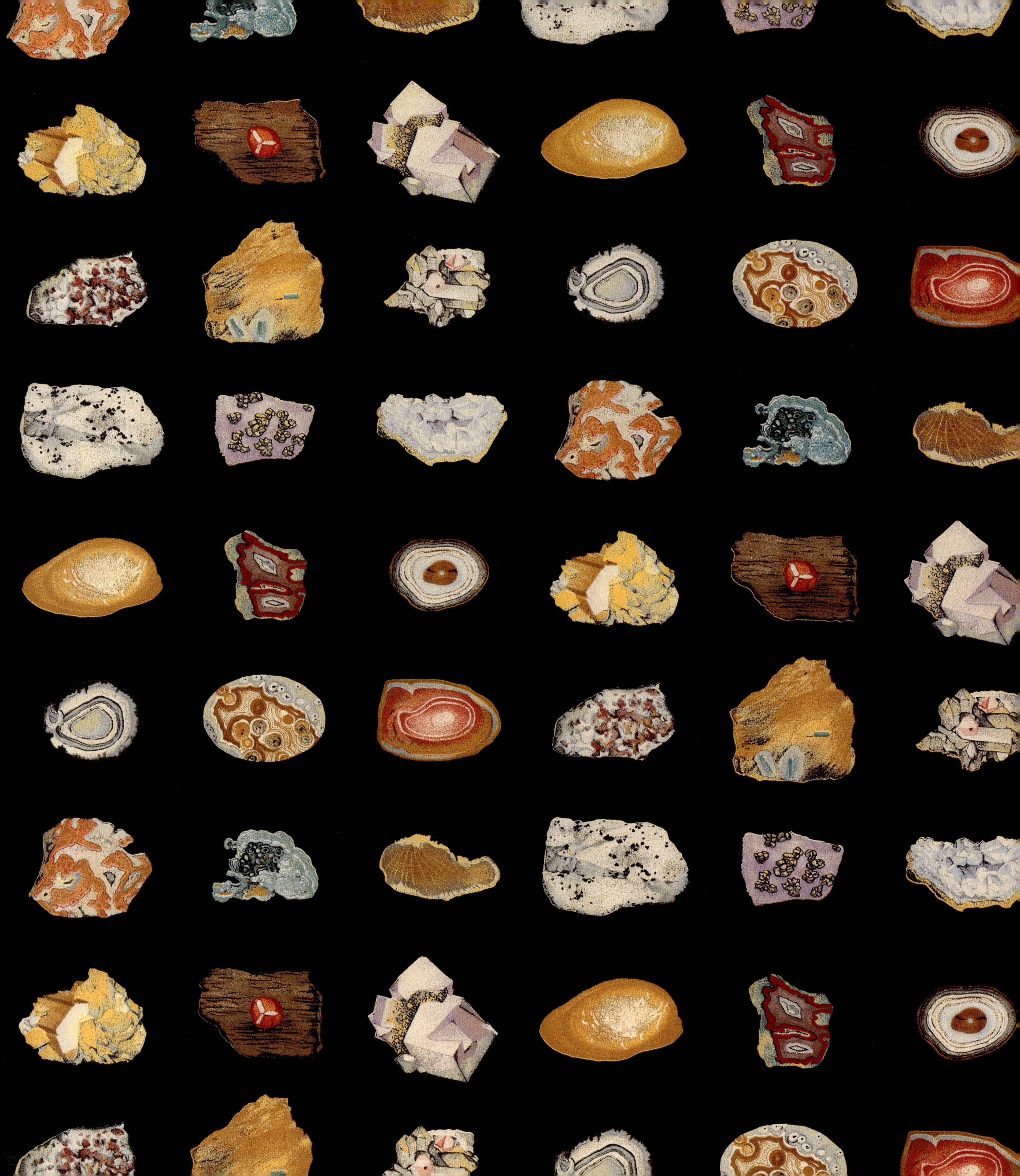

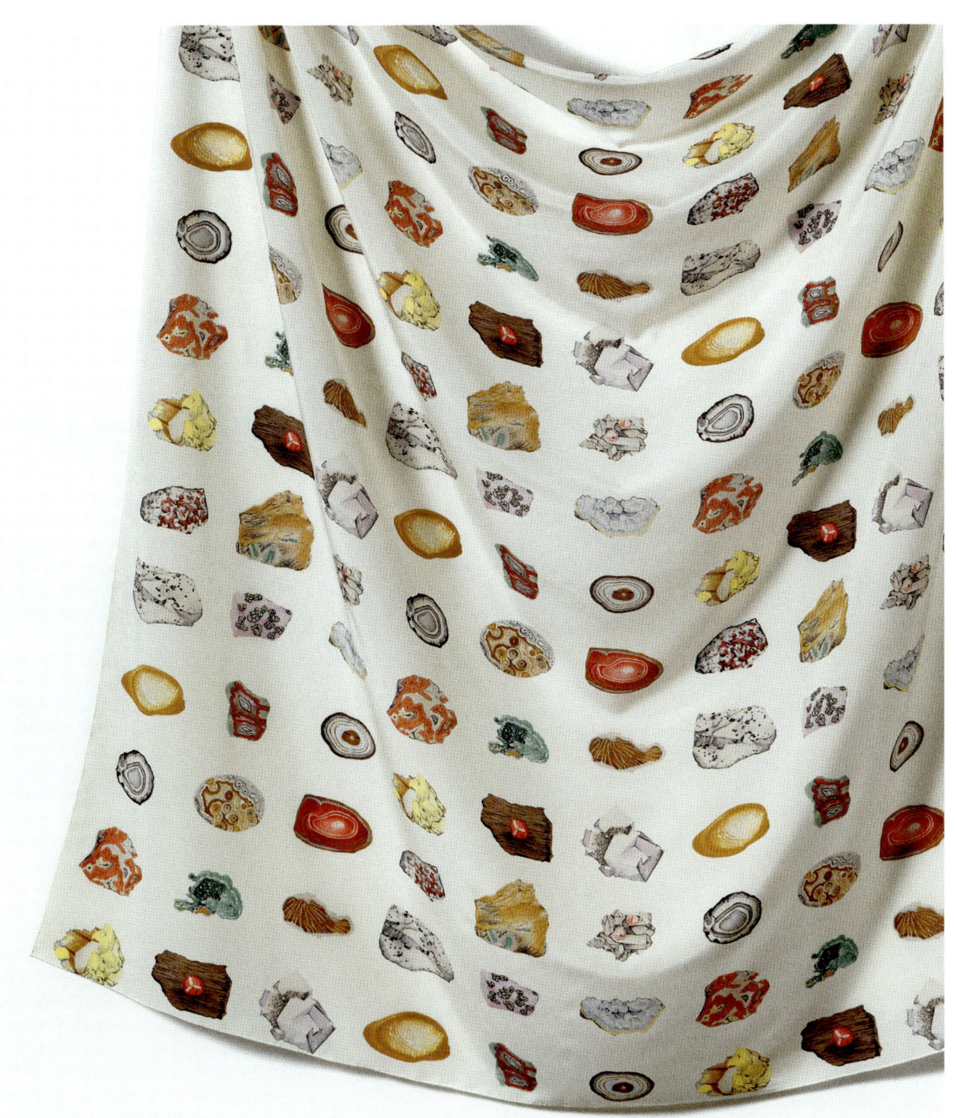

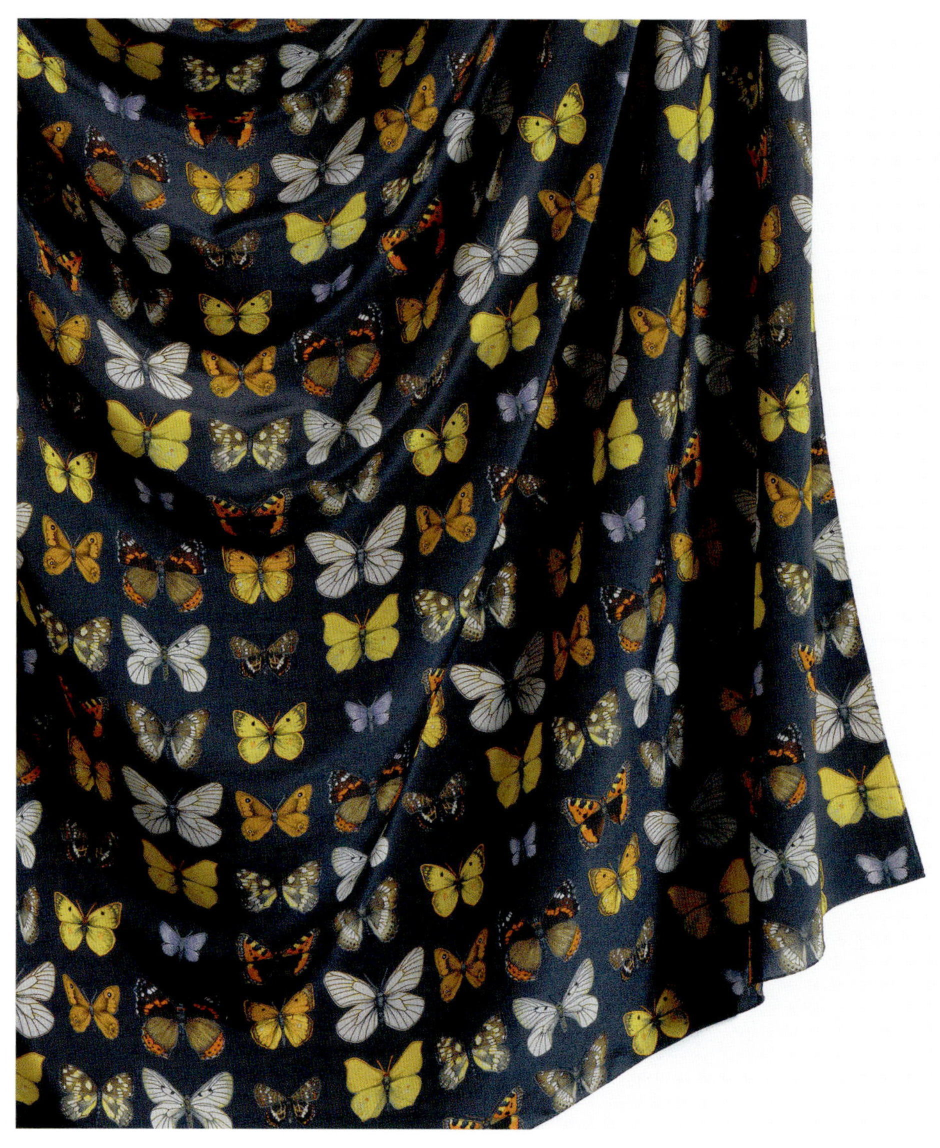

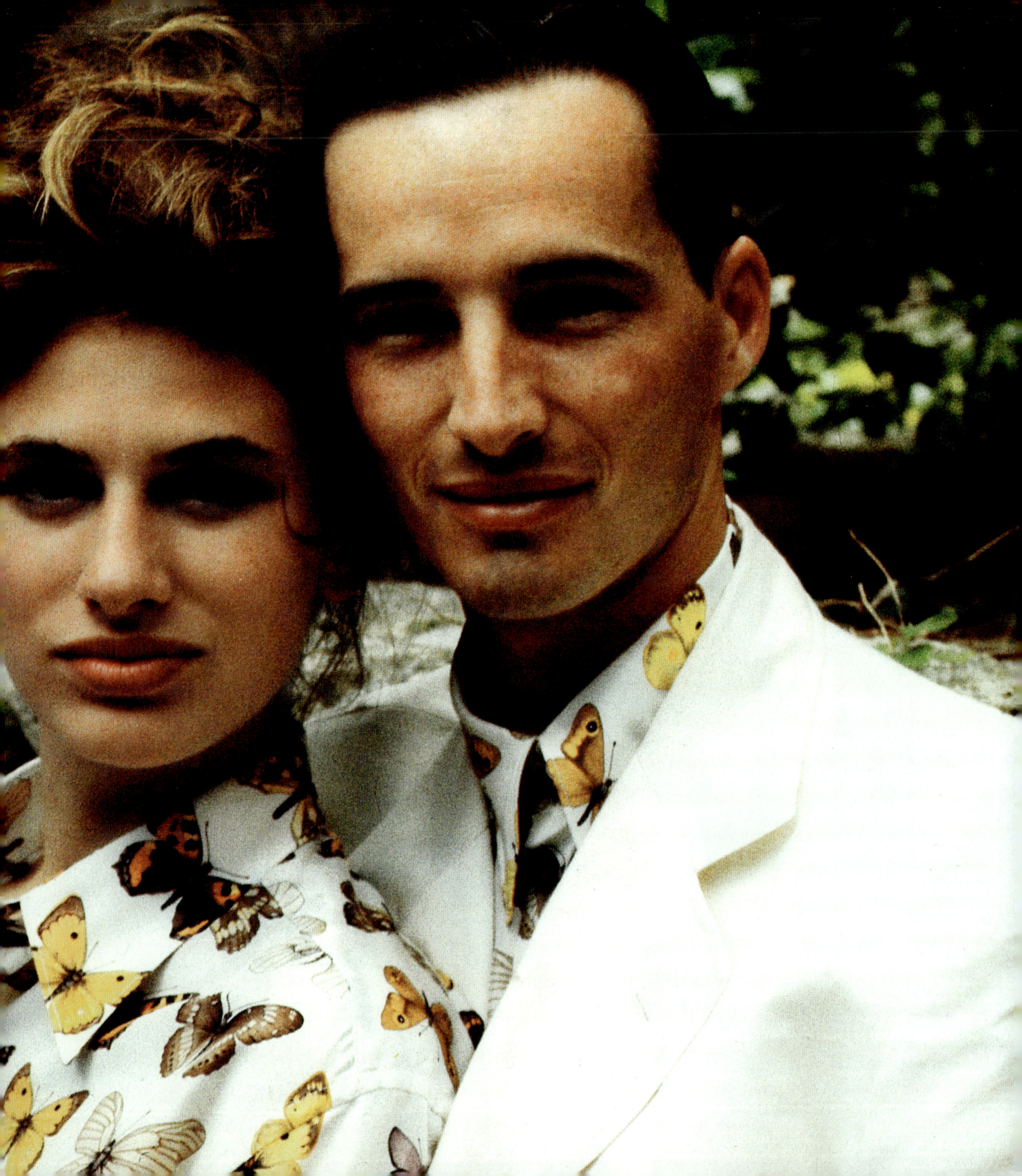

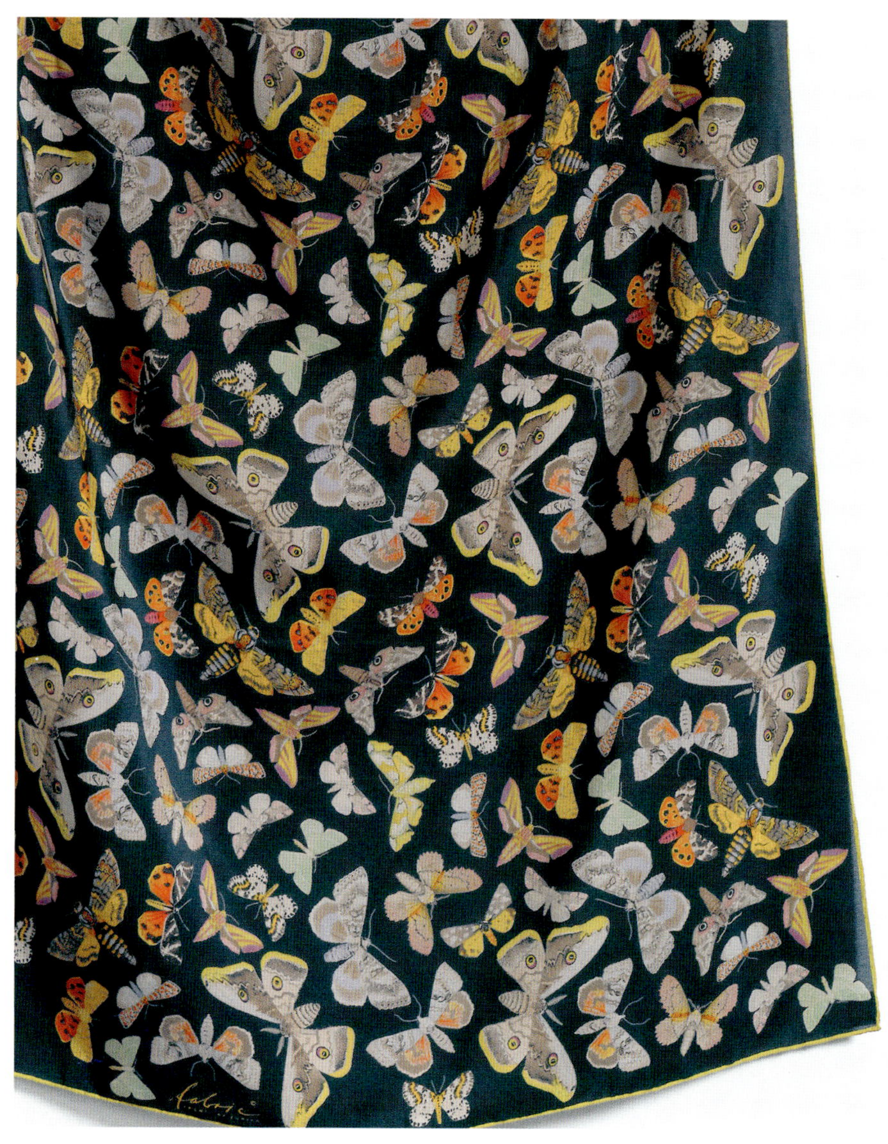

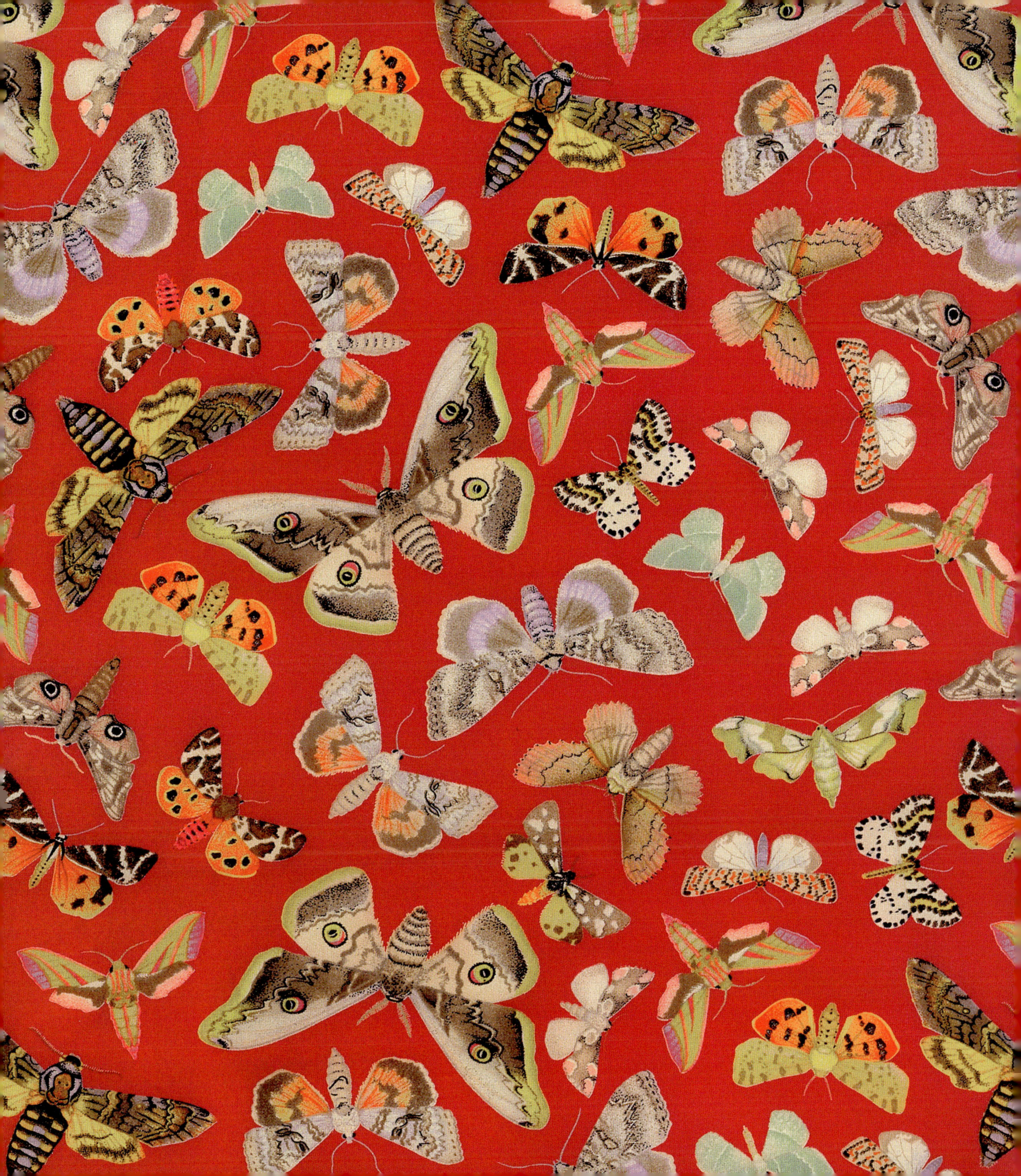

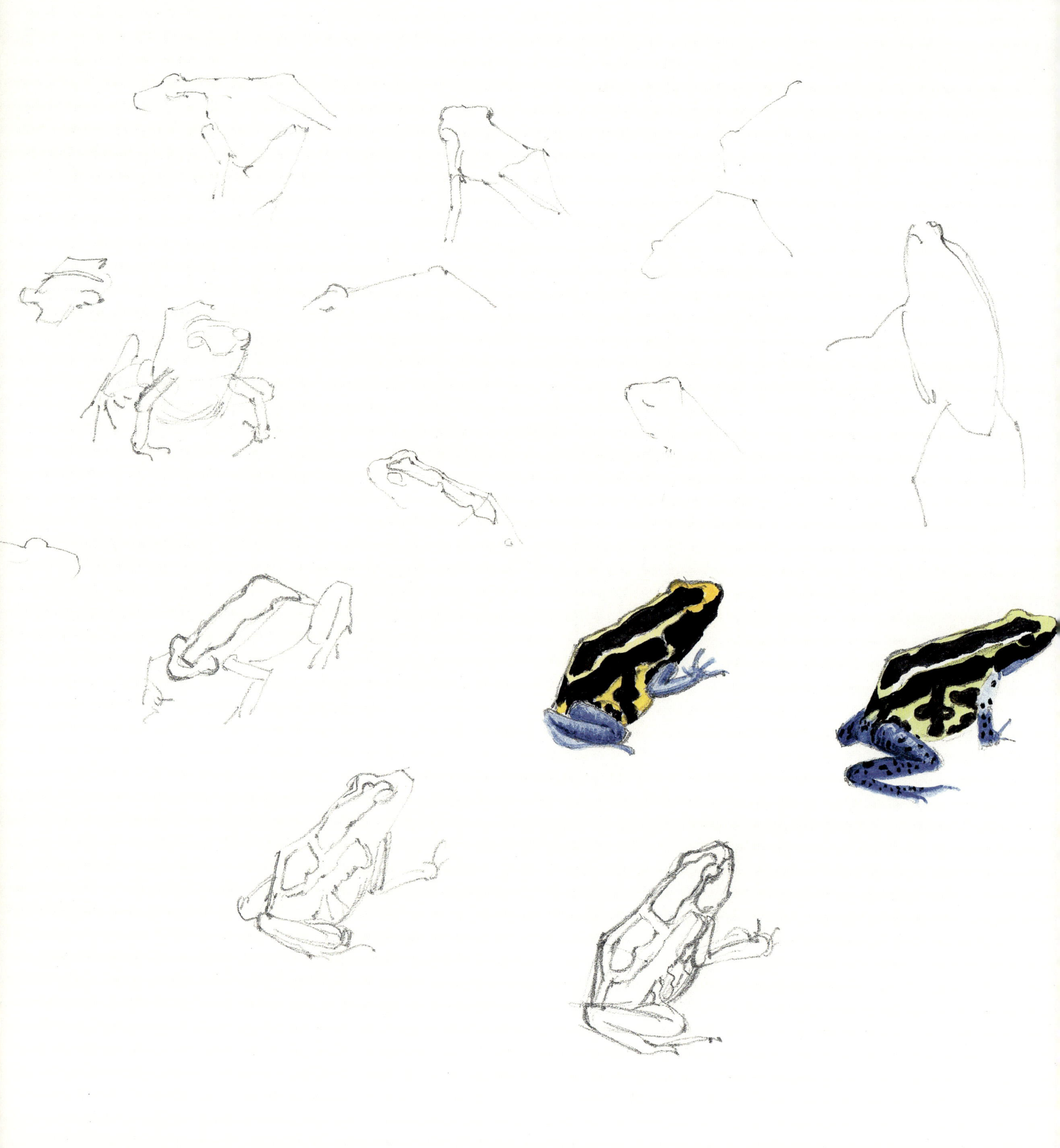

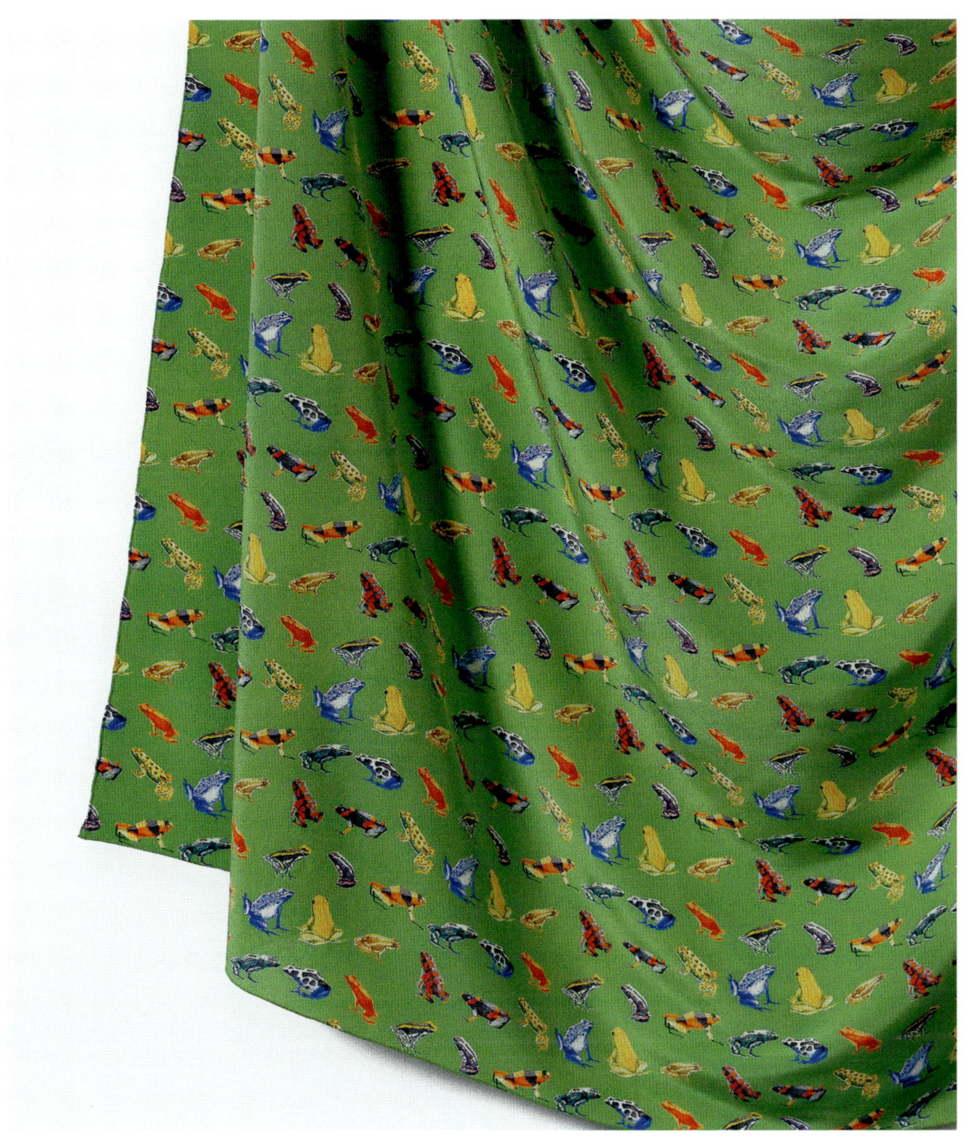

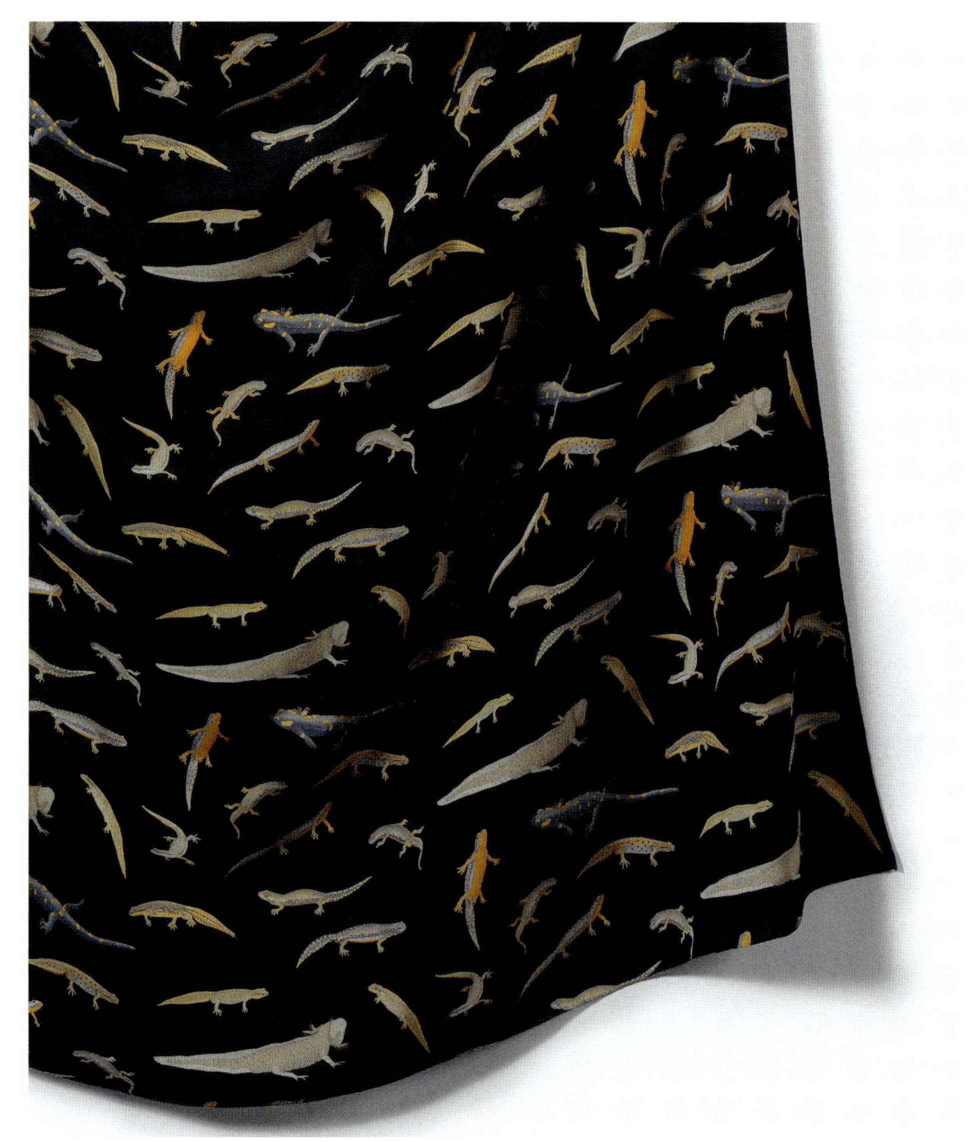

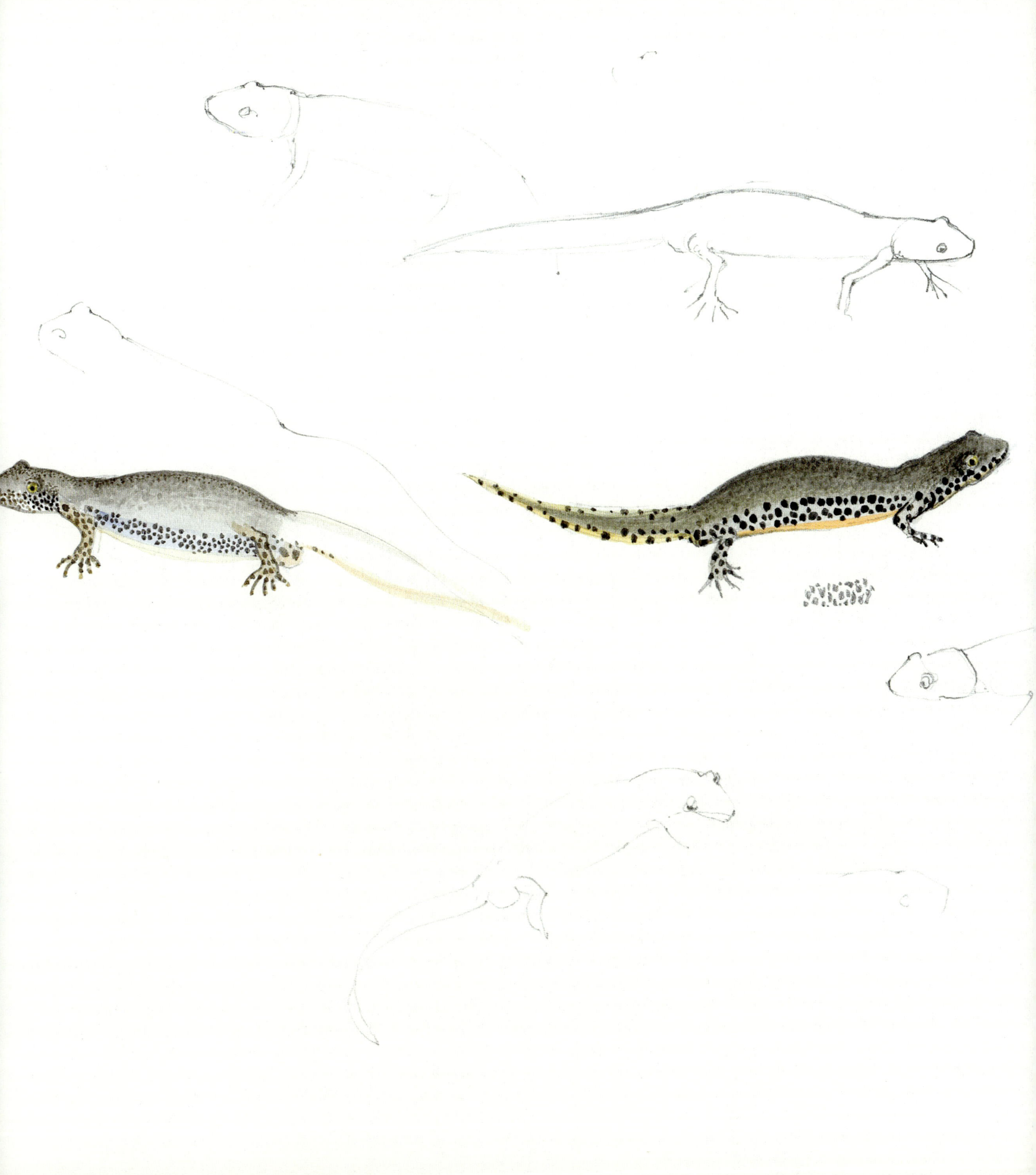

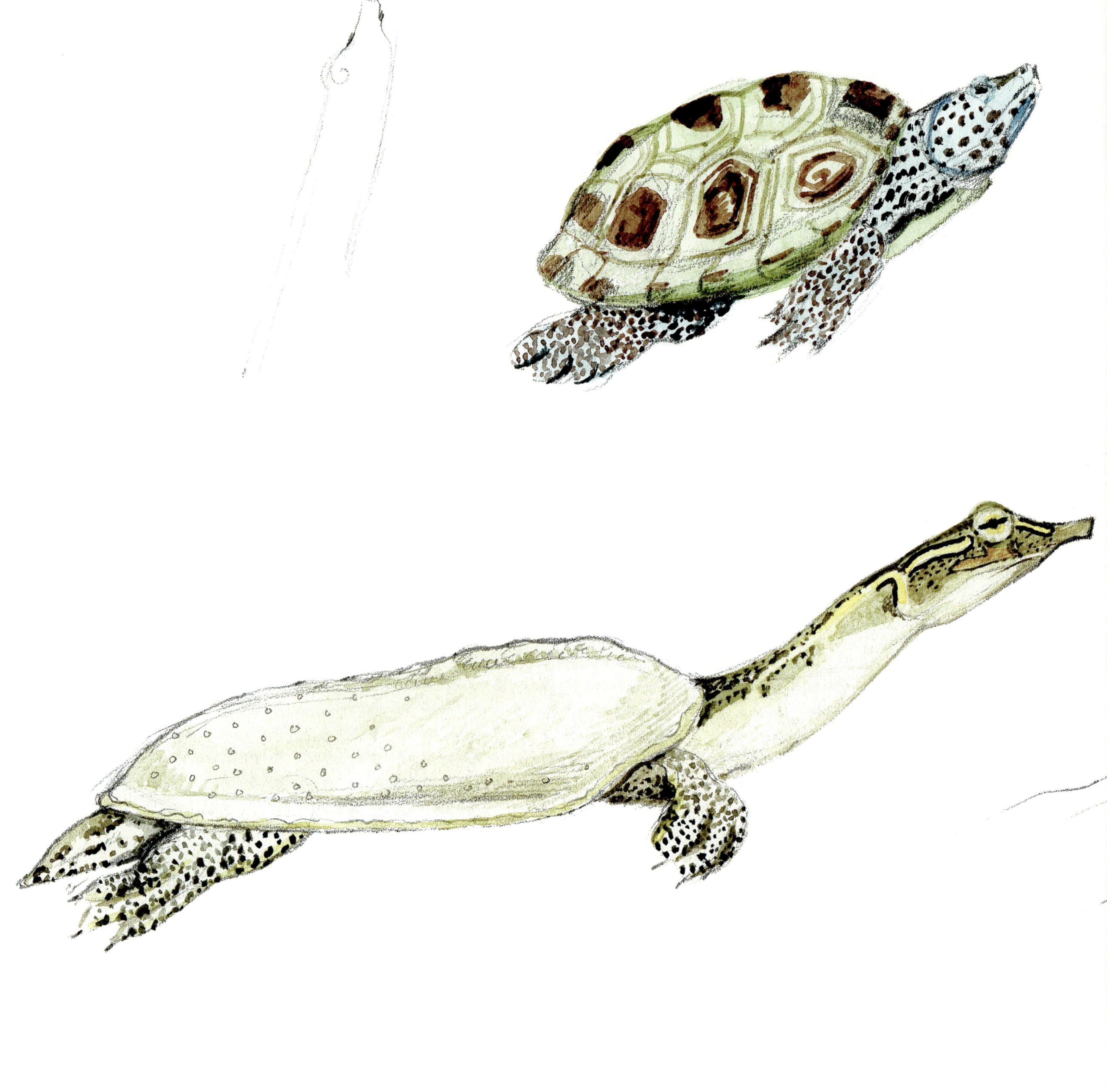

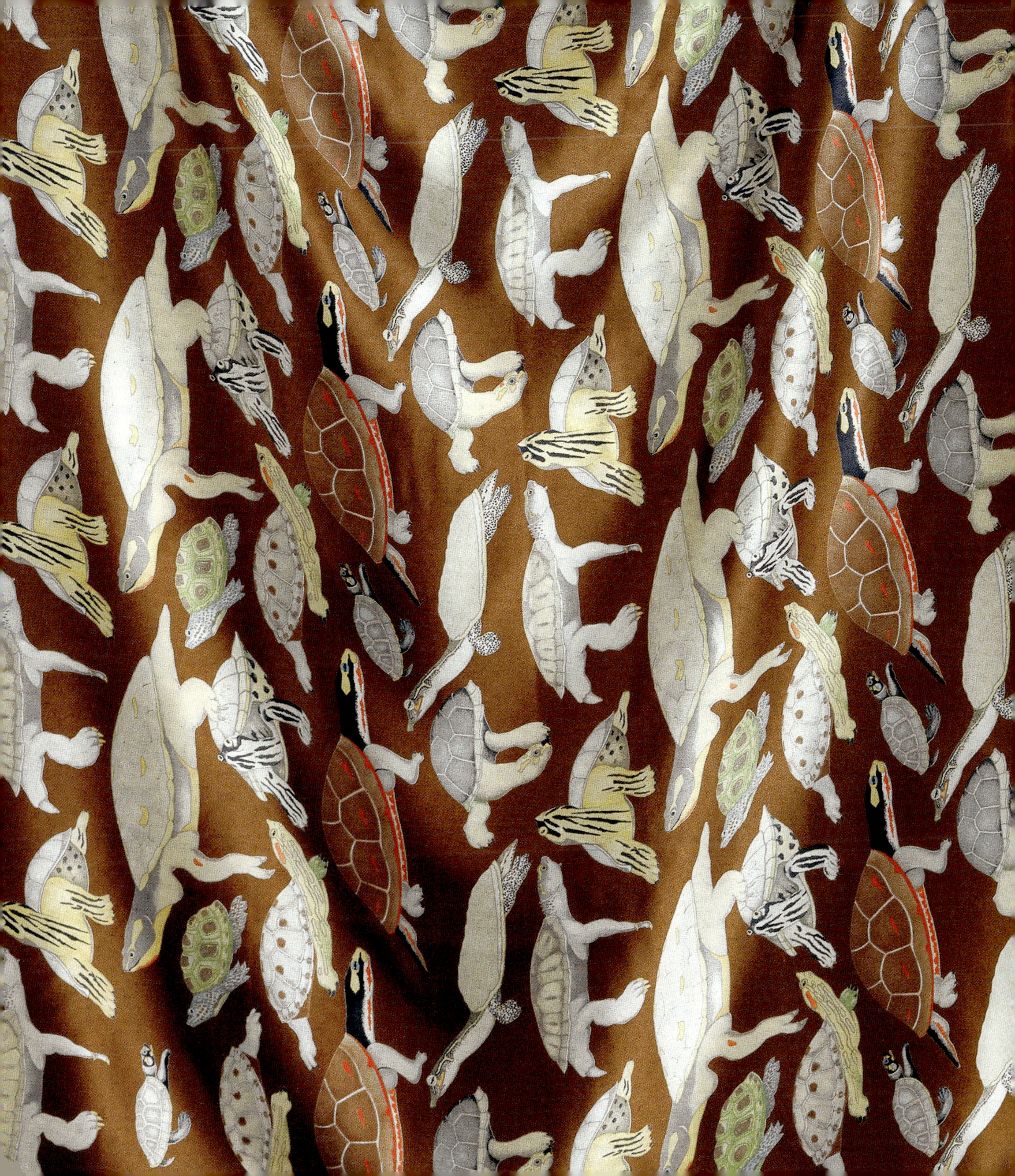

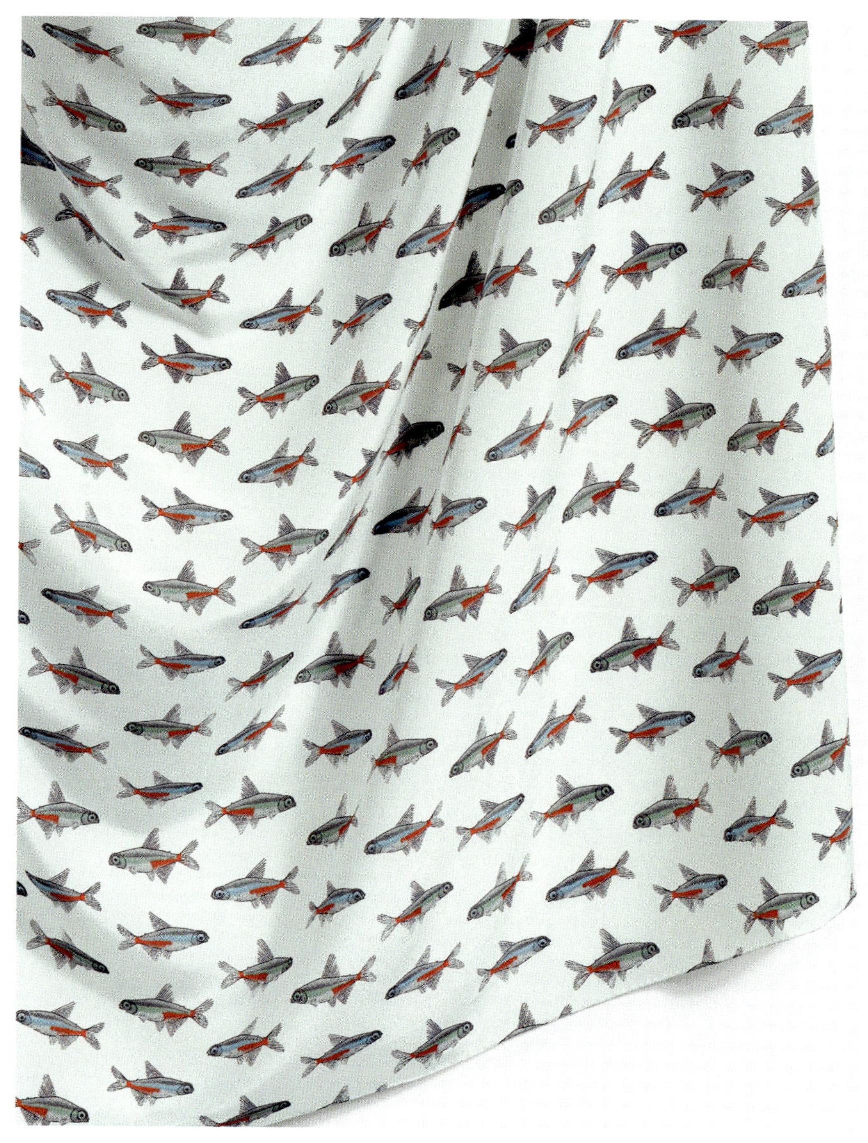

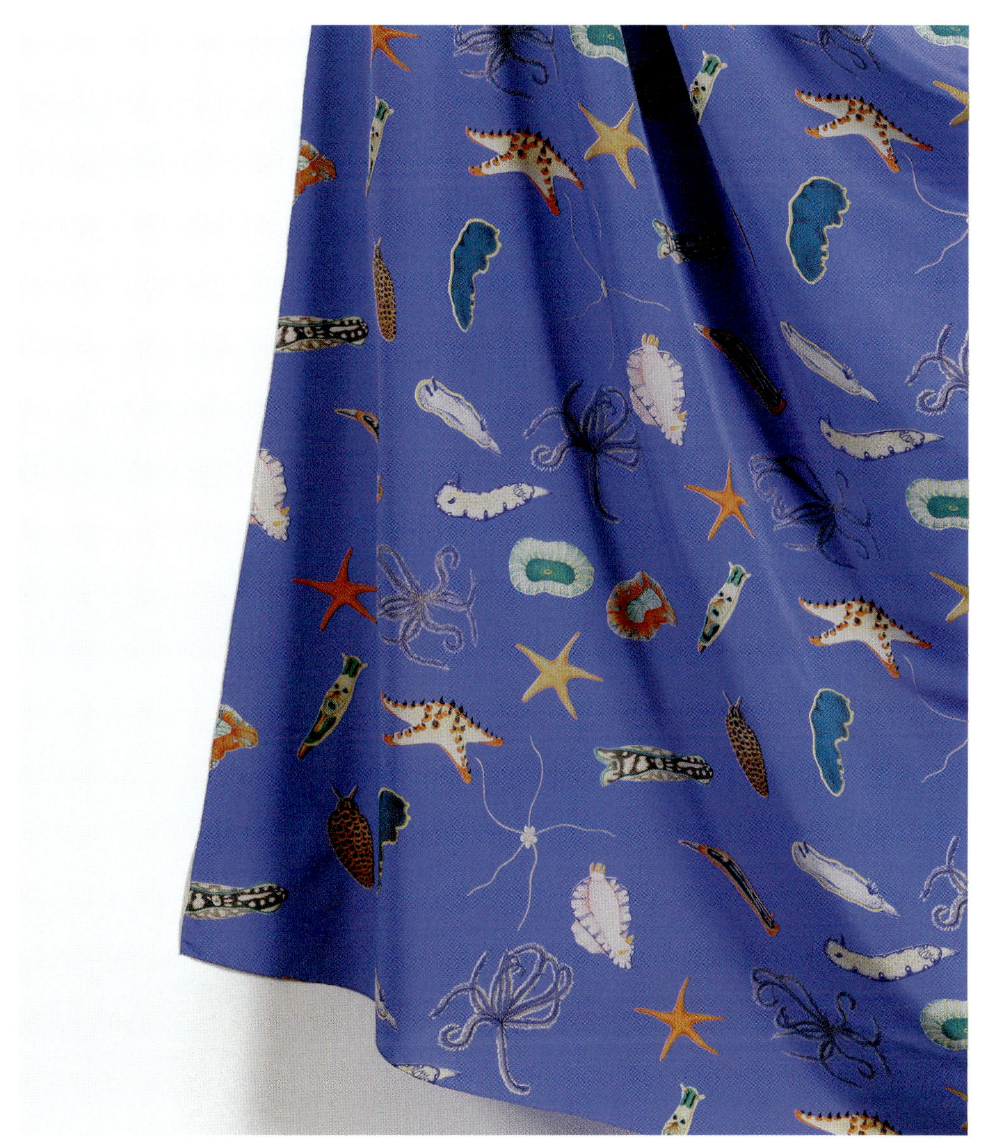

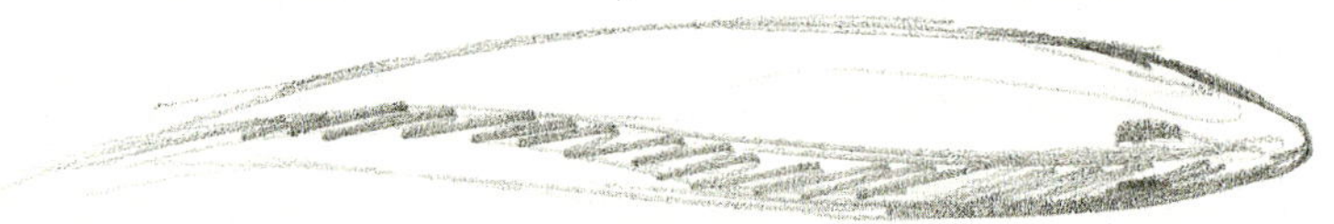
Selectie van de âse

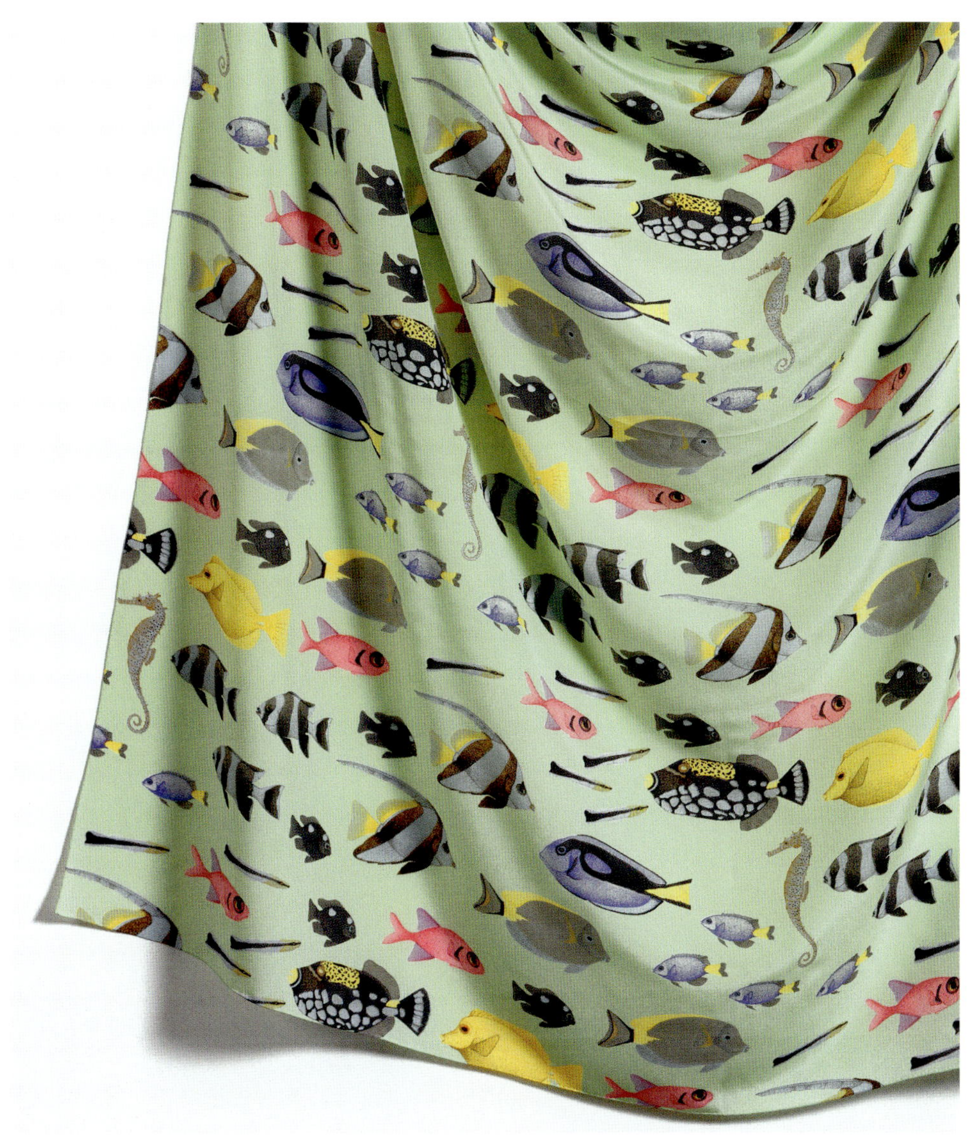

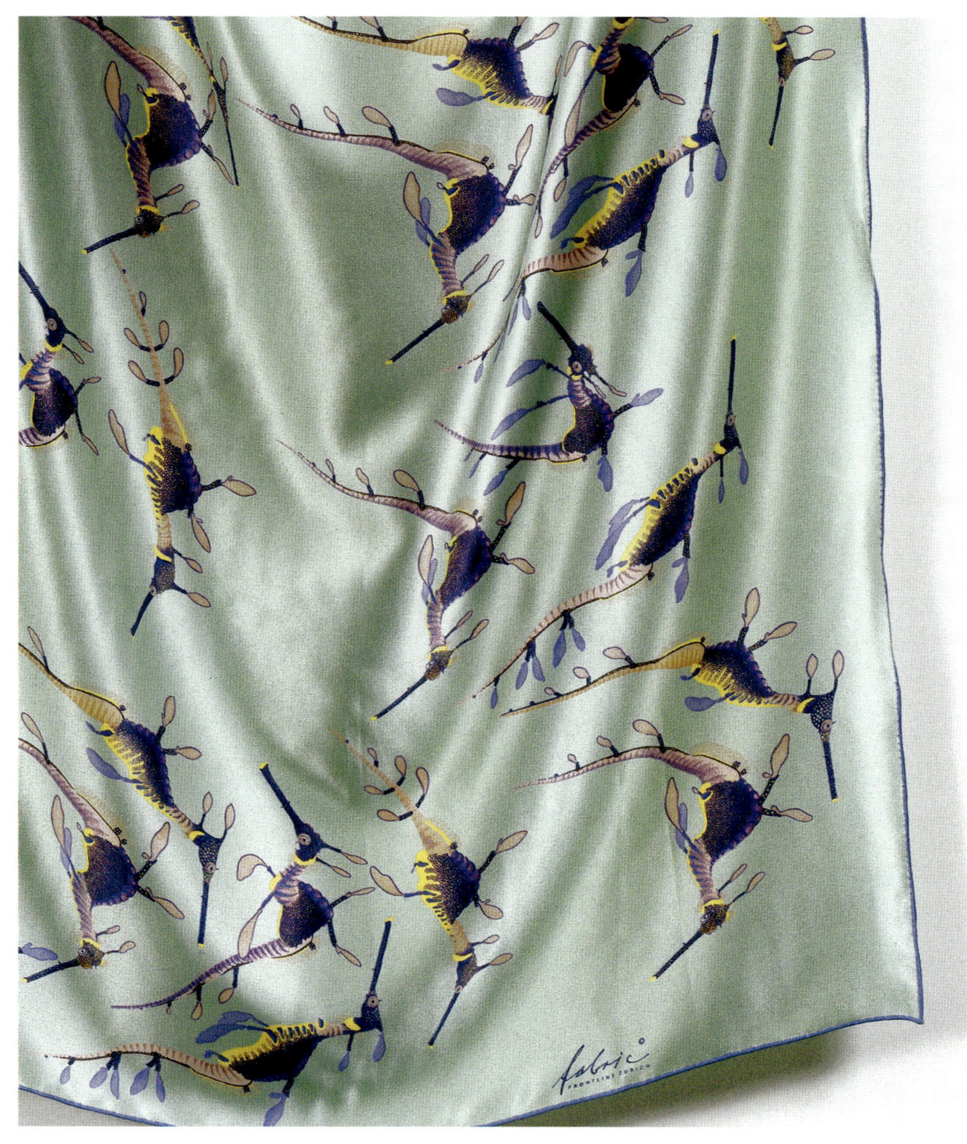

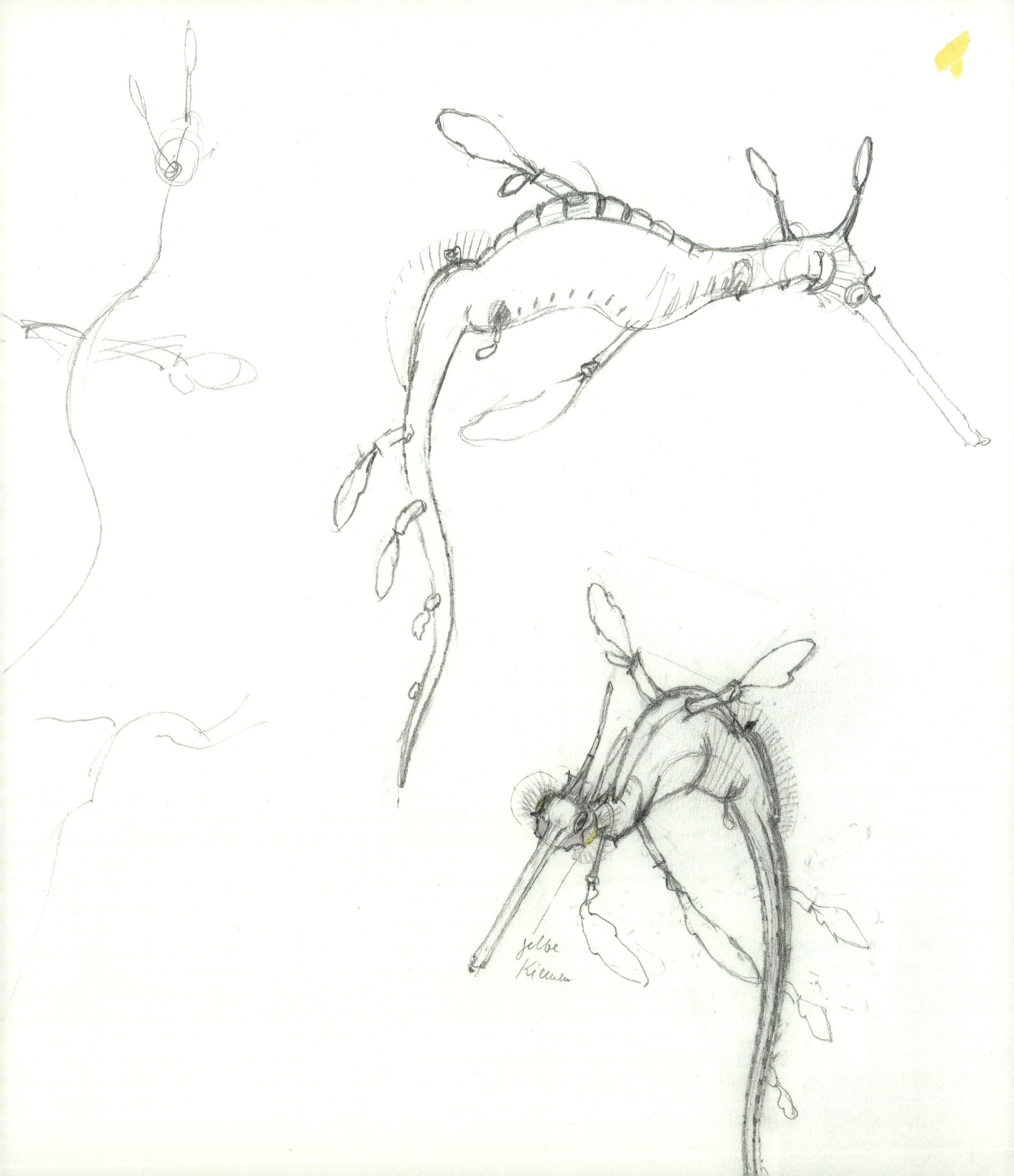
gelbe
Kiemen

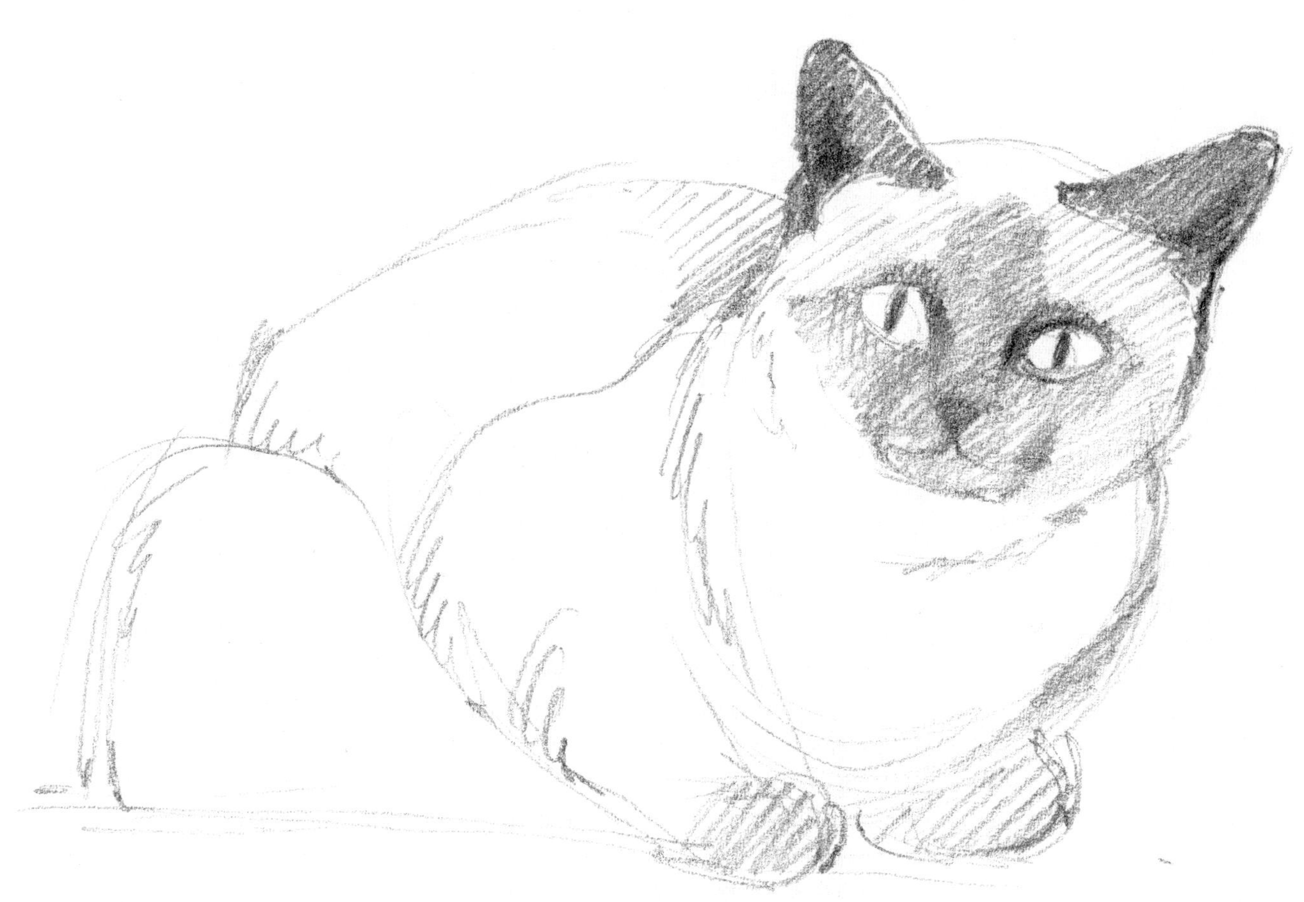

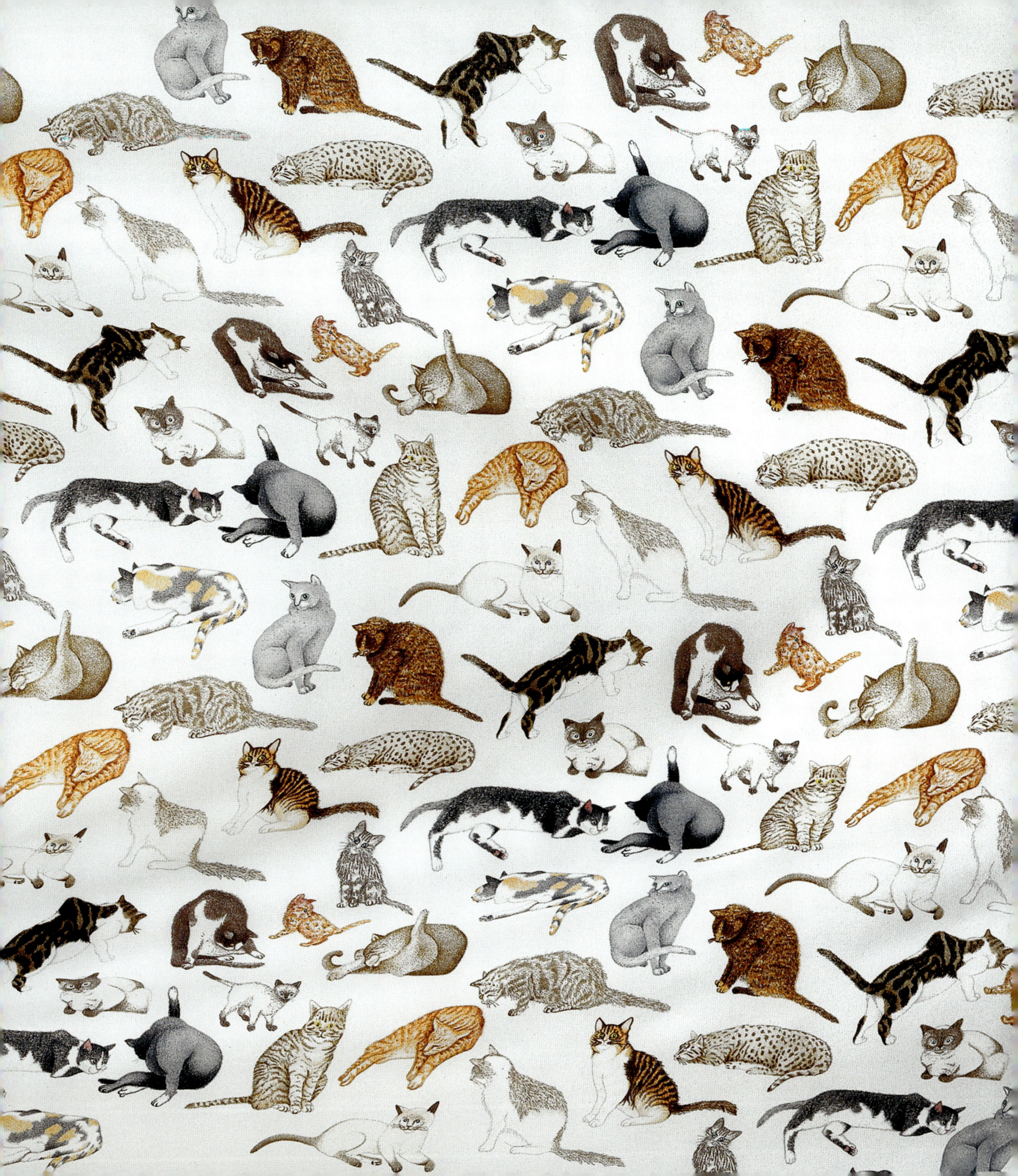

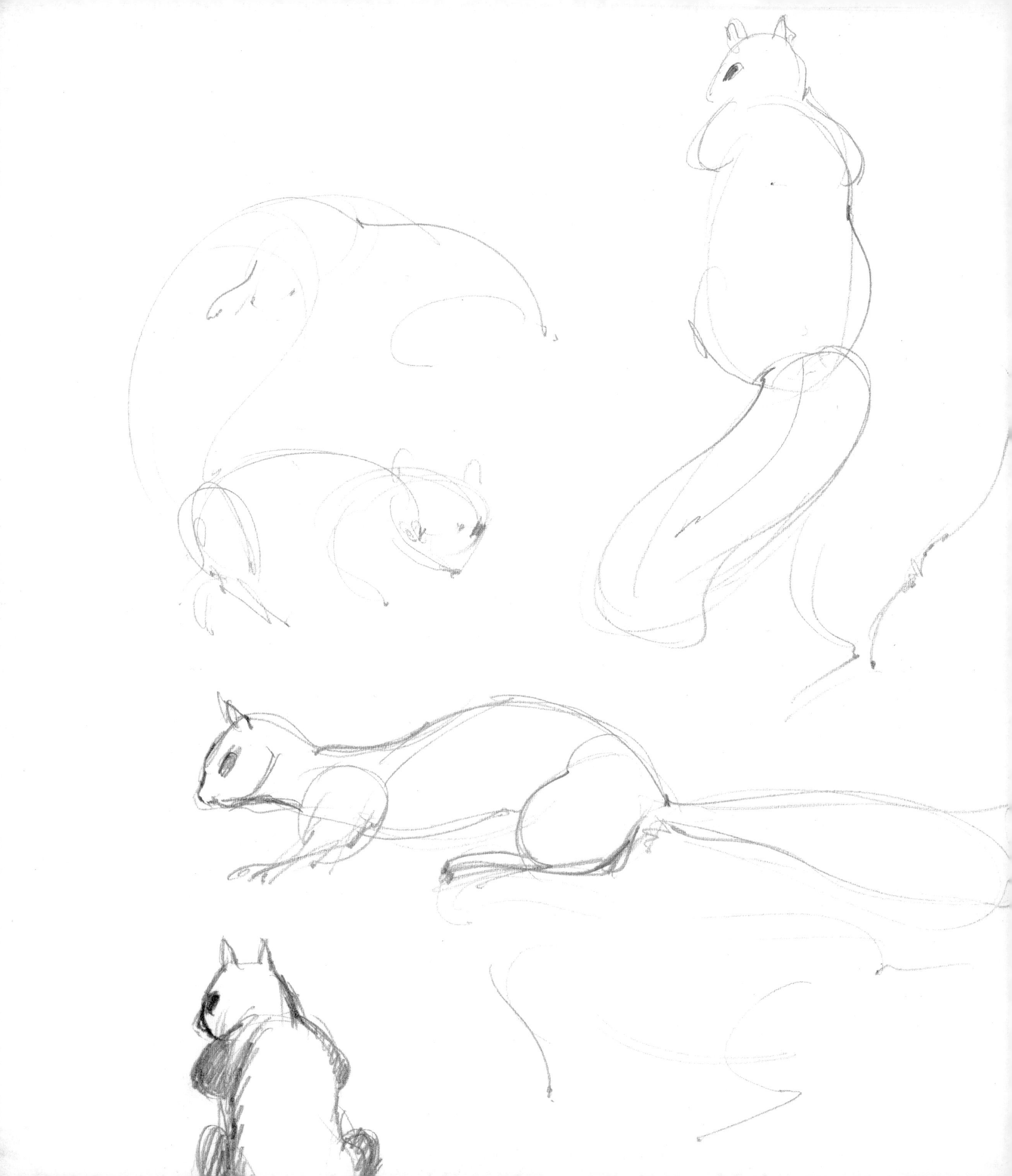

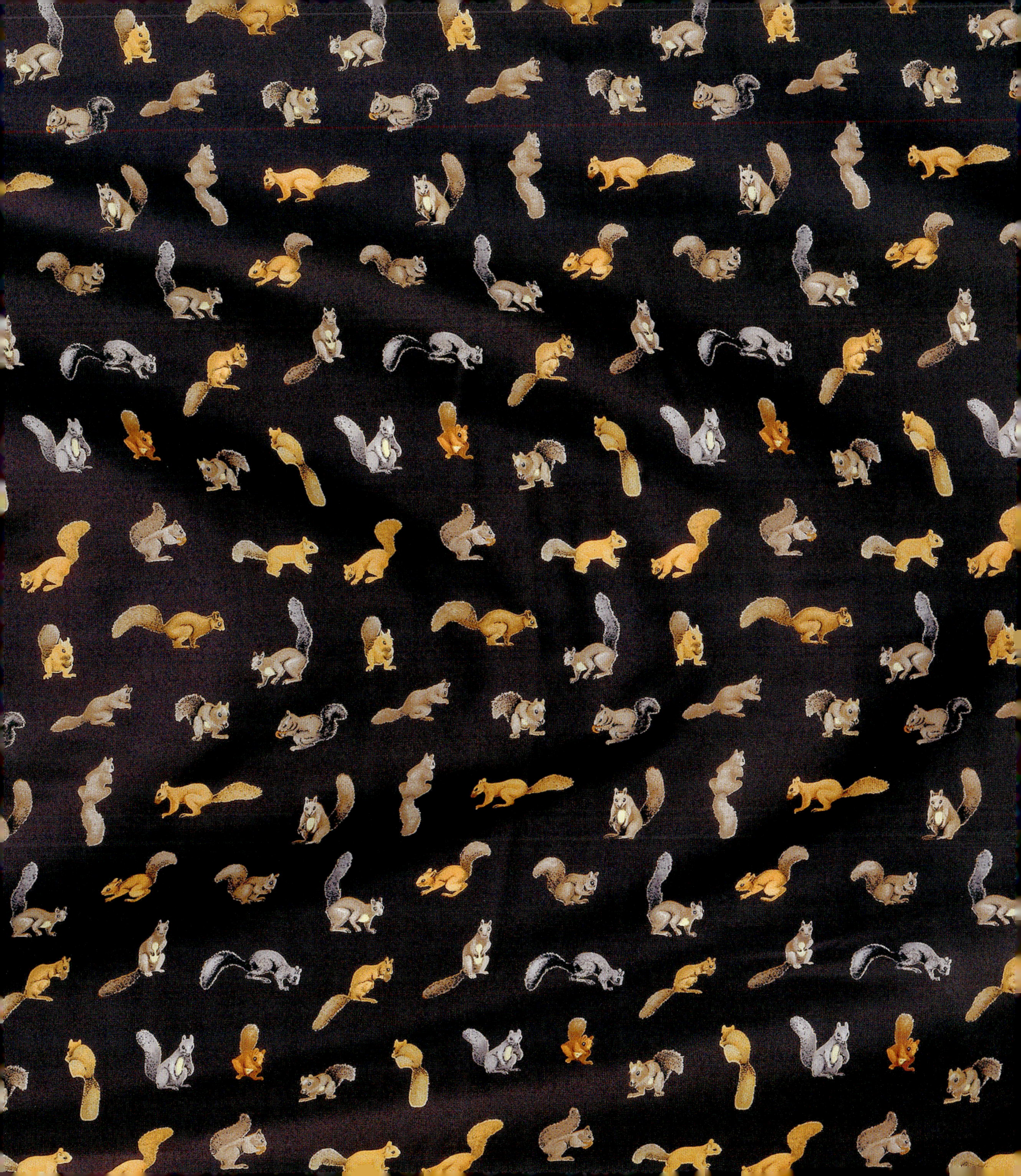

Die Mode ist Abbild einer Zeitkultur.
Fashion mirrors contemporary culture.

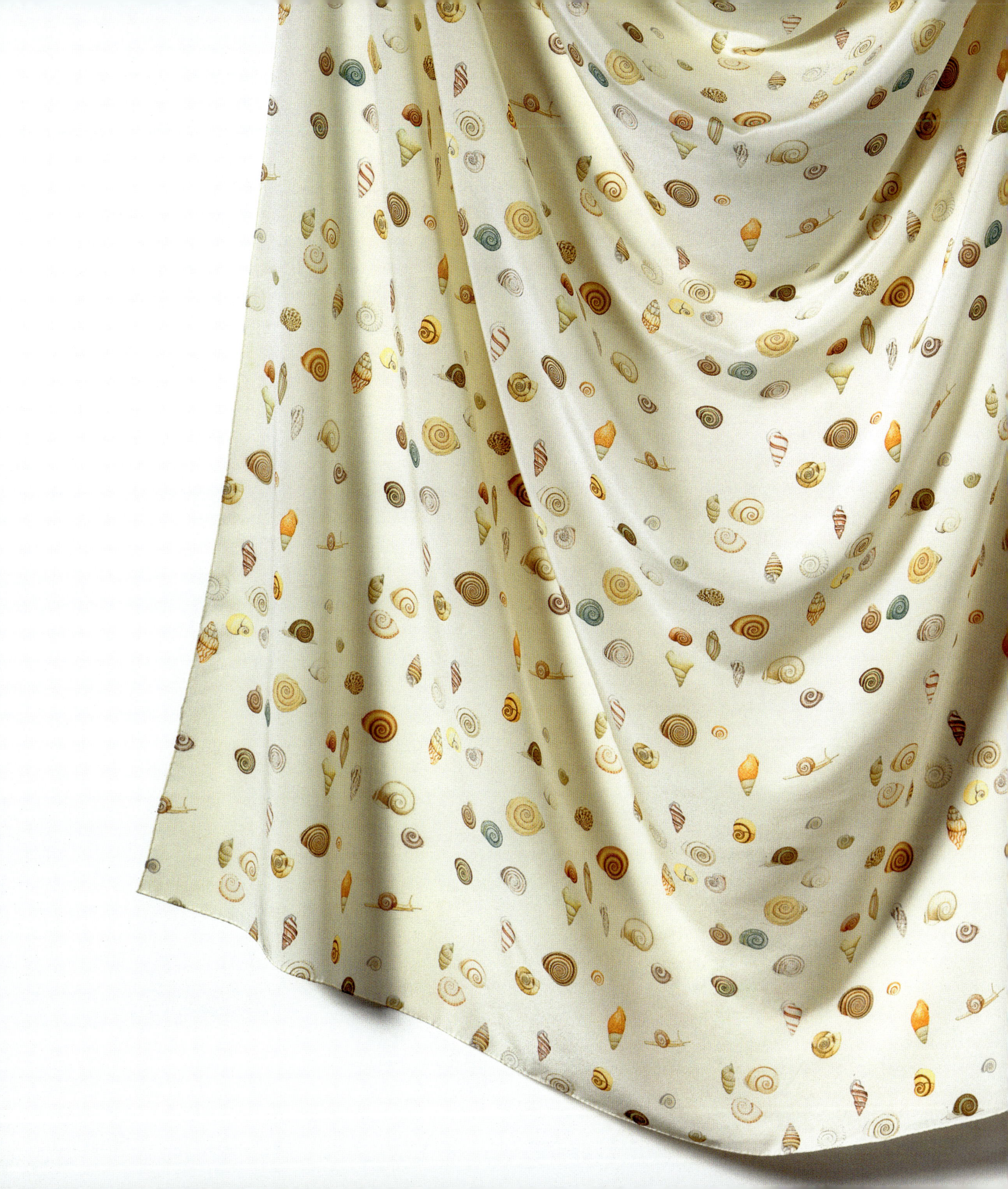

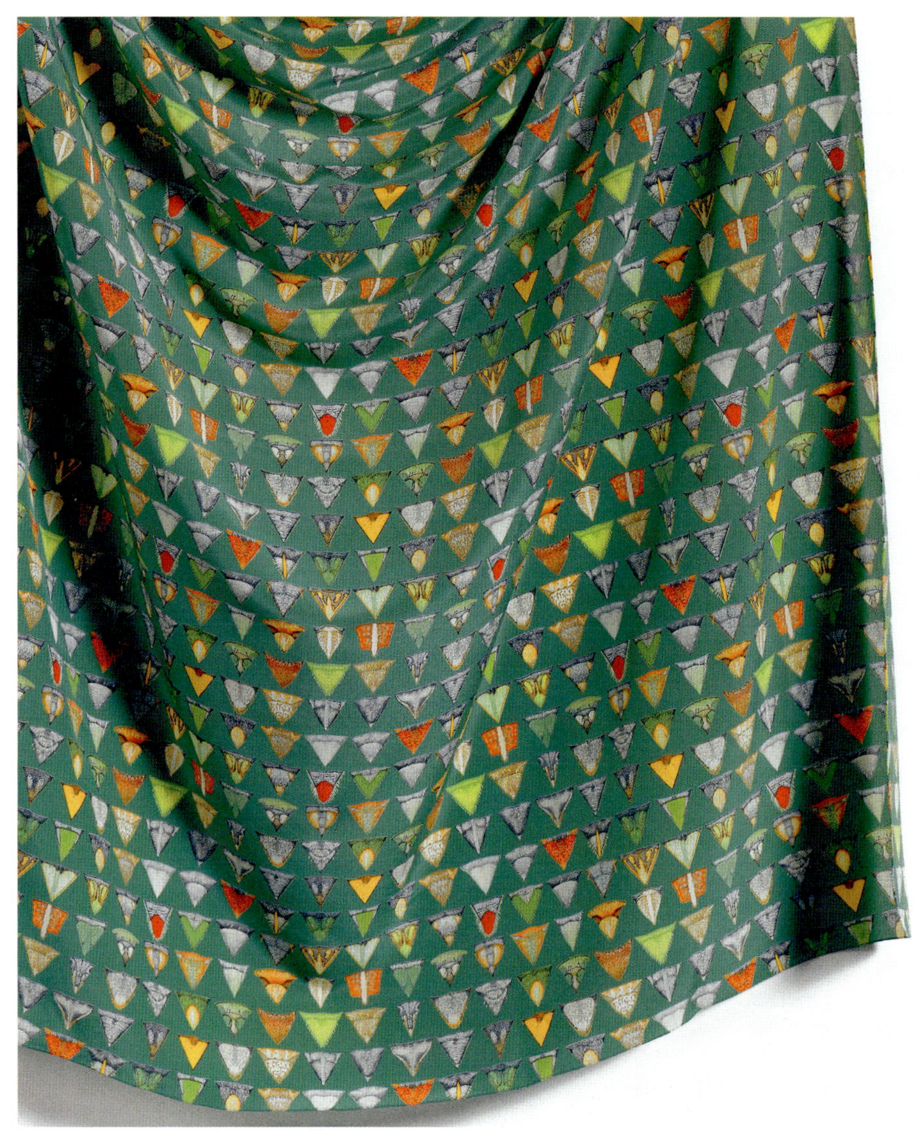

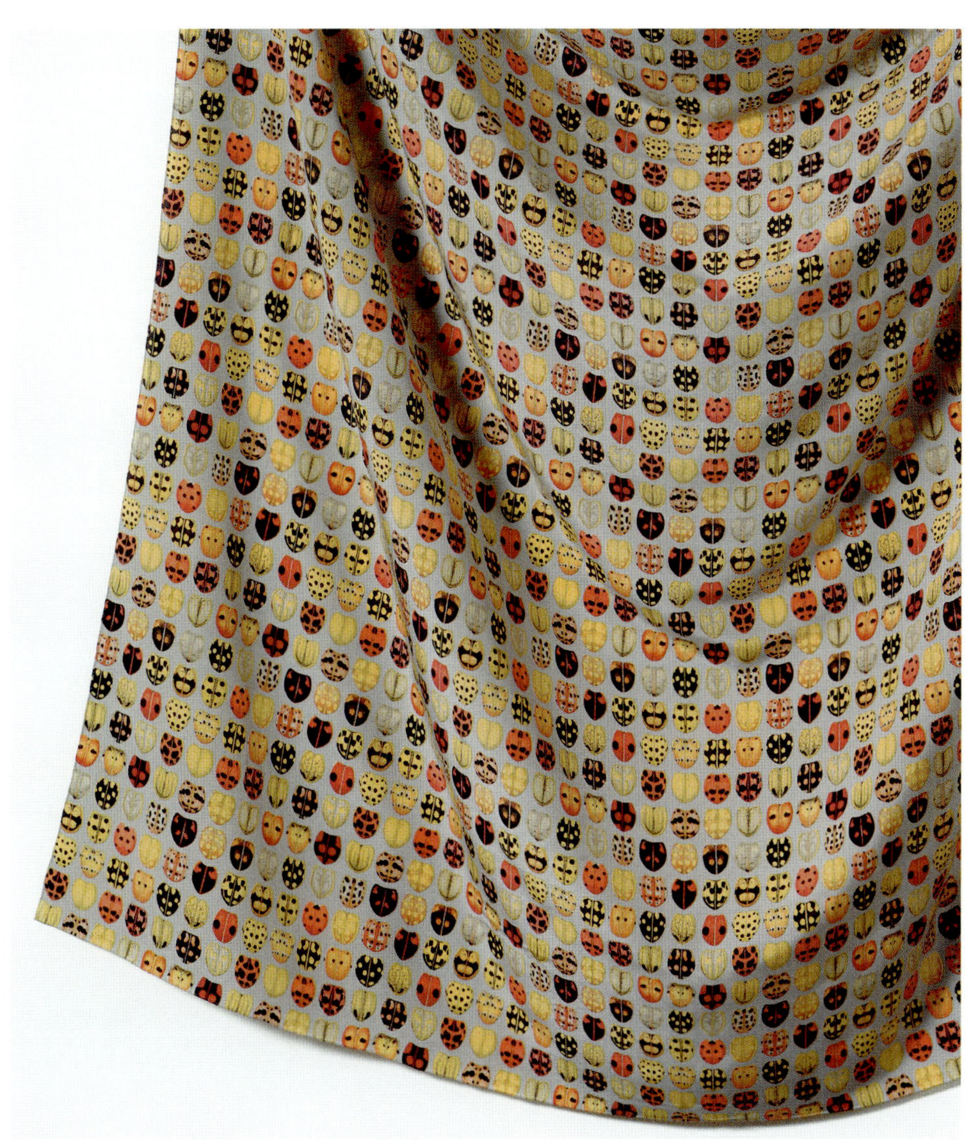

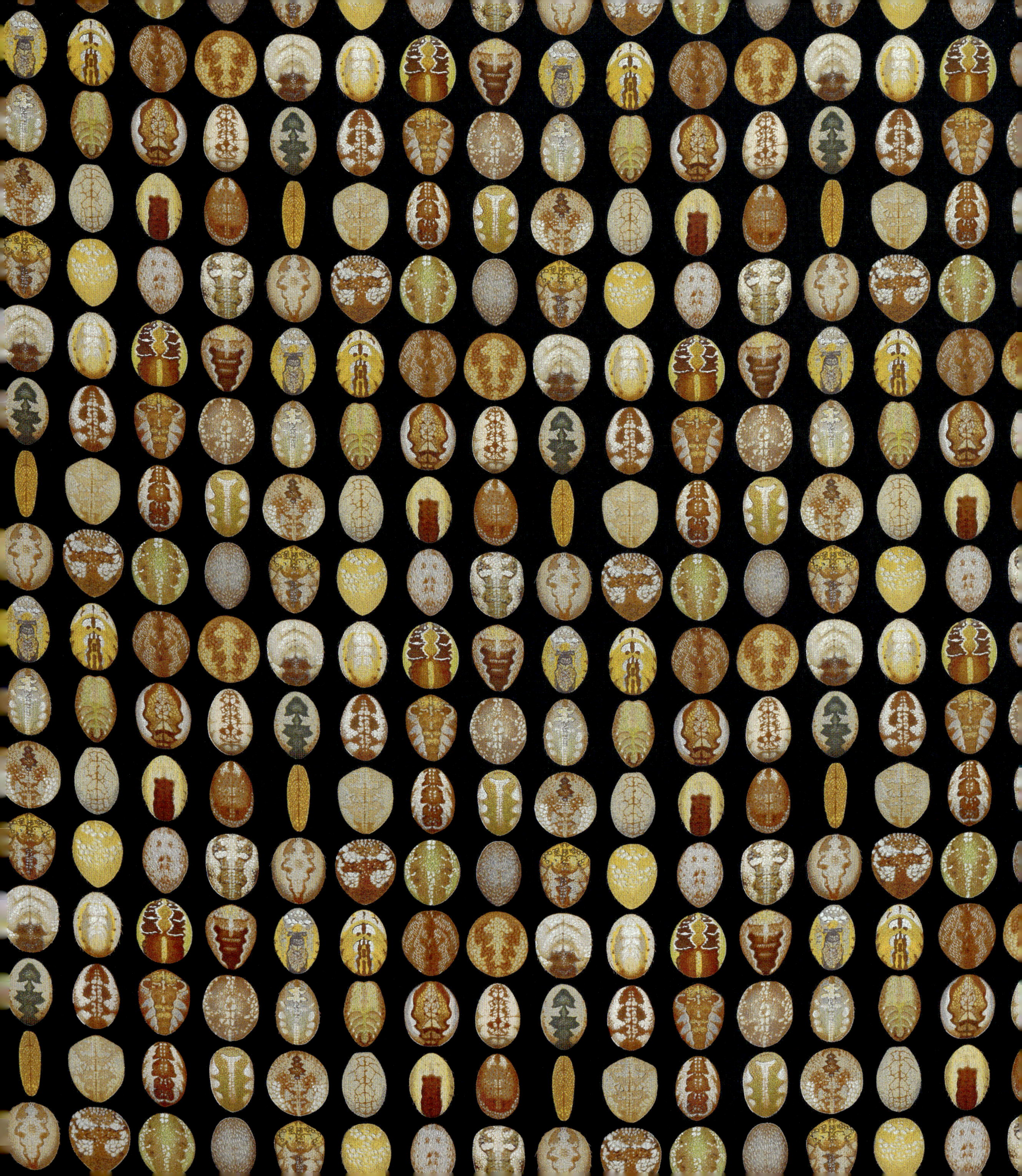

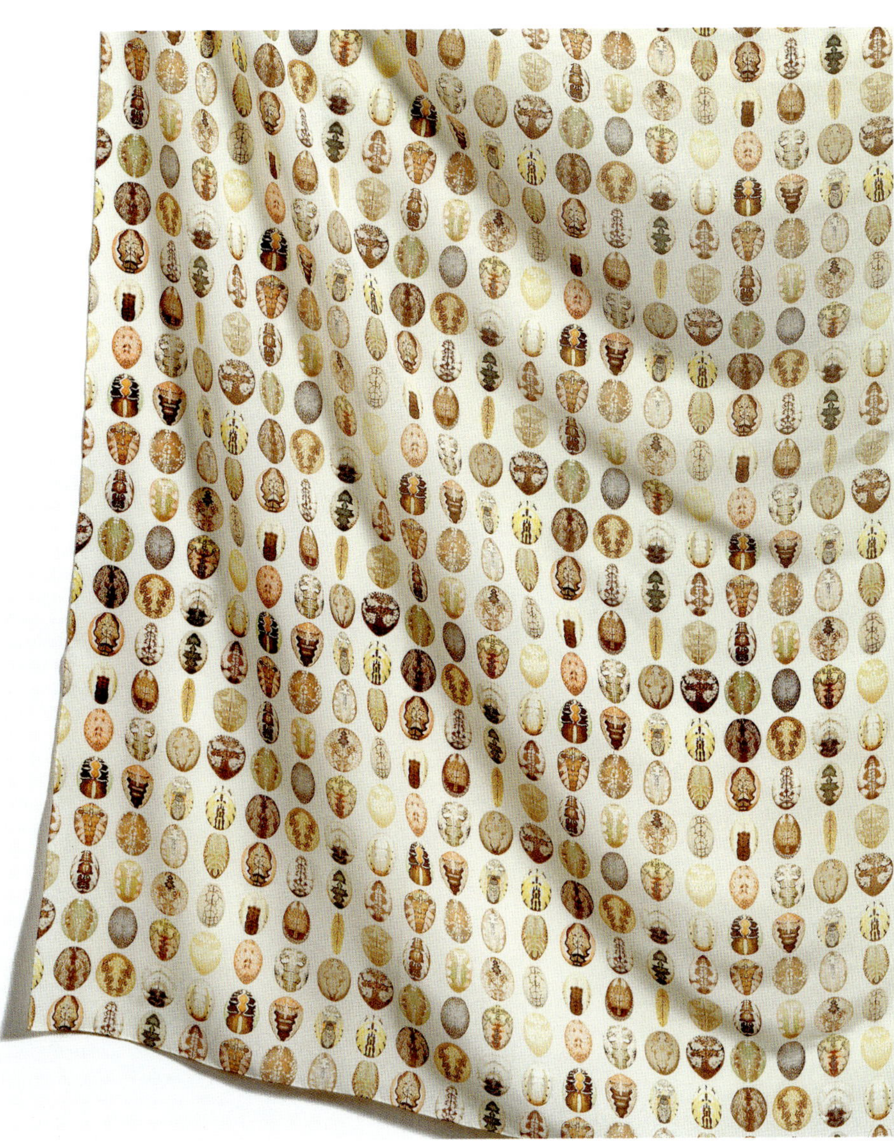

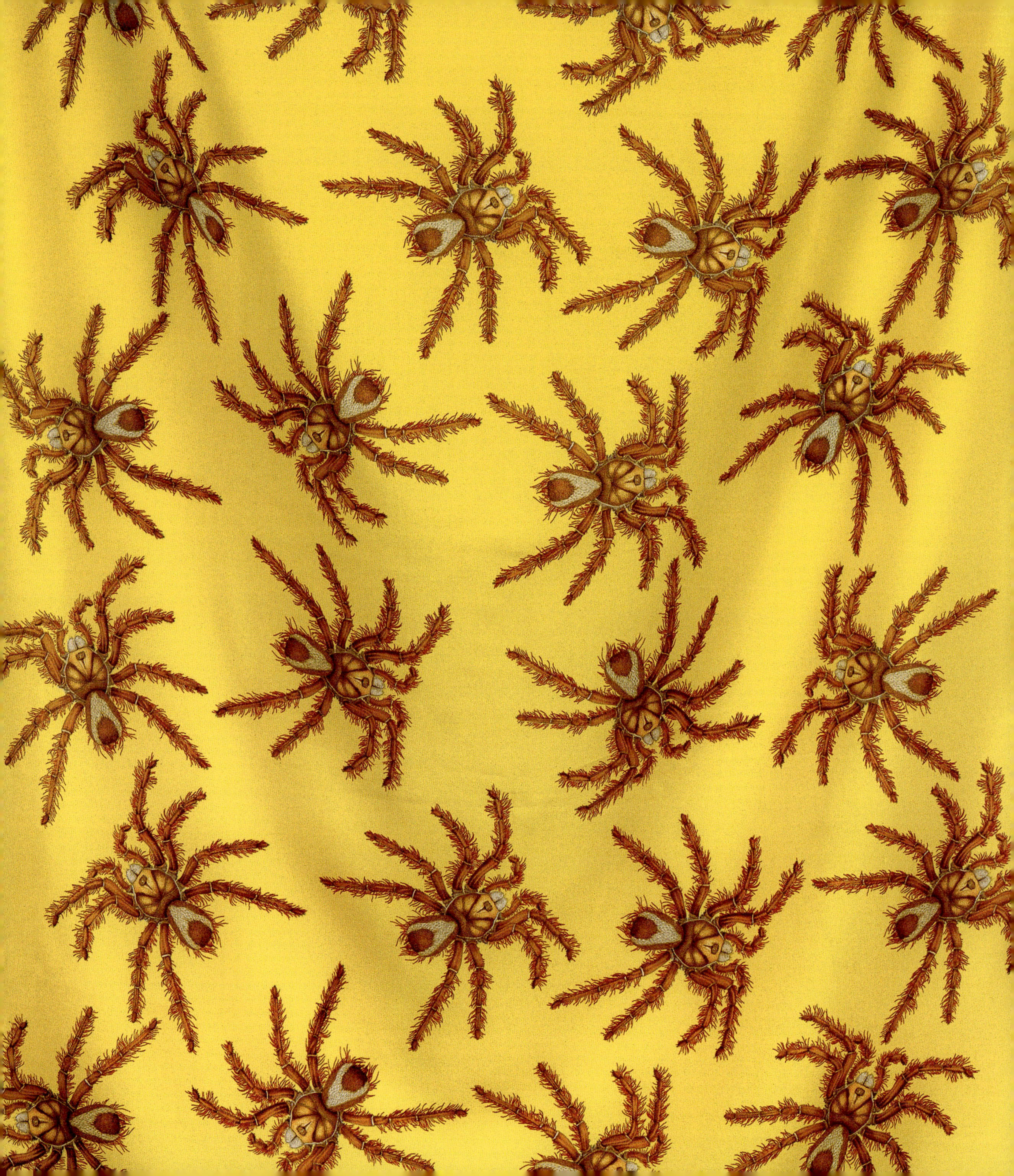

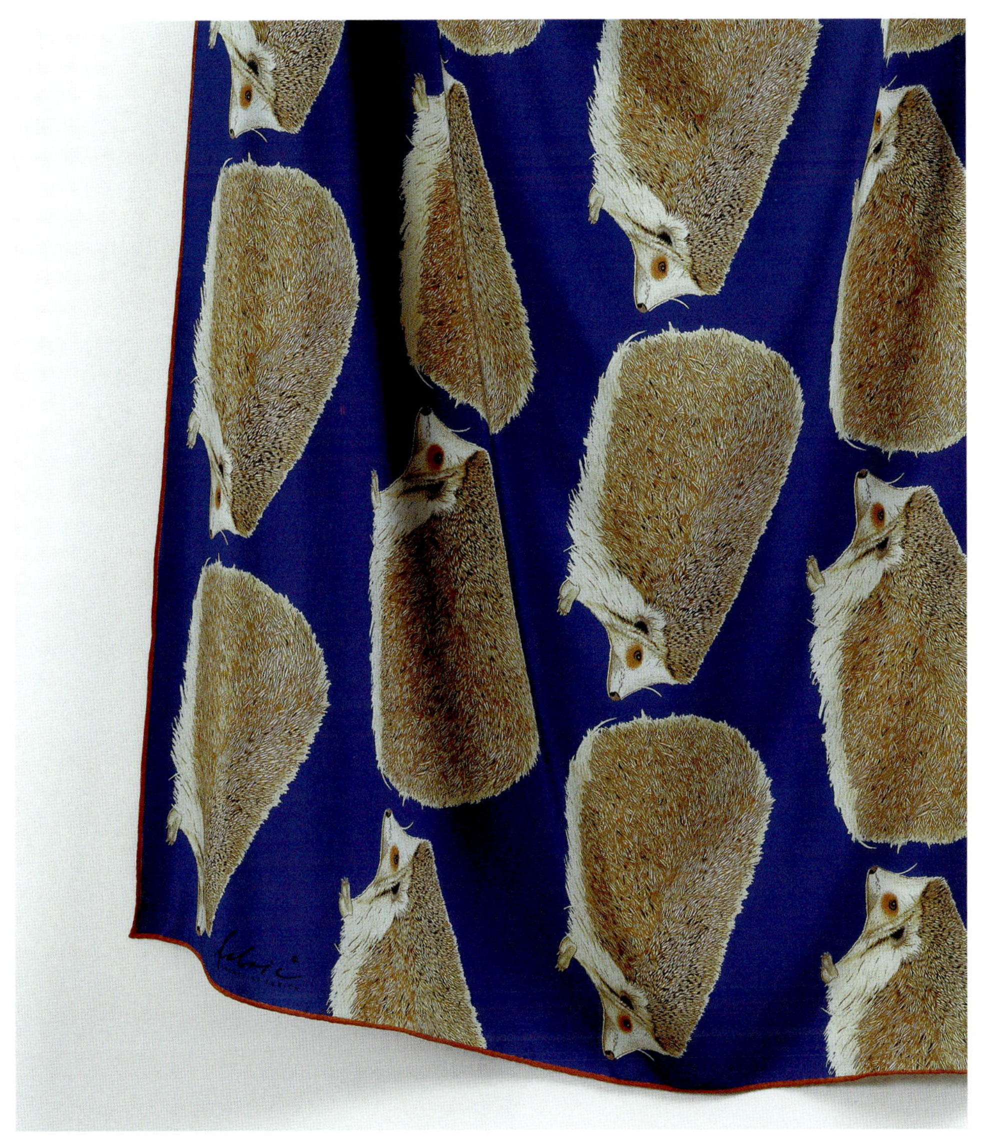

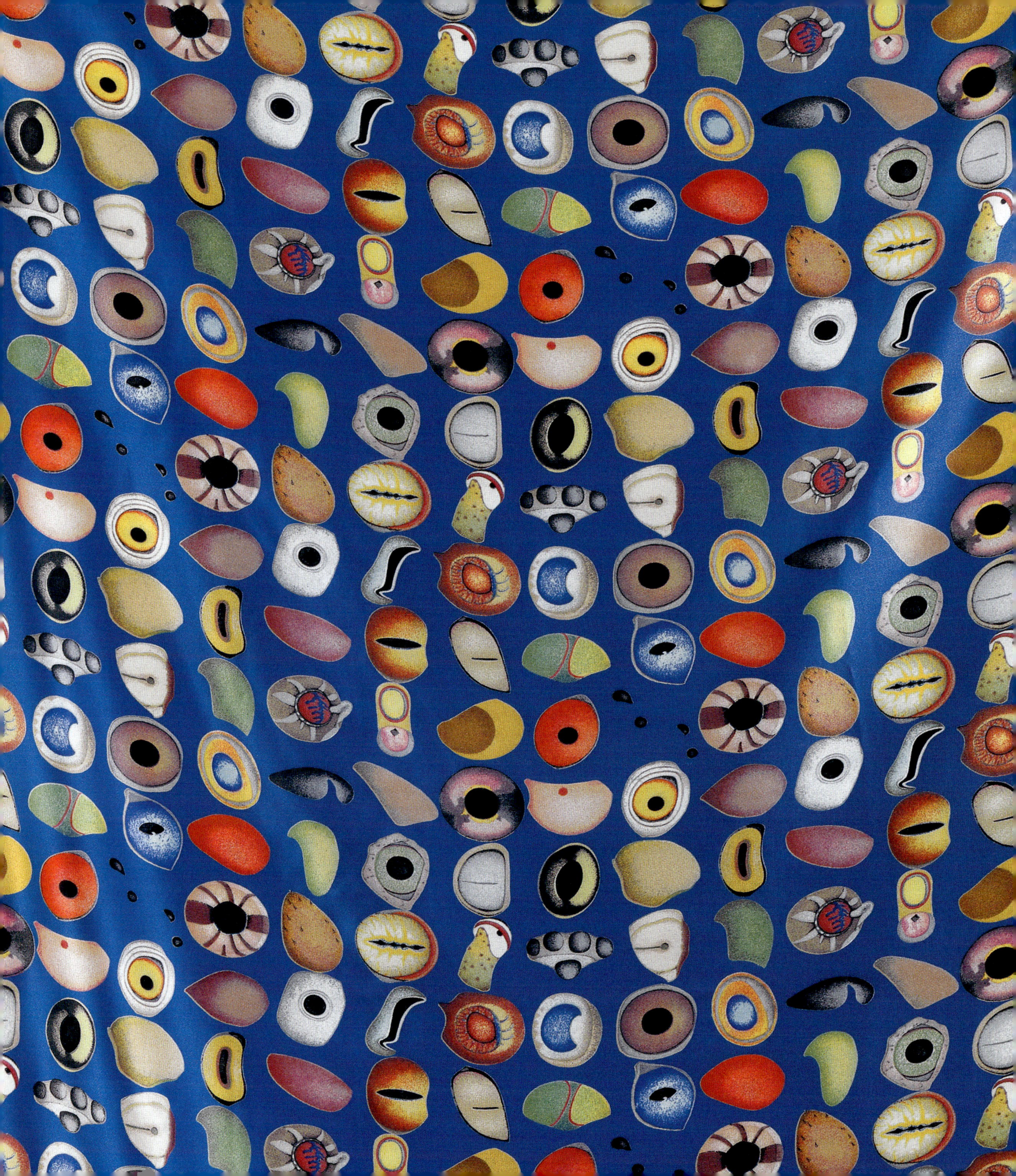

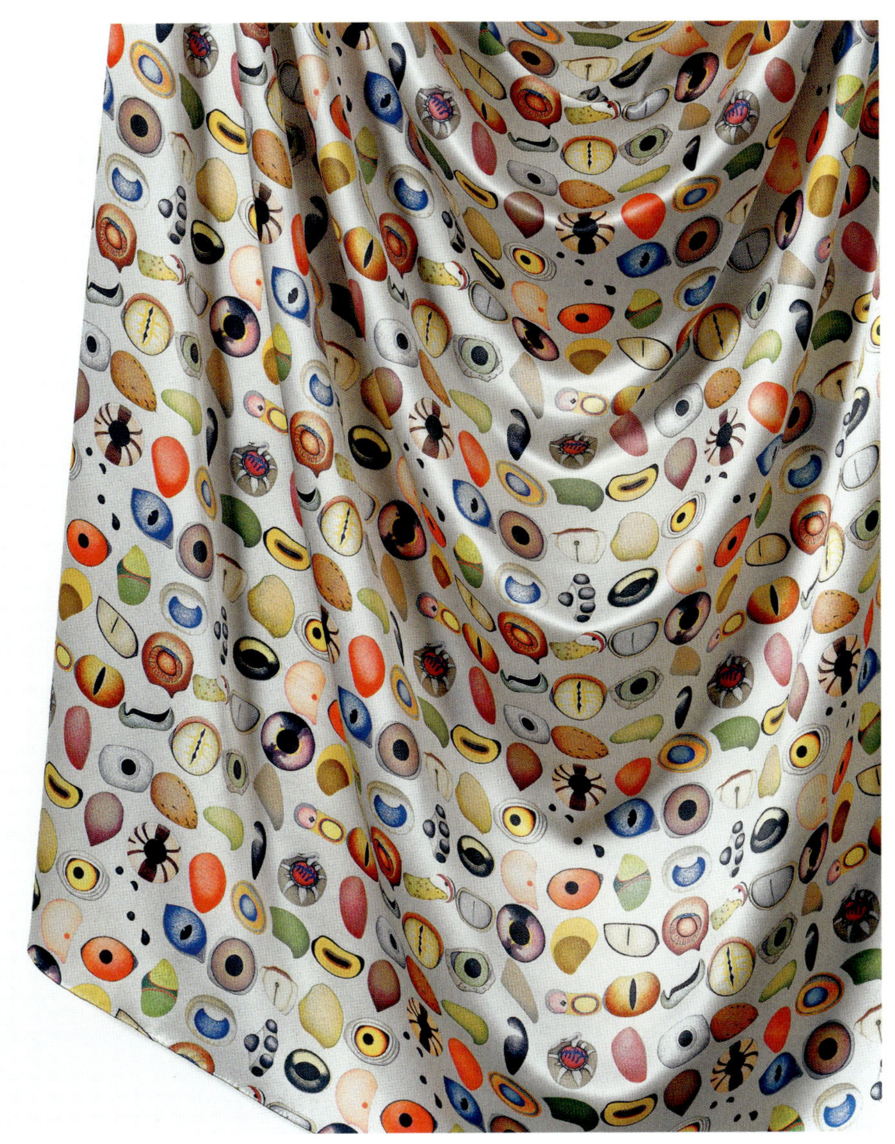

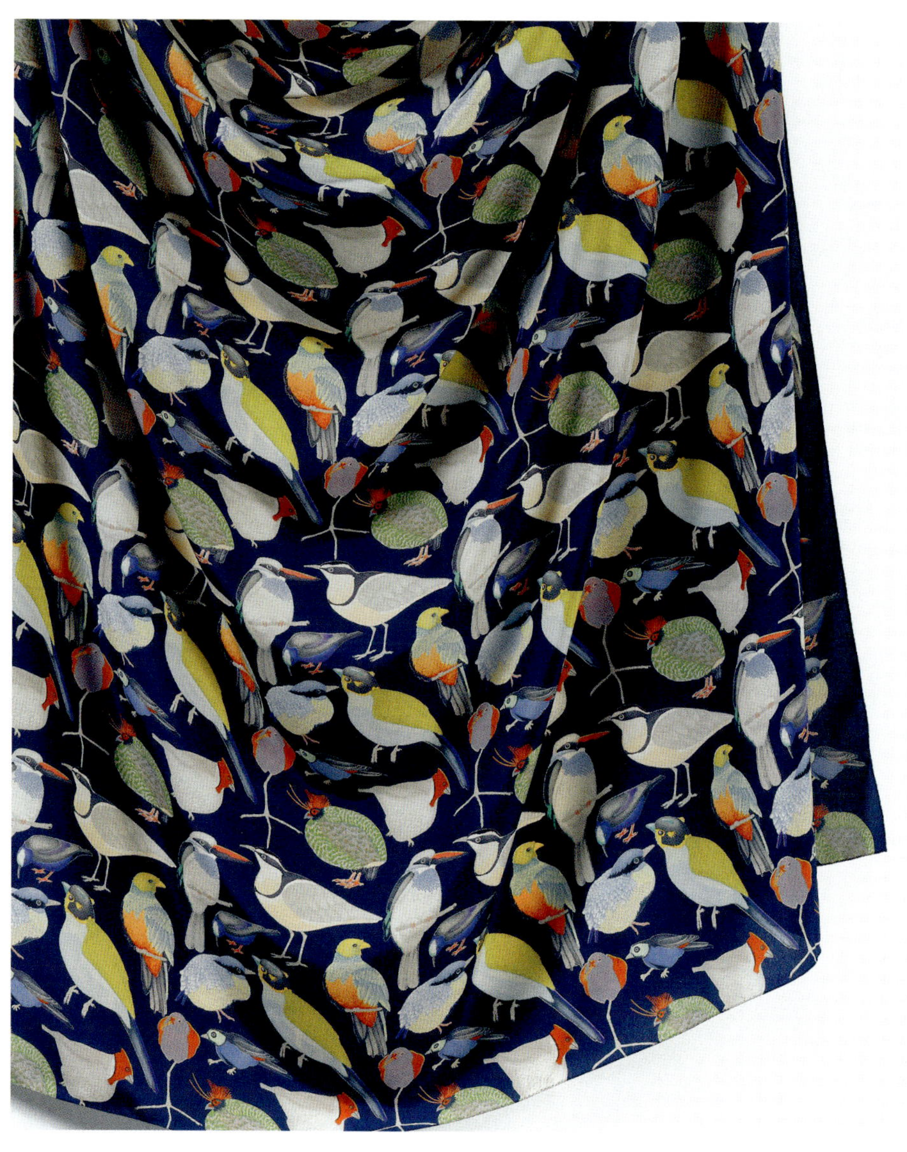

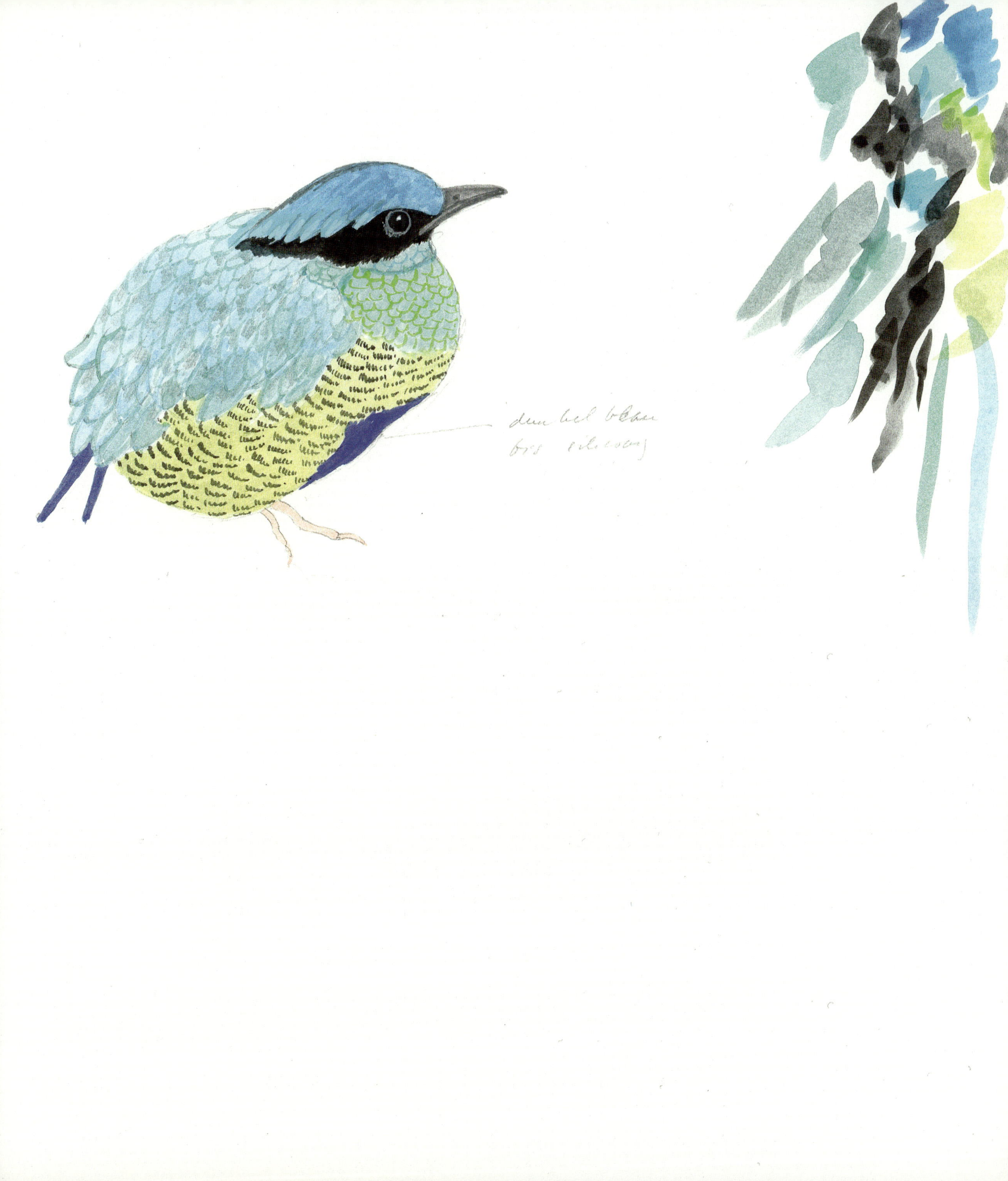

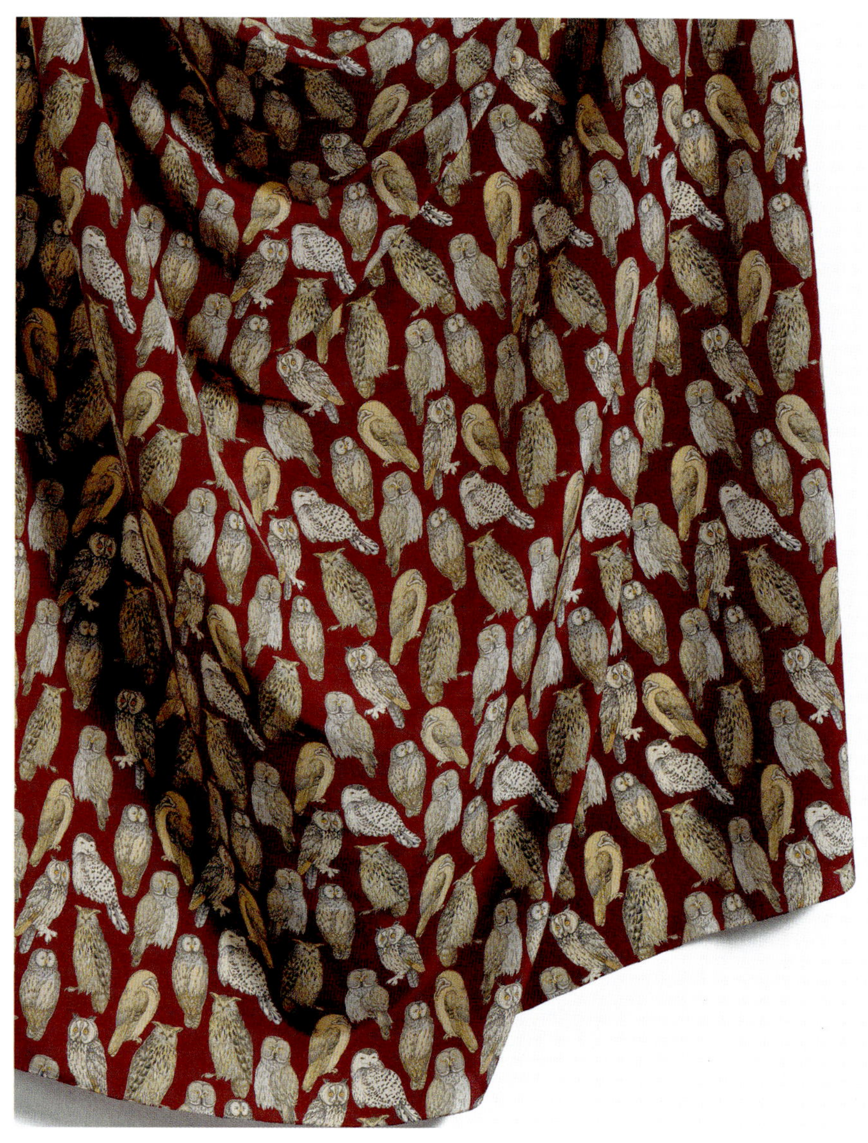

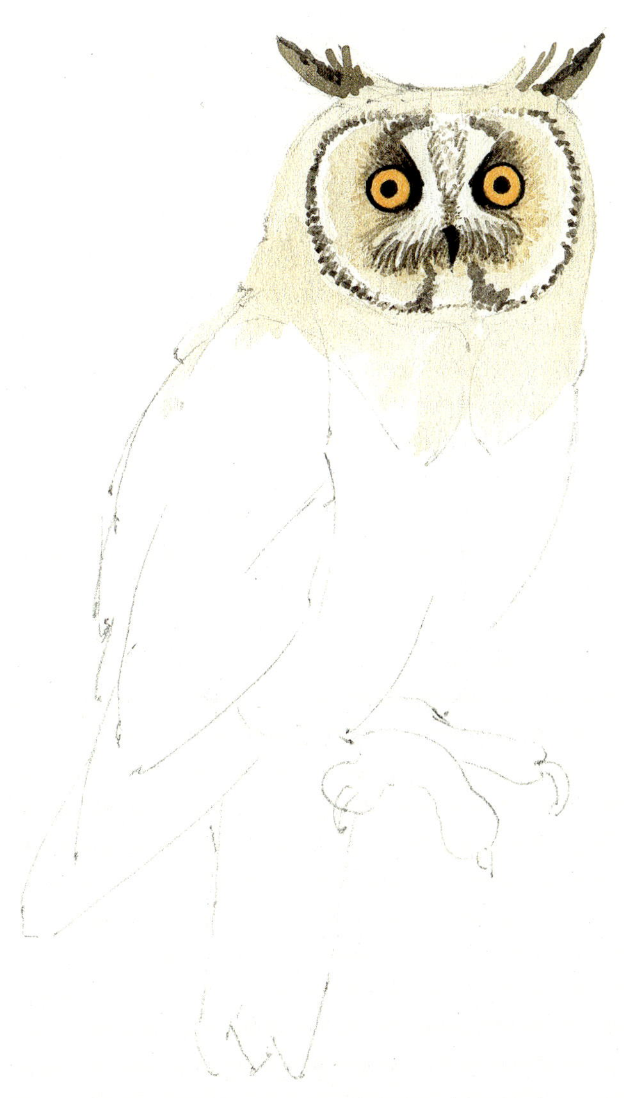
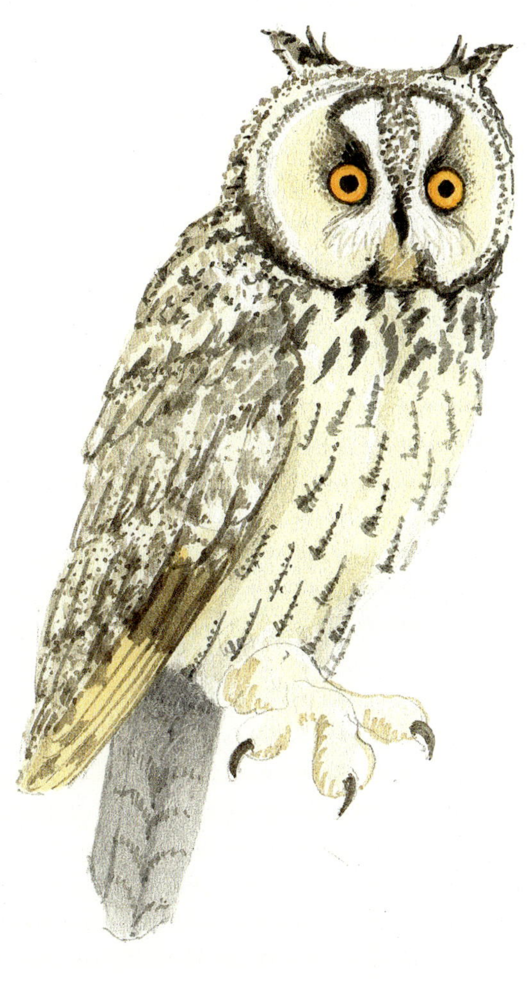

Die Mode ist universell.
Fashion is universal.

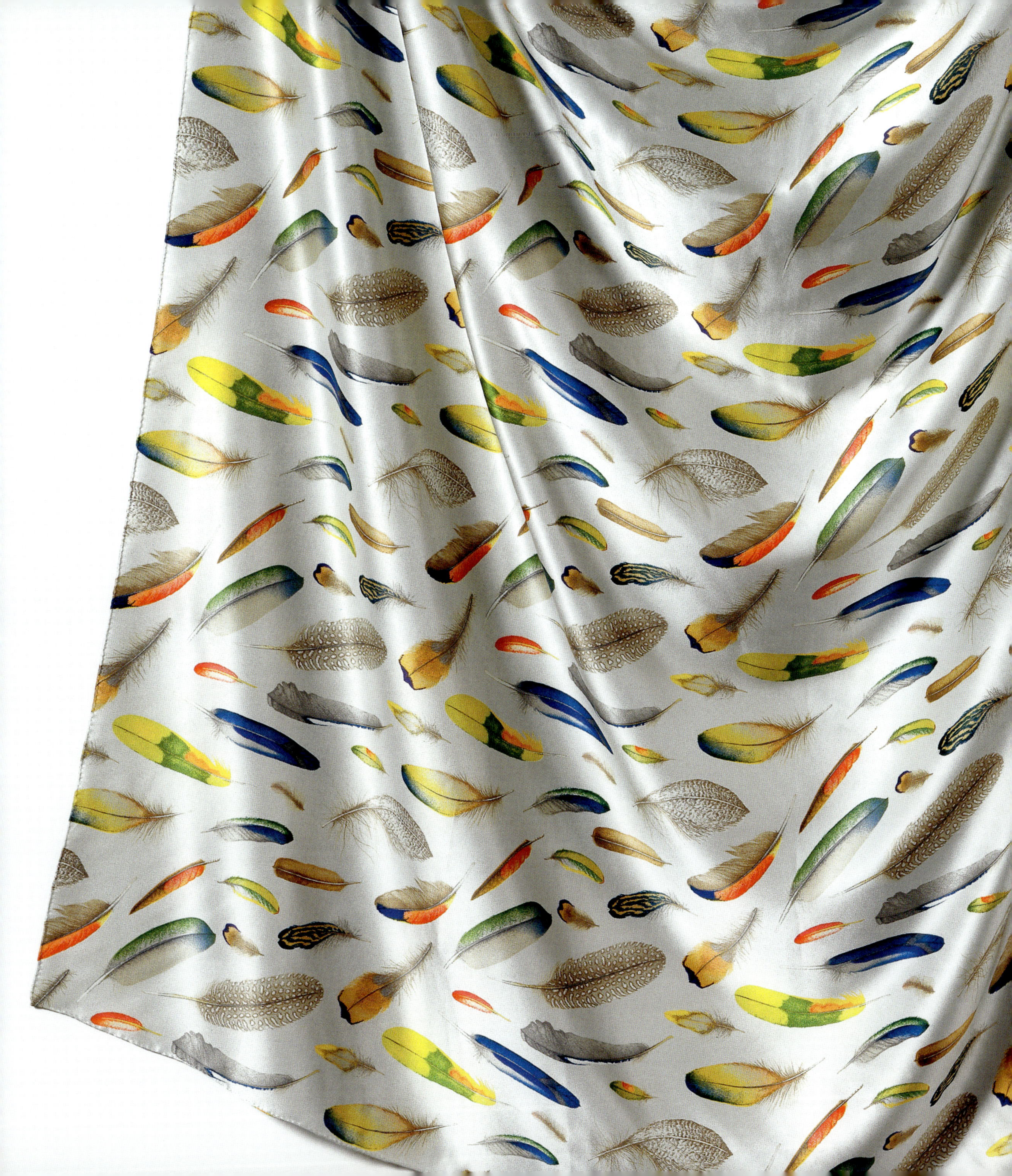

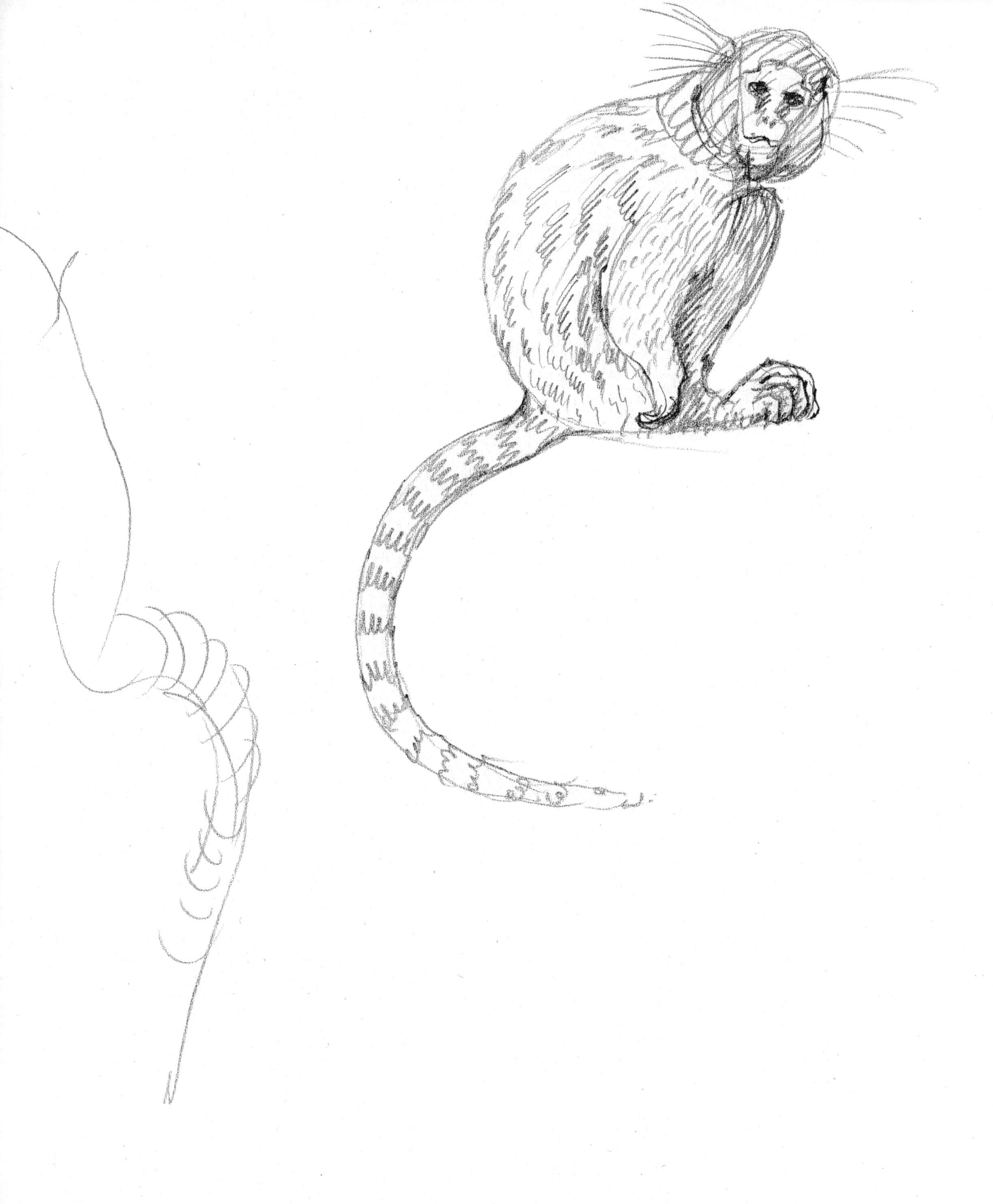

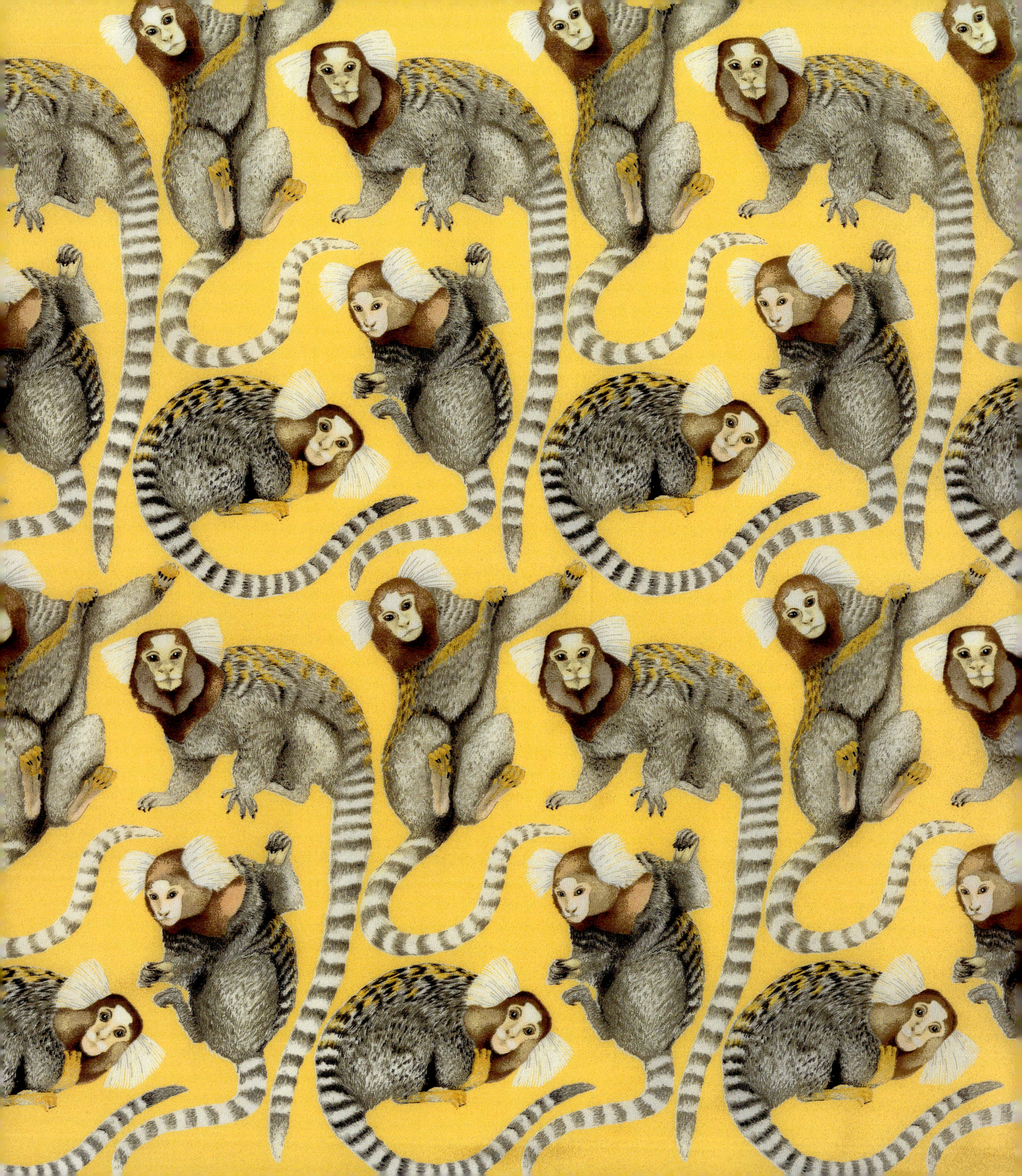

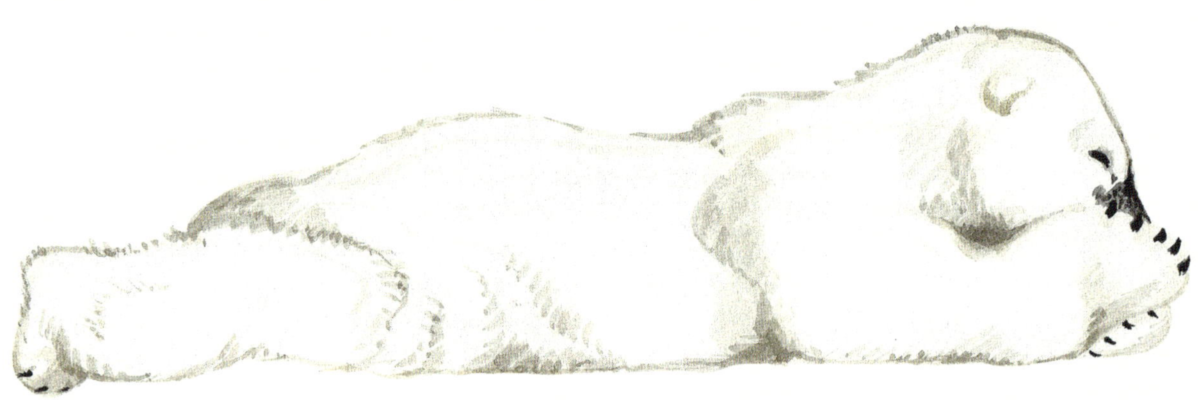

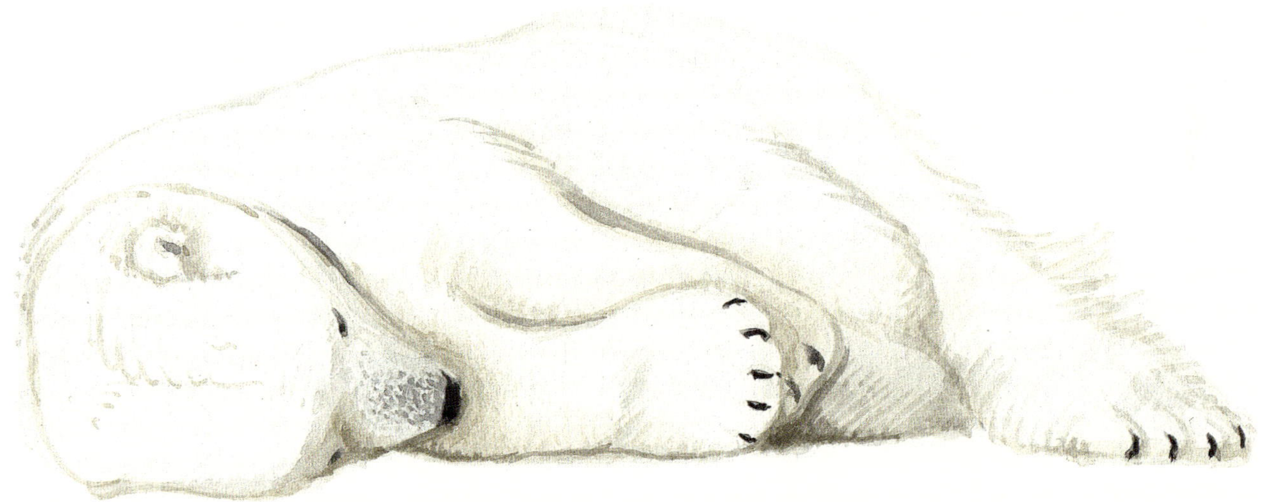

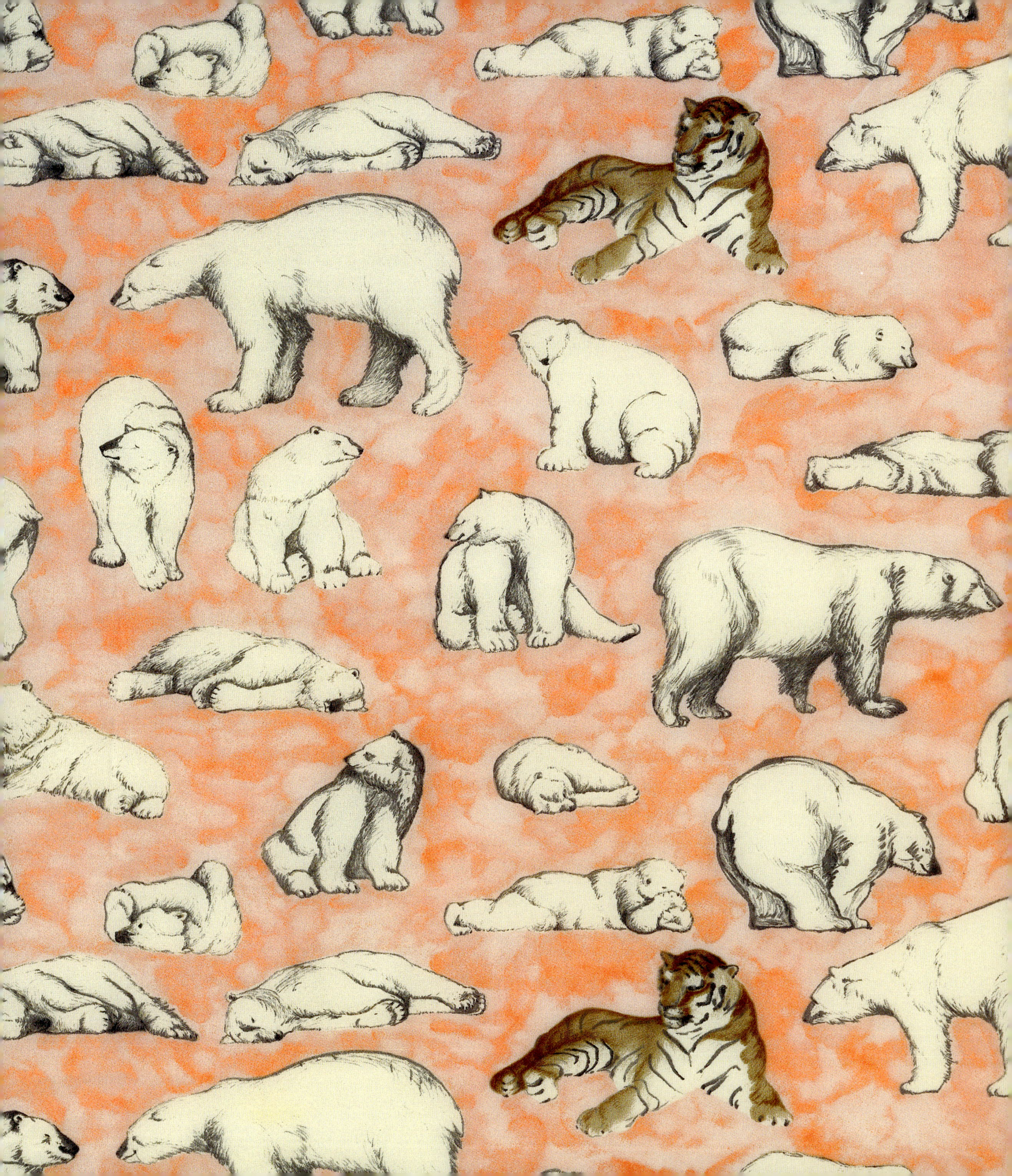

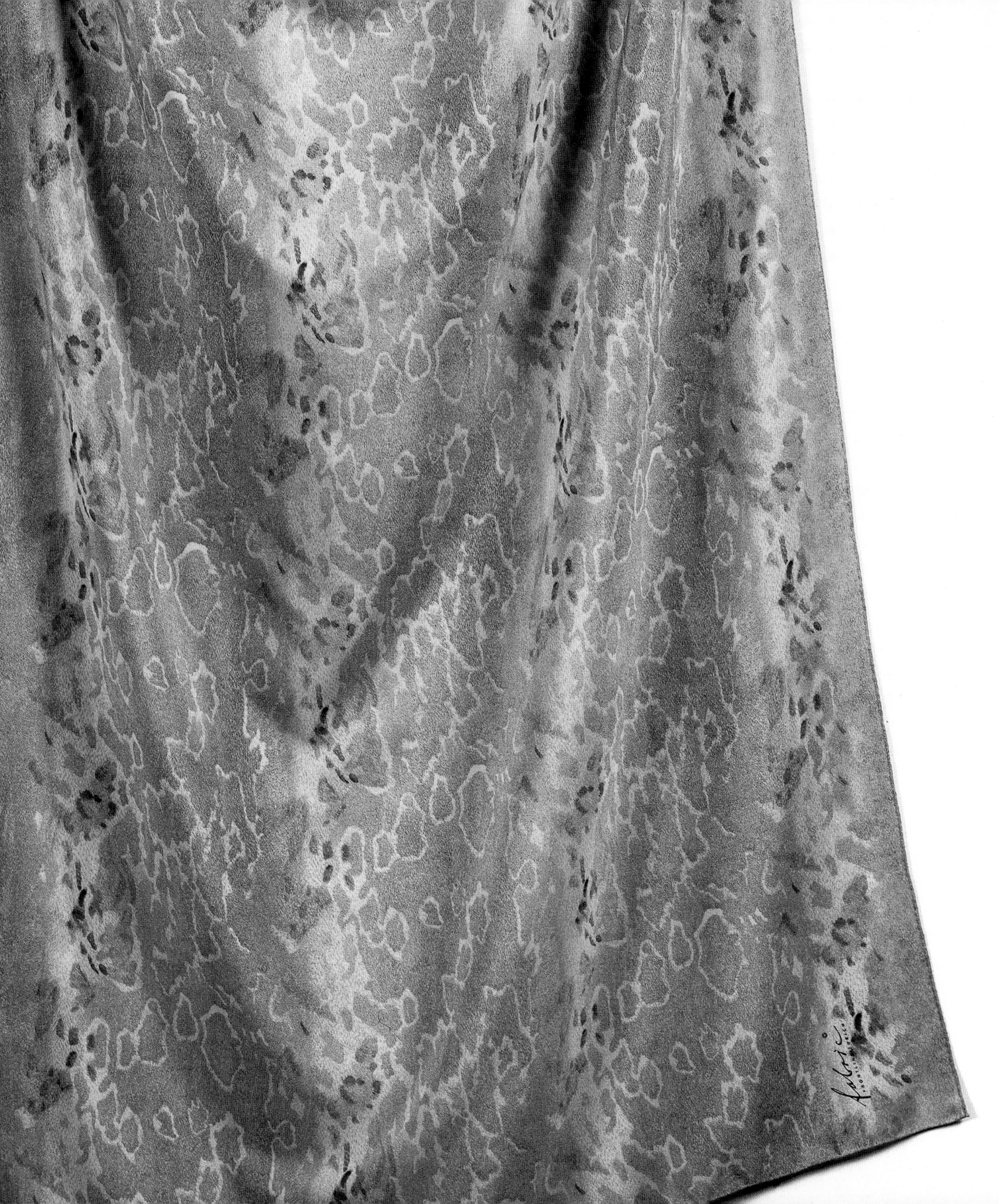

Unser Gehirn denkt in Bildern.
The brain thinks in images.

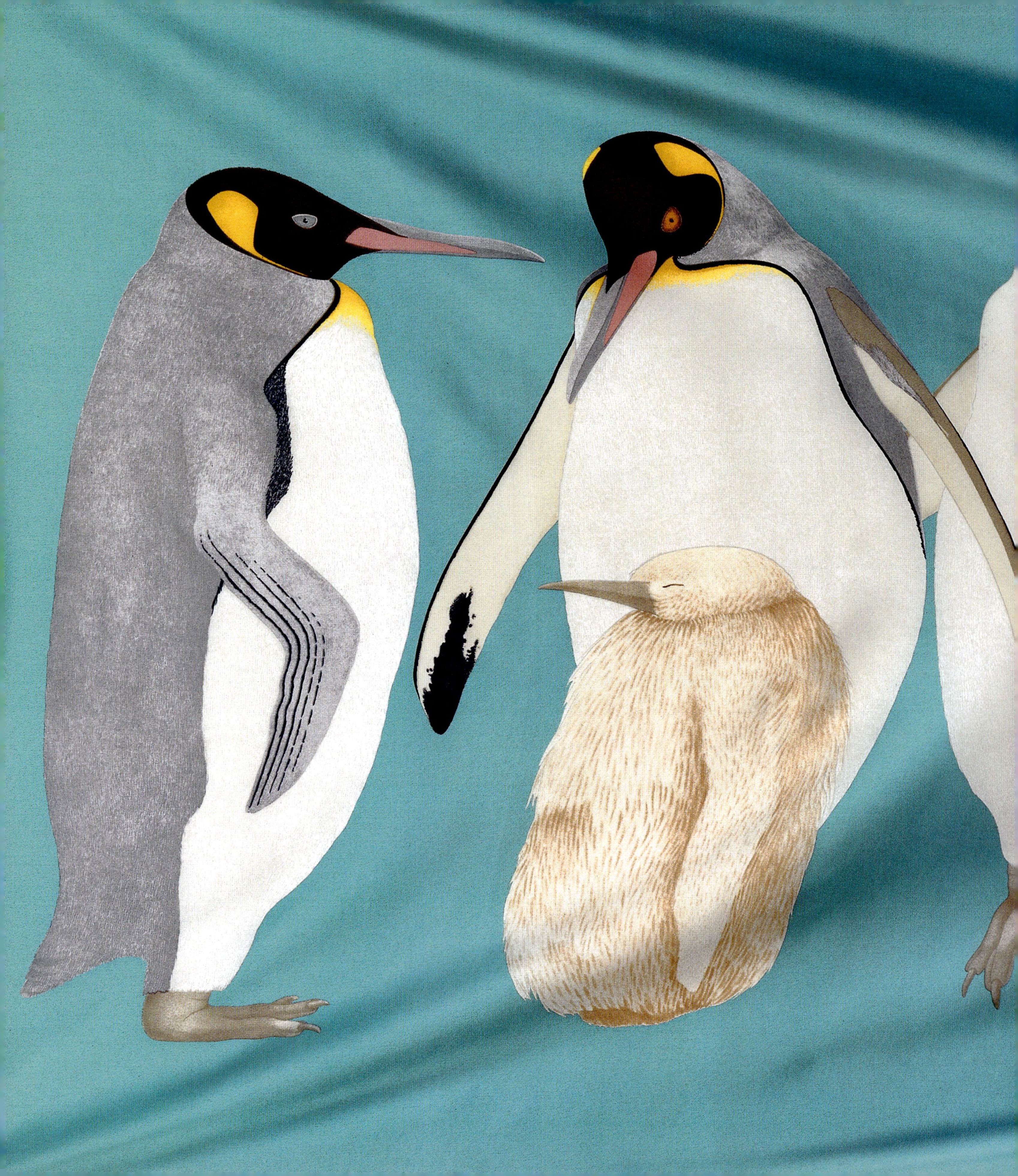

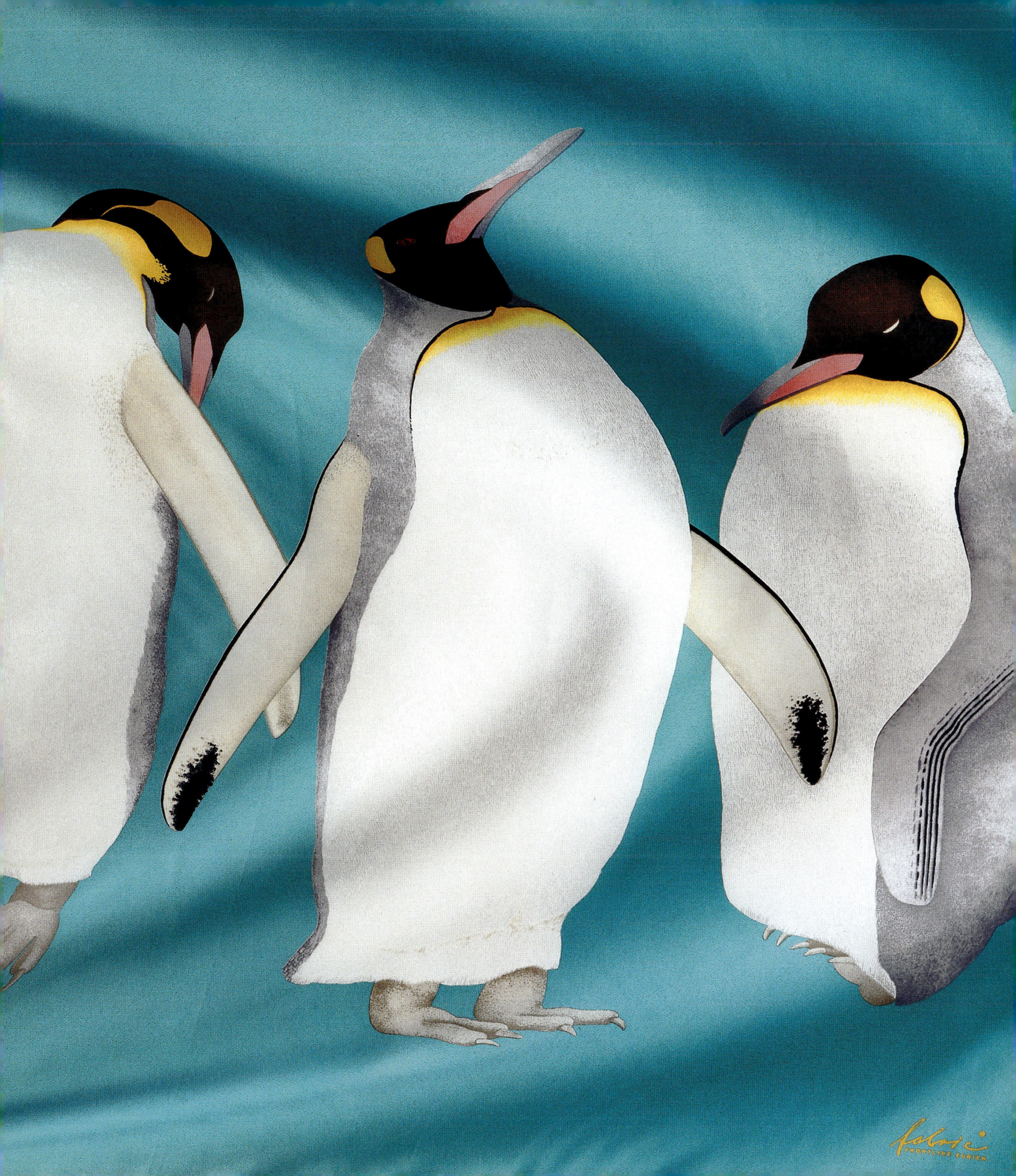

fabri

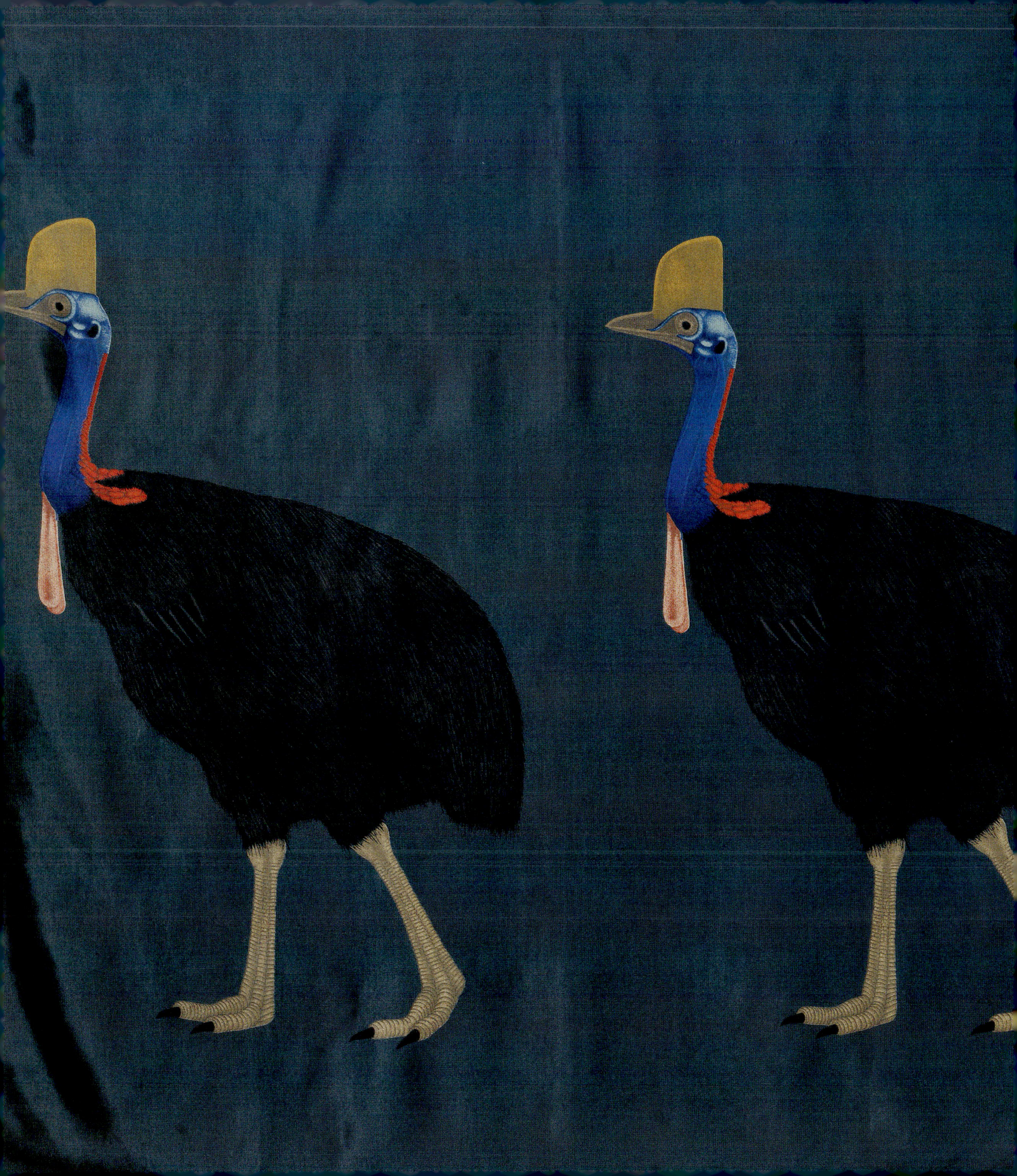

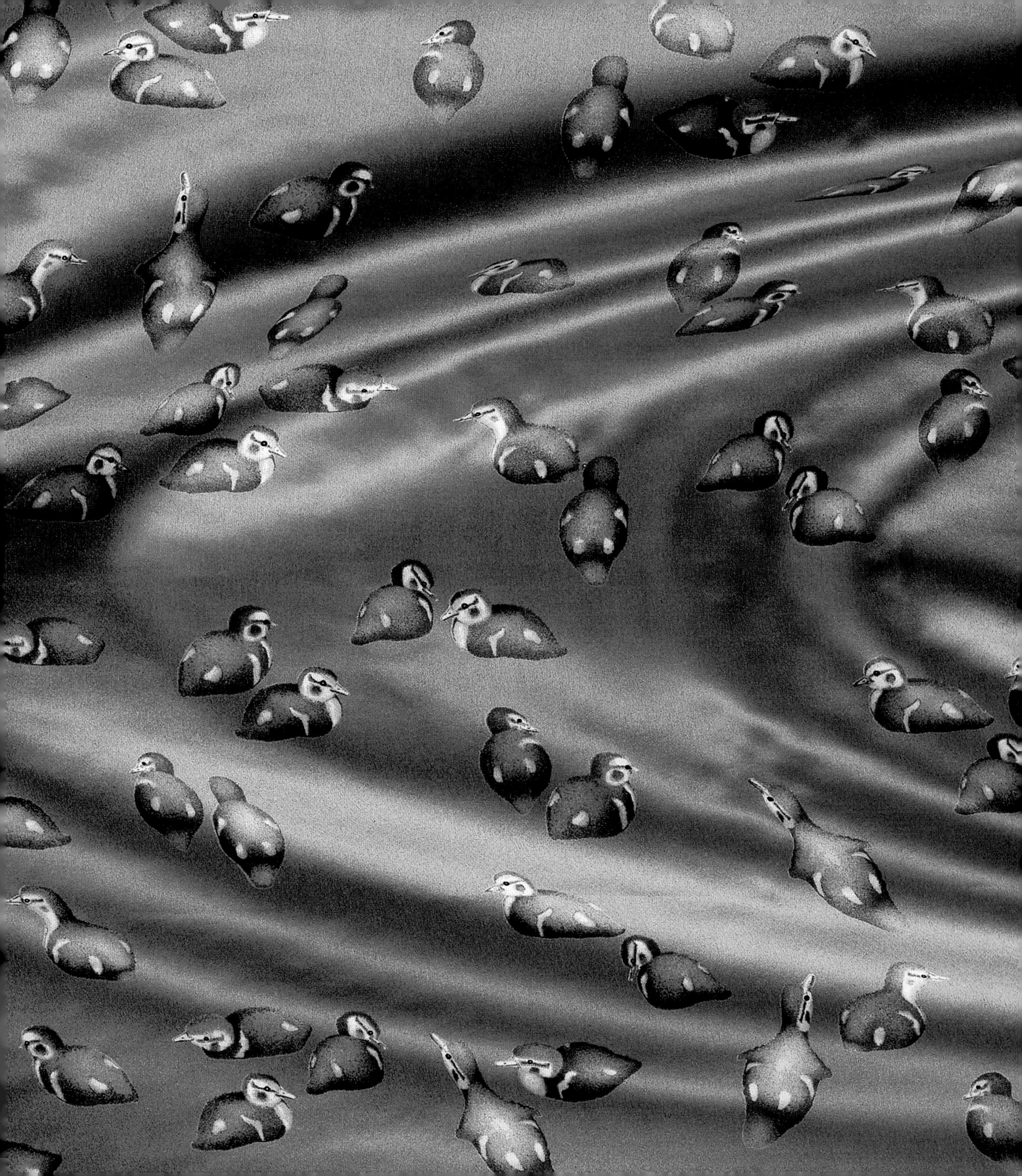

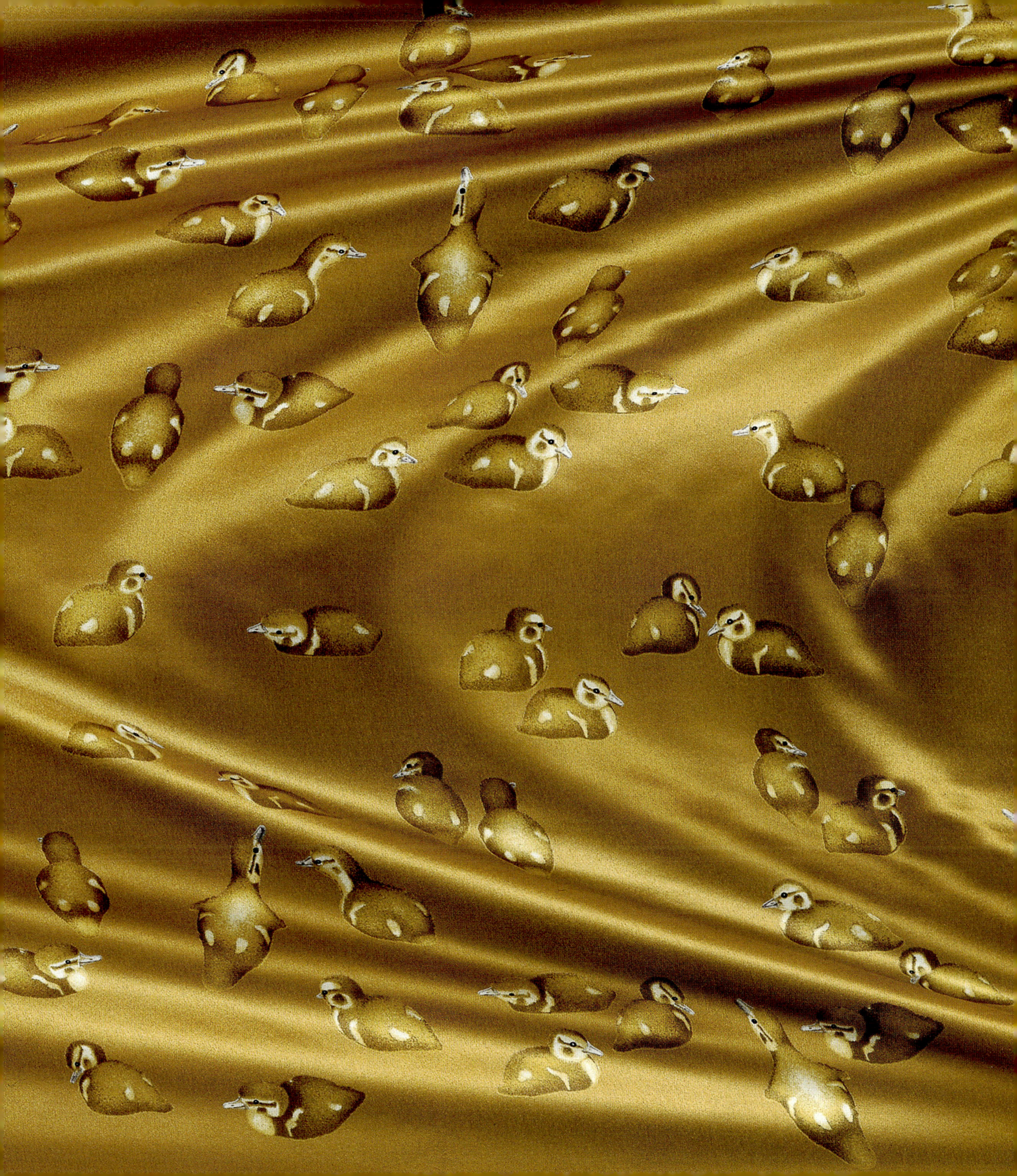

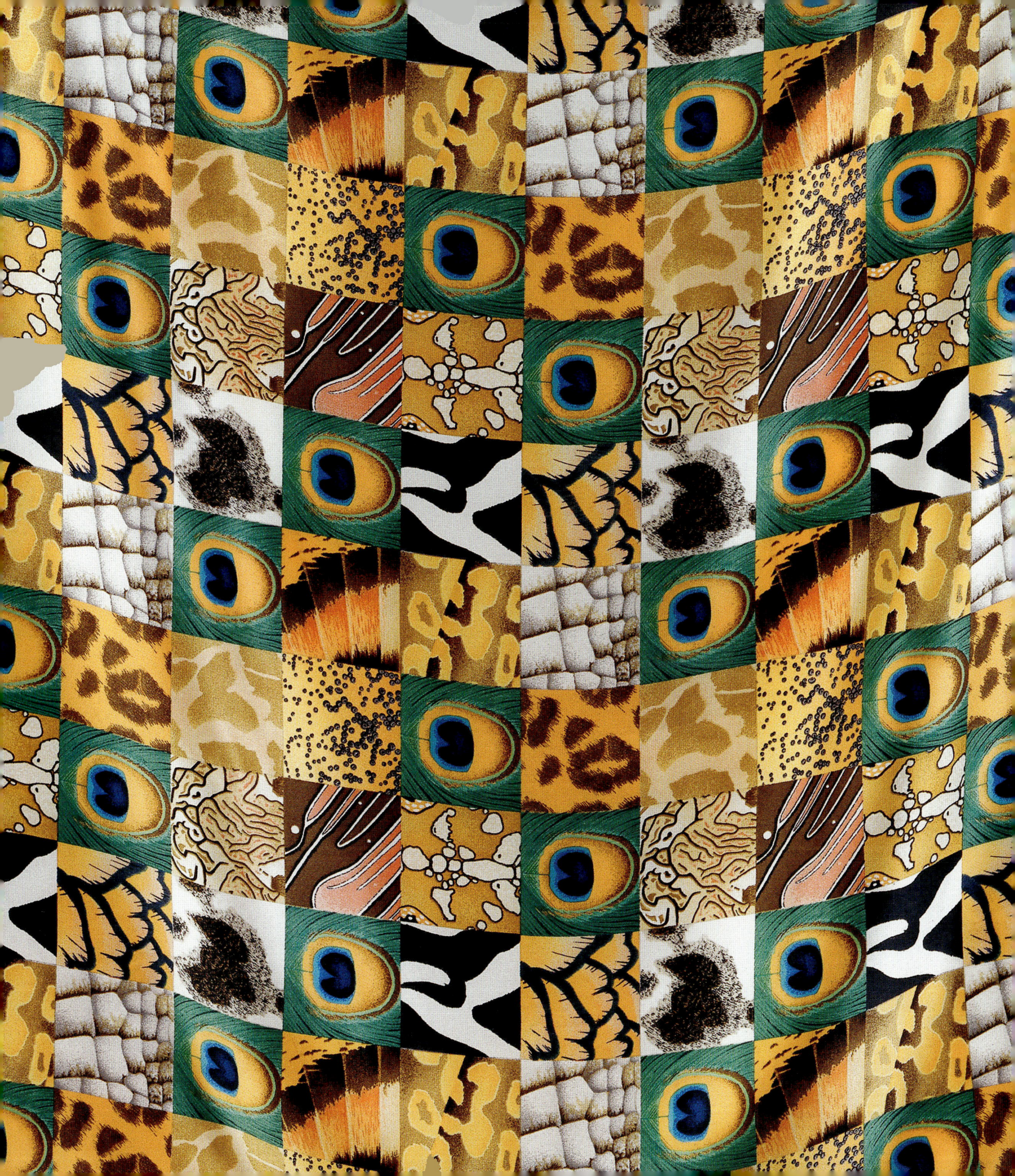

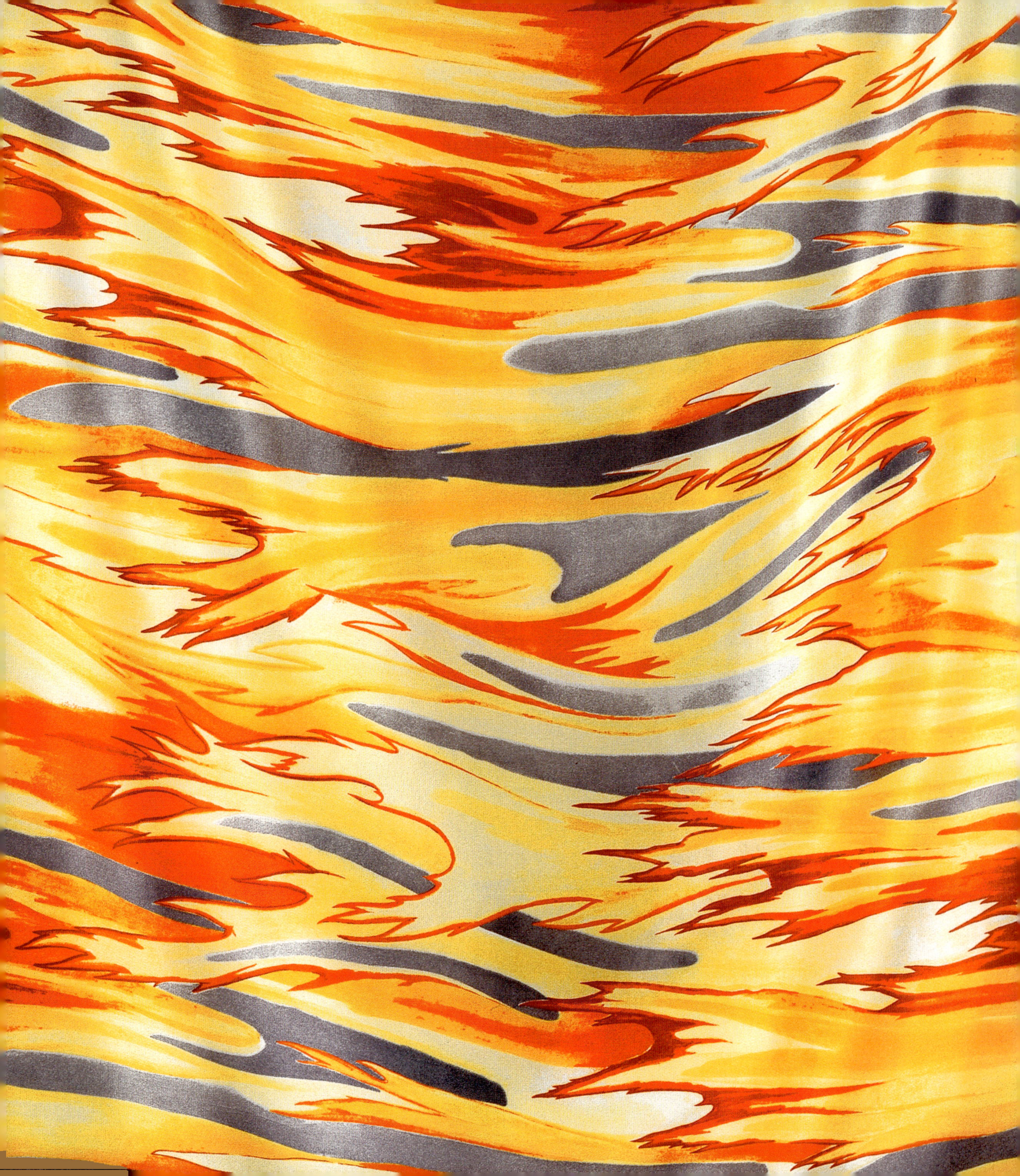

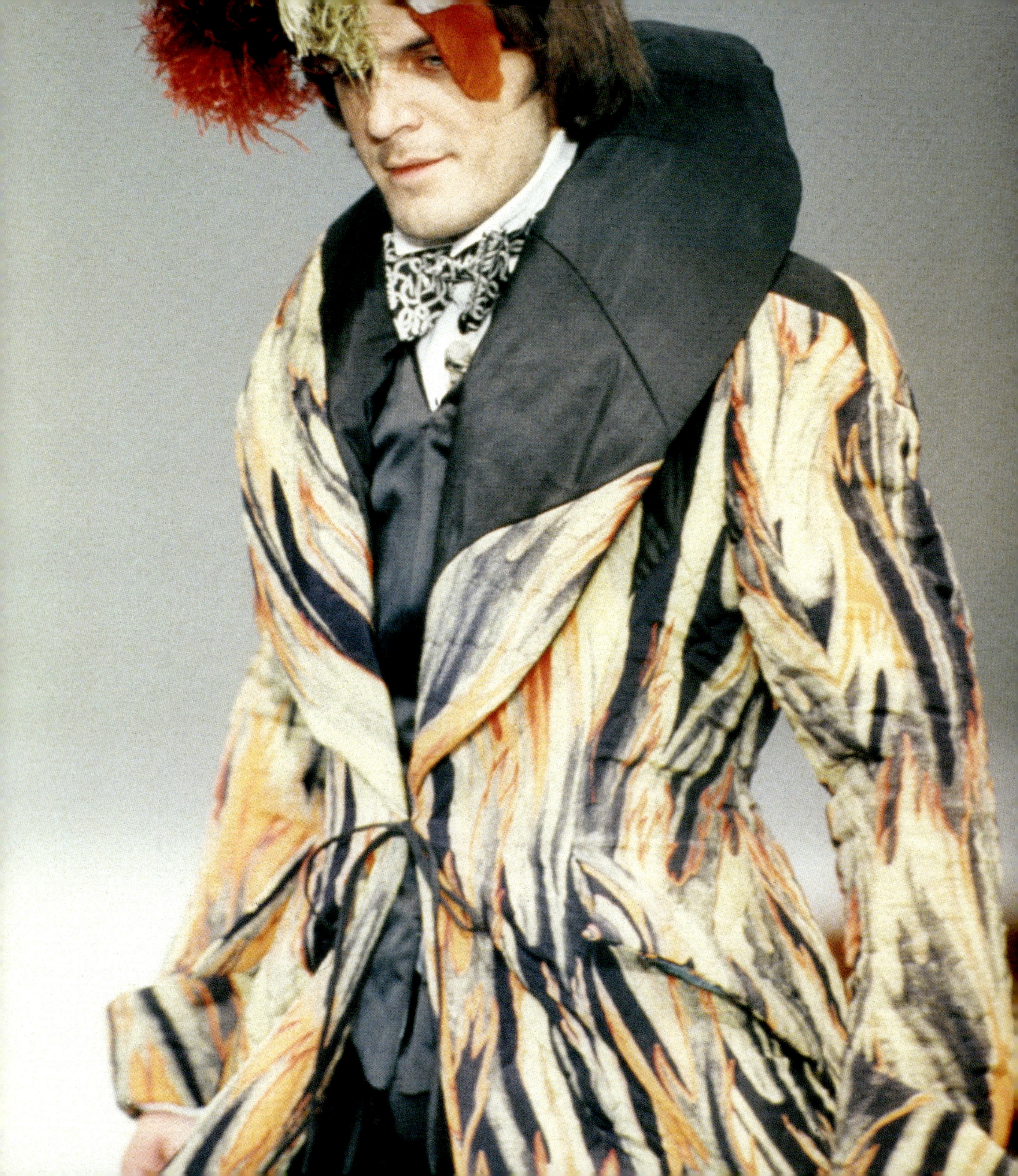

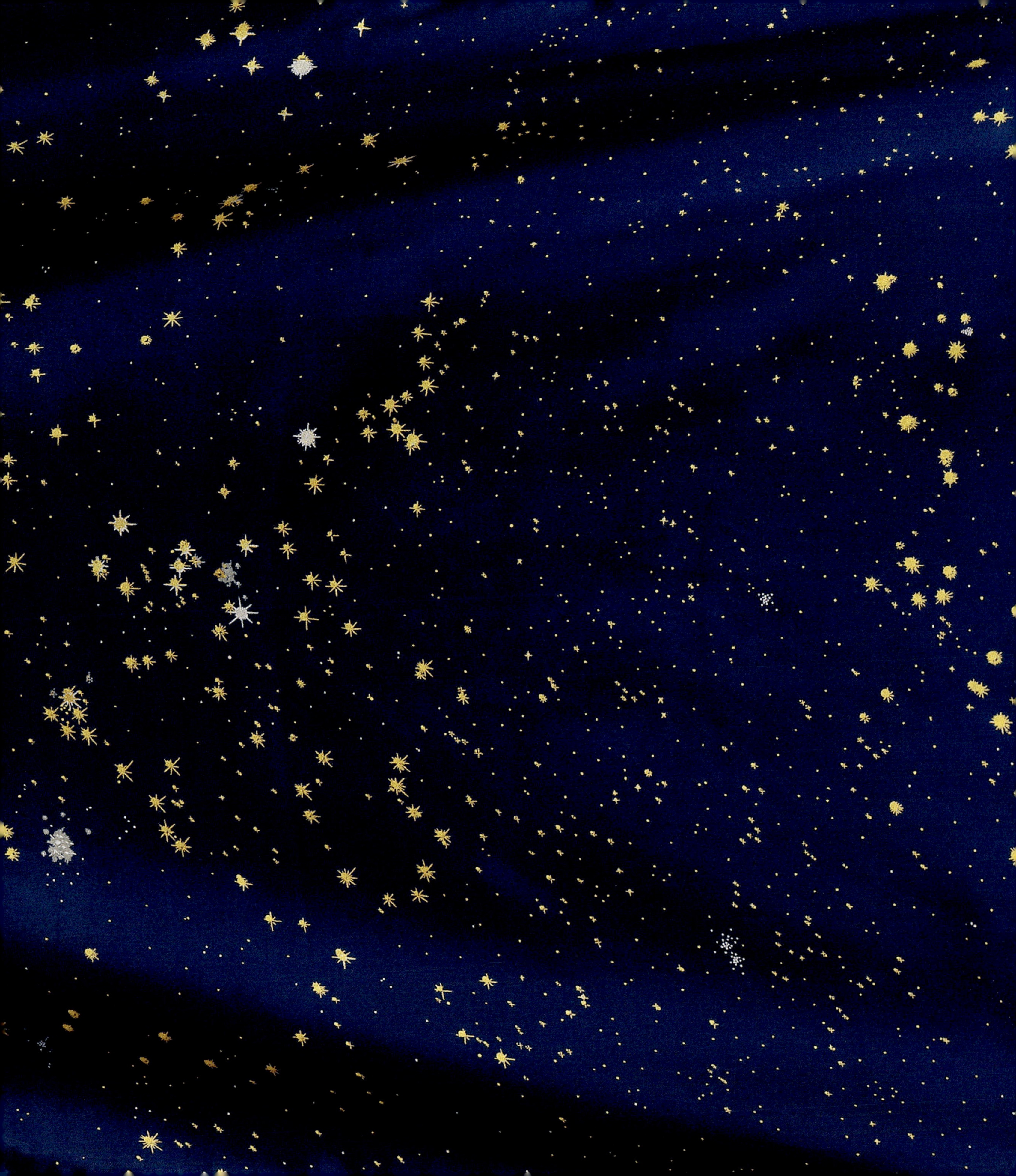

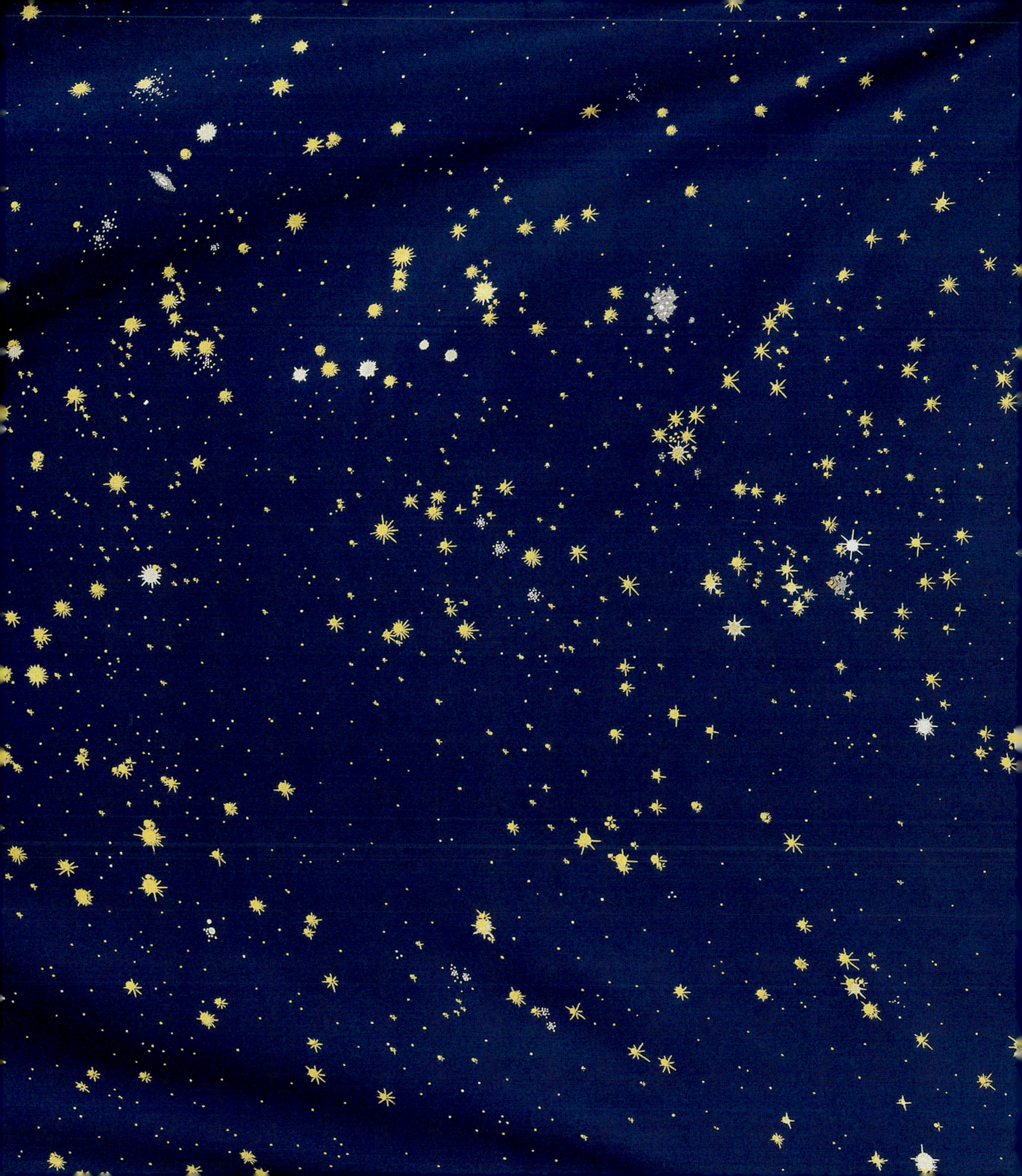

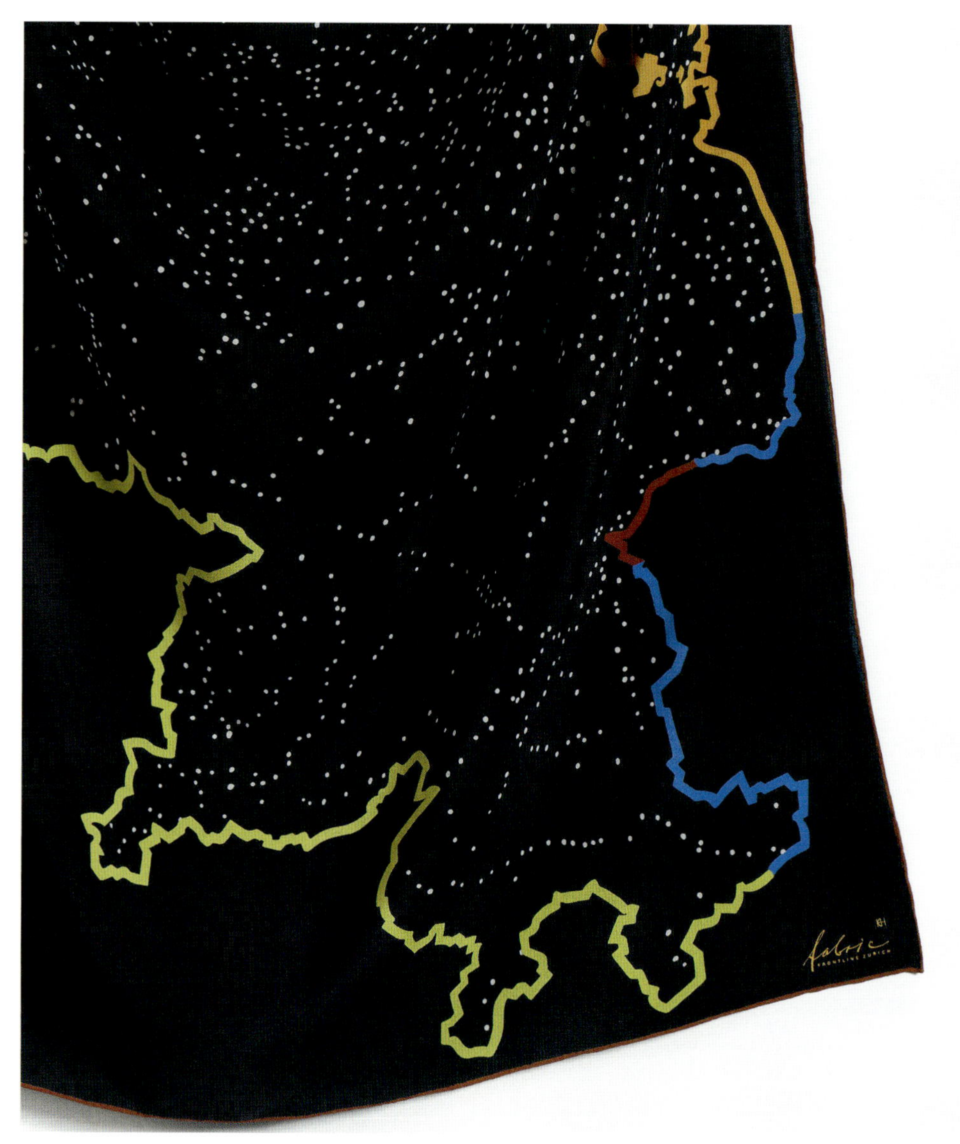

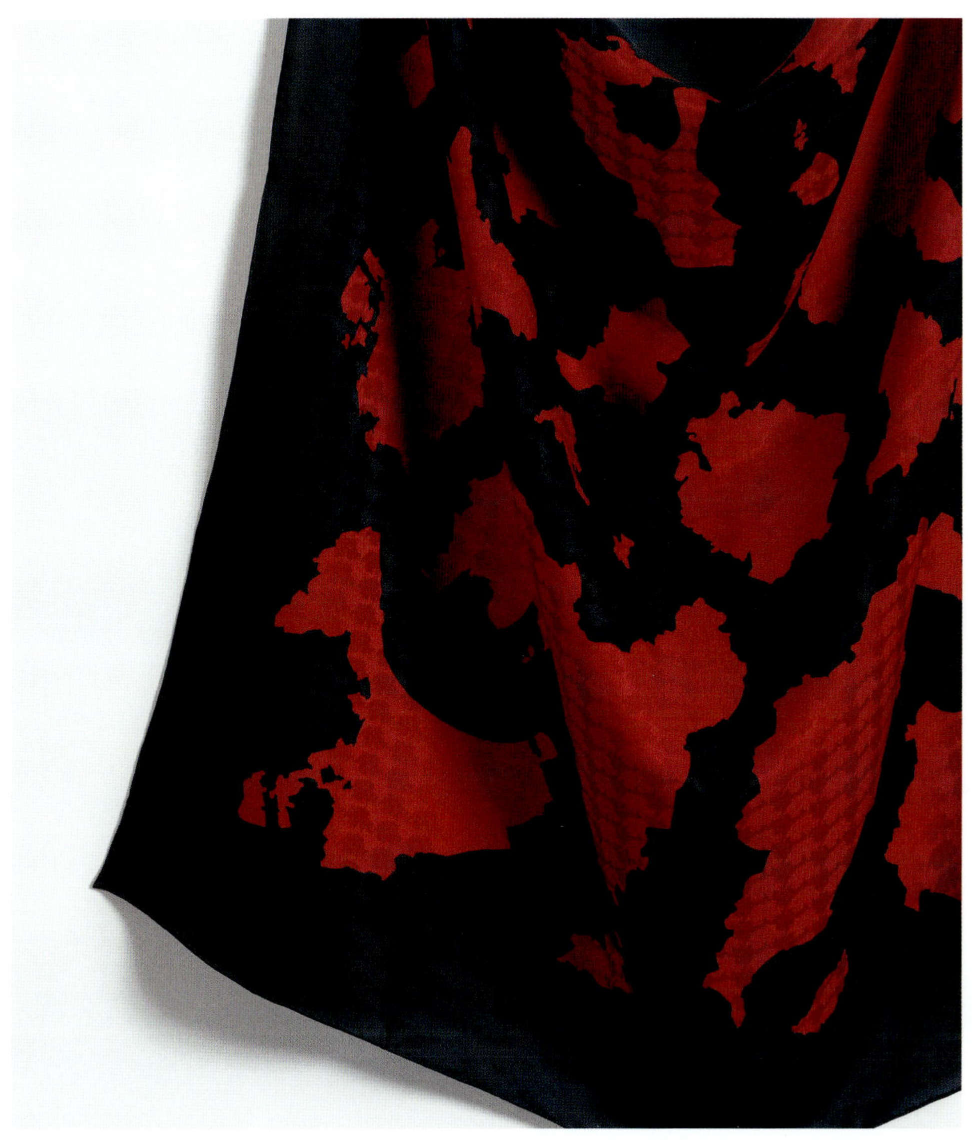

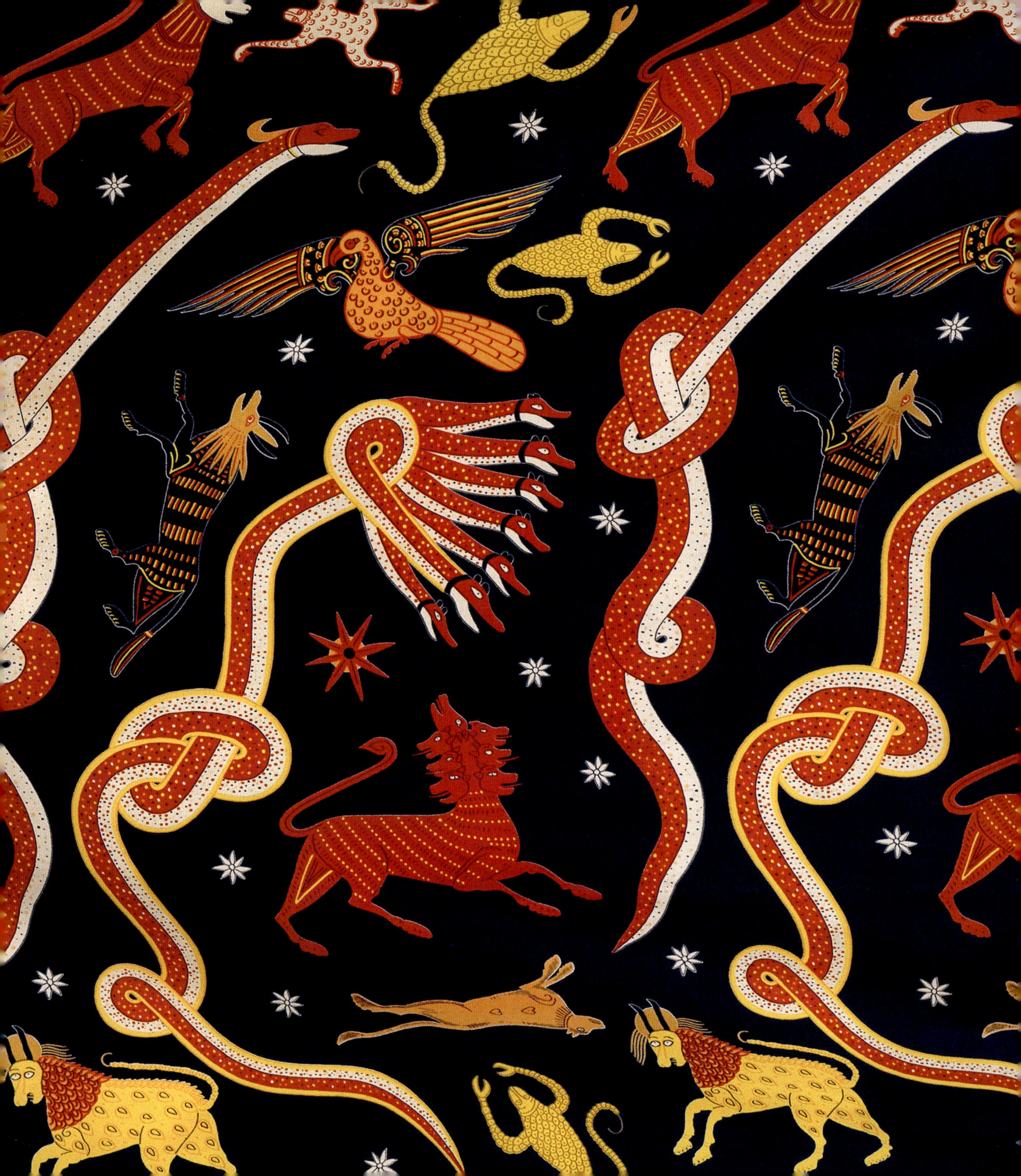

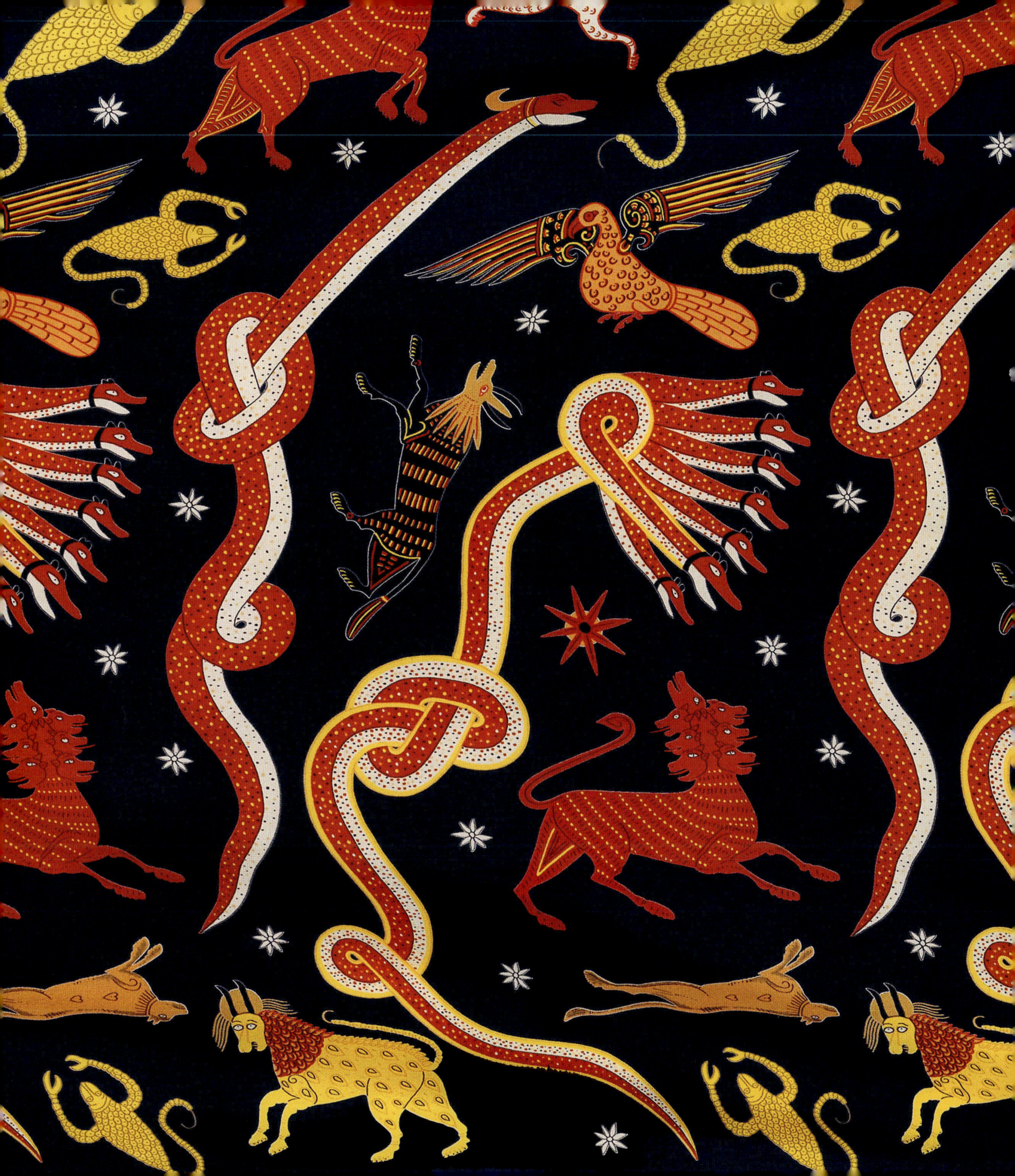

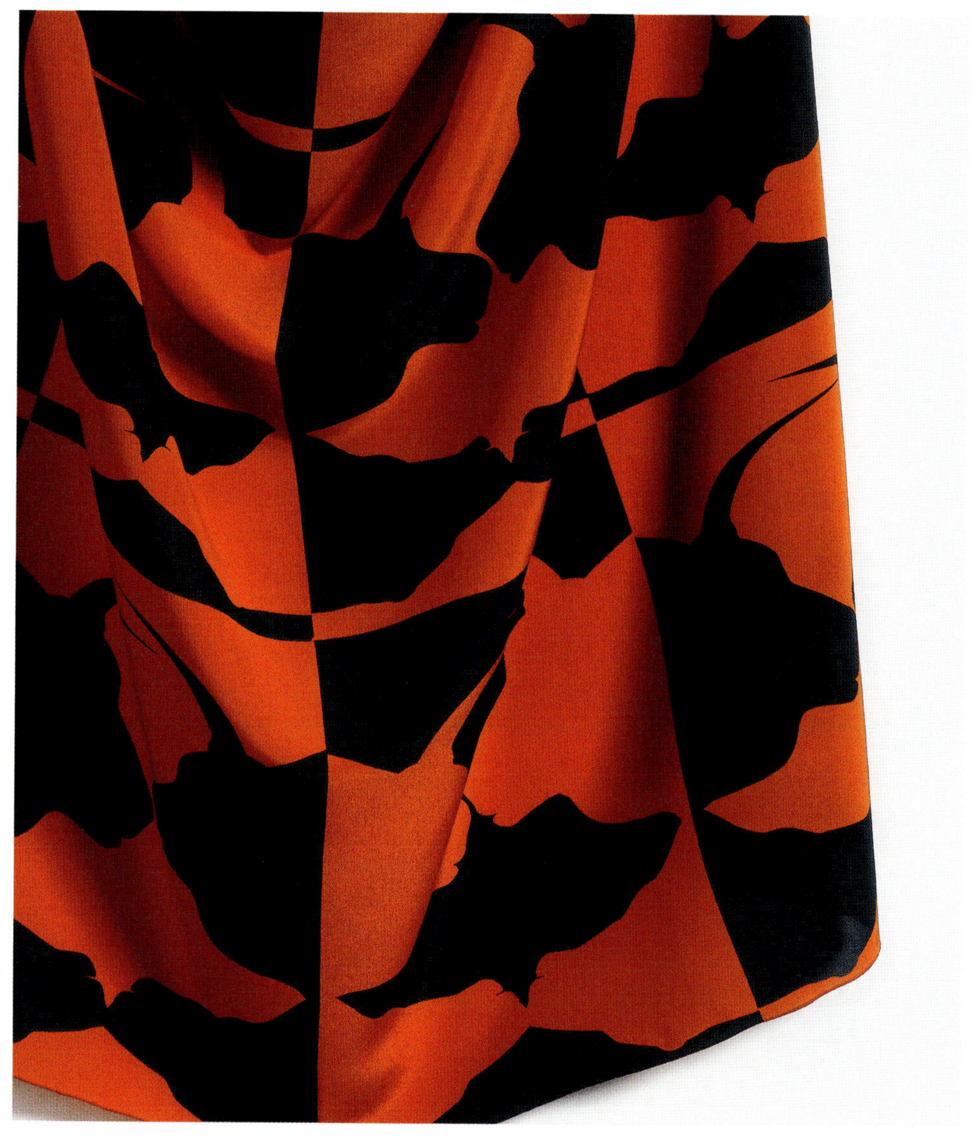

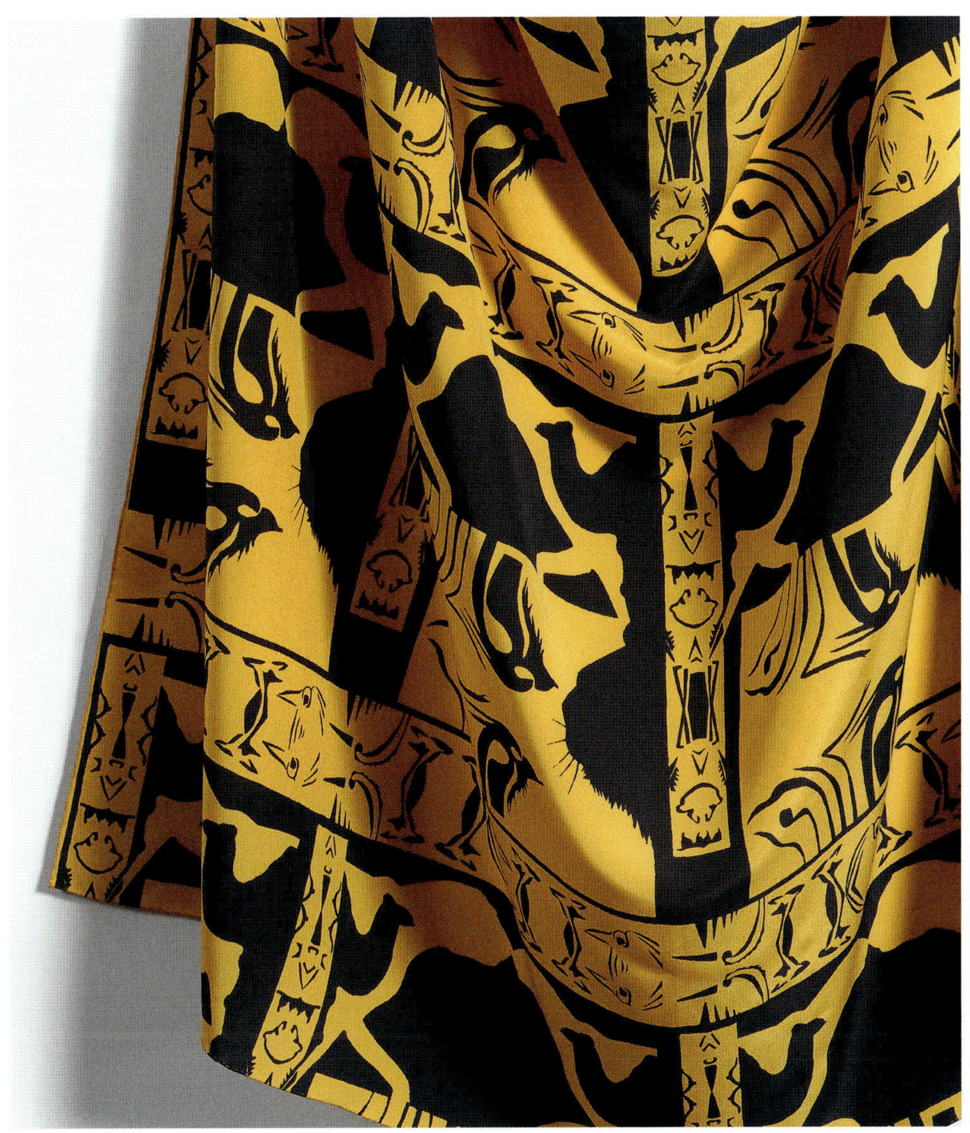

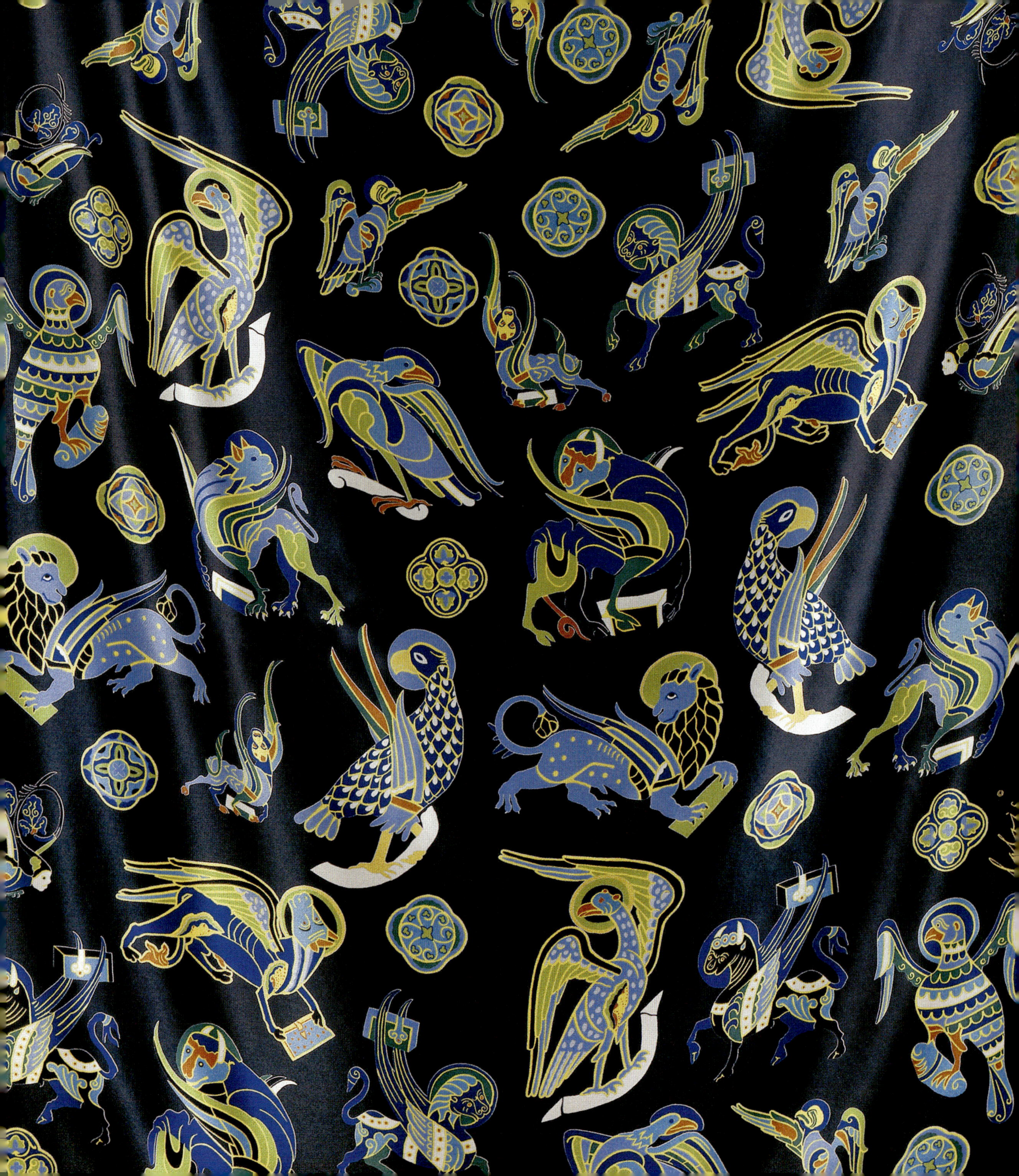

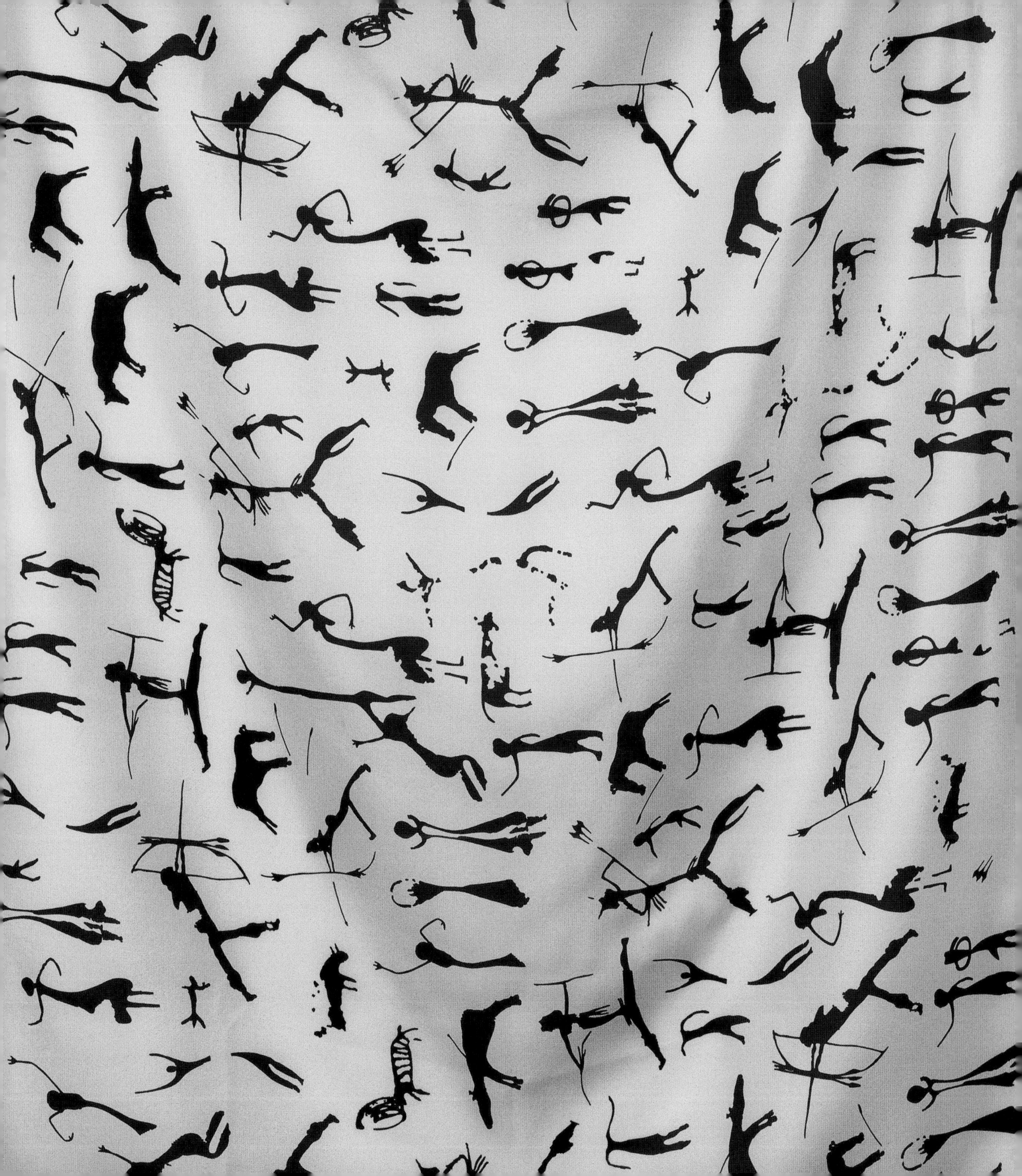

Es begann mit meiner Kunstpostkarten-Sammlung. Wenn ich mich nicht täusche, war ich zehn Jahre alt — meine Eltern sind Künstler — , und so war es ganz natürlich, dass mich die Bilder, dass mich die Kunst interessierte. Ich brachte viele Sonntage mit meiner Sammlung zu. Da gab es aggressive, symbolische, politische, historische, geometrische, aber auch sehr naturalistische Bilder. Ja — ich hatte meine Lieblinge. Eine Abteilung in dieser Sammlung war mein Louvre: Hans Holbein, Jan Vermeer, Paolo Uccello, Leonardo da Vinci bestimmten mein Sehen. Ihnen war ich nah.

So eine Postkartensammlung ist etwas wie ein Porträt, ein Spiegel des Sammlers. Bis heute bestimmt diese Erfahrung mein Denken und Gestalten. Aber auch mein soziales Engagement. In meinem Atelier steht immer noch eine Karte mit einem Stillleben des französischen Künstlers Lubin Baugin (1612–1663), ein Bild, das im Pariser Louvre hängt und das ich dort bewundern konnte.

Später dann wollte ich die Kunst im Original erleben, mit ihr kommunizieren, sie hinterfragen. Der Louvre wurde zu meinem Atelier. Zeichnend entdeckte ich die Geheimnisse des Gestaltens, das Wunder des Kreativen. Ich wurde angeregt, ich wollte und musste dereinst meine eigene Welt schaffen. Ich musste und wollte mein Leben der Kunst widmen, mich ganz und gar in ihr verlieren.

Heute, ein halbes Jahrhundert später, bin ich meiner Kunstpostkarten-Sammlung mehr als dankbar. Sie hat mir den Weg gewiesen, durch sie habe ich mich selbst kennen gelernt, und das, was ich heute erschaffe, entspricht ohne Wenn und Aber meiner Identität.

Ich hatte das Glück — und das Privileg — , an der Universität Zürich im Zoologischen Institut von Herrn Professor Hans Burla in die Welt der Naturwissenschaft eingeführt zu werden. Ich begleitete mit meinen Zeichnungen die wissenschaftlichen Arbeiten, ich wurde angewiesen, selbst zu experimentieren — und zu beobachten. Diese Jahre im Zoologischen Institut haben mein Sehen geschärft, dort versöhnte sich für mich die Kunst mit der Naturwissenschaft.

Ich heiratete, habe zwei Söhne erzogen, lebte mit meiner Familie an der Peripherie von Zürich auf einem wunderbaren Stück Erde. Hier entstanden meine ersten Zeichnungen von Insekten. Vor allen Dingen faszinierte mich die formale und farbige Vielfalt der Wanzen (Heteroptera). Ich entdeckte so eine Welt, die wir heute leider zu wenig ernst nehmen und doch in ihrer Existenz bedrohen. Ich sammelte, ich beobachtete, ich lebte mit meinem Mikroskop in einer Welt ohne Sünde, in einer Welt reiner Schönheit. Und weil dem so war, war mein Entsetzen entsprechend gross, als ich entdeckte, dass im Laufe der Jahre mehr und mehr geschädigte Insekten — mehr und mehr deformierte Wanzen — meine Untersuchungen bestimmten.

1986 kam Tschernobyl, eine weltweite Katastrophe, die mich ganz und gar in die Pflicht nahm. Meine Reise nach Schweden, das vom Fallout besonders betroffen war, sowie an den Ort des Unglücks in der Ukraine war meine erste Begegnung mit einer Vielfalt geschädigter Wanzen. Nun gab es für mich kein Zurück mehr. Meine Arbeiten zeigten mir und belegten, welch grosse Gefahr Atomkraftwerke auch im Normalbetrieb für die gesamte Natur und für uns Menschen sind.

Ich wollte es wissen. Bis heute untersuche und visualisiere ich Insekten, besonders Wanzen, im Umkreis von Atomreaktoren und anderen Atomanlagen. In der Schweiz kenne ich heute Gösgen, Leibstadt sowie das Paul Scherrer Institut, in England Sellafield, wo die Not besonders gross ist. Ich konnte es kaum glauben, wie sehr Radioaktivität, selbst geringer Strahlung, Leben bedroht. Meine Arbeiten führten mich nach Three Mile Island in den USA, wo ein Fast-GAU stattgefunden hat, dann nach Frankreich, La Hague, aber auch nach Deutschland zu den Atomkraftwerken Krümmel und Gundremmingen. 2004 reiste ich nach Vietnam: Auch dort, wo die Amerikaner während des Vietnamkriegs Agent Orange versprüht hatten, begegnete ich immer und immer wieder demselben Drama. Ich suchte Hilfe an den Forschungsinstituten und bei Naturwissenschaftlern. Leider blieb ich bis heute ohne Antwort.

Um diesem gesellschaftlichen Auftrag nachzukommen, brauchte ich ein Einkommen. Und so war ich denn überglücklich, als meine Freundin, die Modeschöpferin Eri Székely, mich 1986 mit dem Zürcher Seidenfabrikanten André Stutz bekannt machte. Fabric Frontline wurde zu meinem Arbeitgeber und André Stutz zu einem guten Freund. Dank ihm konnte ich meine Sehnsucht nach dem Schönen, dem Nützlichen erfüllen. Es war mir eine Wohltat, mein Denken und Fühlen auch im angewandten Bereich zu befriedigen. In 16 Jahren Zusammenarbeit haben wir gemeinsam eine Kollektion geschaffen, die mehr ist als nur Konsumware. Wir ernteten viel Lob und Anerkennung. Auch wirtschaftlich war unsere Arbeit ein Erfolg. Ein Highlight sicherlich, dass weltbekannte Modeschöpfer wie Yves St. Laurent, Jil Sander und Vivienne Westwood meine Dessins für ihre Kollektionen wählten. Amüsiert hat mich natürlich auch, als ich der Zeitung entnahm, dass sich der Sänger

Elton John auf seiner Europatournee 1989 mit meinen auf Seide gedruckten Marienkäfern schmückte.

Schon die Seide als Grundmaterial hat ja etwas Edles, etwas Besonderes, und sie stammt aus der Welt der Insekten. Einer Welt, die ich kannte, einer Welt, die weit zurückgreift in die Geschichte von uns Menschen. Und zu allen Zeiten etwas Aussergewöhnliches gewesen ist.

André Stutz gab mir die Freiheit und die Mittel, meine Phantasie, meine Sehnsüchte, aber auch meine Fragen auszuleben, sie sichtbar, sie lesbar zu machen.

Natürlich freue ich mich heute, wenn ich in Gesellschaft bin, hier einen Schal und dort eine von mir gestaltete Krawatte zu sehen. Für mich aber ist Kunst nicht «l'art pour l'art». Kunst hat einen Auftrag, einen Sinn: nebst der natürlichen eine künstliche Schönheit zu schaffen. Heute, da wir in einer zunehmend künstlichen Umwelt leben, ist künstliche Schönheit mehr denn je die einzige Alternative, um unsere Umwelt als humanes Ganzes zu erleben. Wir wissen es: Hässlichkeit macht uns krank, Schönheit schafft Hoffnung, Identität.

Ich bin stolz, dass meine Arbeiten eine Symbiose aus Denken und Fühlen sind. Ich glaube an die Aufklärung, ich bin glücklich, Dinge geschaffen zu haben, die Freude, die Harmonie ausstrahlen.

Dafür bin ich André Stutz und seiner Schwester Elsa Stutz dankbar, aber auch dem Drucker Claudio Milesi in Como, der meine Bilder auf Seide mit so viel Liebe und Fachkenntnis vervielfältigt hat.

So war es… Ich wollte es wissen. Ich wollte es verstehen. Ich wollte wirken. Heute… glaube ich. An die Schönheit. An die Wirkung der Kunst.

Cornelia Hesse-Honegger

It started with my collection of art postcards. If I'm not mistaken, I was ten years old — my parents are both artists — so it was quite natural that painting and art interested me. I spent many Sundays poring over my collection. There were aggressive, symbolic, political, historical, geometric, but also very naturalistic paintings. Yes, I had my favorites. A section of the collection was my Louvre: Hans Holbein, Jan Vermeer, Paolo Uccello, Leonardo da Vinci shaped my way of seeing. I was close to them.

A postcard collection like this is something like a portrait or reflection of the collector. To this day, that collection influences my thinking and my designs, and my social engagement as well. A card with a still life by the French artist Lubin Baugin (1612–1663) is still pinned up in my atelier, a painting that is hanging in the Louvre and that I could admire in the museum.

Later, I wanted to experience the artworks in person, communicate with them, scrutinize them. The Louvre became my atelier. Through sketching, I discovered the secrets of design, the wonder of the creative. I was inspired; I wanted to, had to create my own world. I wanted to and had to dedicate my life to art, to lose myself absolutely and completely in art.

Today, half a century later, I am more than grateful for my postcard collection. It showed me the way. Through the collection I got to know myself, and understood that what I create today corresponds without exception to my identity.

I had the good fortune — and privilege — to be introduced to the world of natural sciences at Professor Hans Burla's Zoological Institute at the University of Zurich. I followed the scientific activities there with my drawings and was instructed to do experiments myself, and to observe. The years at the Zoological Institute sharpened my ability to see; it was there that art and science were reconciled.

I married, raised two sons, lived with my family on the outskirts of Zurich on a wonderful piece of earth. It was here that I made my first drawings of insects. What fascinated me above all were the myriad shapes and colors of true bugs (Heteroptera). This is how I discovered a world that these days we unfortunately do not take seriously enough and thus still endanger its existence. I collected, observed, lived with my microscope in a world without vice, in a world of pure beauty. That was why my horror was commensurately large when I discovered that the number of deformed heteroptera in my investigations was increasing every year.

Then Chernobyl happened, a global catastrophe that made action imperative. My trip to the site of the accident in the Ukraine, as well as to Sweden, which was particularly affected by the fallout, was my first encounter with a variety of deformed bugs. For me there was no turning back. My work showed and proved to me that even nuclear power plants functioning normally are a threat to humans and to all of nature.

I wanted to know. Even today, I continue to examine and draw insects, true bugs in particular, in areas surrounding atomic power plants and other atomic facilities. In Switzerland, I am familiar with Gösgen, Leibstadt, and the Paul Scherrer Institute; in England, Sellafield where the situation is especially grave. I could hardly believe how radioactivity (even the most minimal radiation) threatens life. My work also took me to Three Mile Island in the US where a partial meltdown took place, then to La

Hague in France, but also to the Krümmel and Gundremmingen nuclear plants in Germany. In 2004 I traveled to Vietnam and encountered time and again the same drama in places where the Americans had sprayed Agent Orange during the Vietnam War. I sought help from research institutes and scientists. But to this day, I have unfortunately received no response.

In order to be able to pursue this social mission, I needed an income. When, in 1986, my friend the fashion designer Eri Székely, introduced me to the Zurich silk manufacturer André Stutz, I was ecstatic. His company, Fabric Frontline, became my employer, and André Stutz a good friend. Thanks to him I could combine the pragmatic with my aspiration to the beautiful. It was wonderful for me to be able to put my thoughts and feelings to practical use. In 16 years of collaboration we have produced collections that are more than just consumer goods. We have received much praise and recognition and financially, our work has been a success. That internationally recognized designers like Yves St. Laurent, Jil Sander and Vivienne Westwood have chosen my designs for their collections is without doubt a highlight. I was also amused to see in the newspaper that the singer Elton John wore one of my ladybug print scarves on his 1989 European tour.

Even as a basic material, silk has something precious, something special, and it comes from the world of insects. A world that I know, a world that goes back far into human history and has always been something extraordinary.

André Stutz gave me the freedom and the means to live out my fantasies and aspirations, but also to make my questions visible, to make them legible.

Of course I am pleased when I am out in the city and here or there spot a scarf or necktie that I designed; but for me art does not exist for art's sake. Art has a task, a meaning: to create artificial beauty next to the natural. We live in an increasingly artificial environment, and manmade beauty is fast becoming the only alternative to experiencing our environment as a humane entirety. We know that ugliness is not healthy for us, beauty gives hope and identity. I am proud that my works are a symbiosis of thinking and feeling. I believe in enlightenment; I am happy to create things that radiate joy and harmony.

Thus I am grateful to André Stutz and his sister Elsa Stutz, as well as to Claudio Milesi, the printer in Como who reproduced my drawings on silk with such care and expertise.

So this is how it began… I wanted to know. I wanted to understand. Today I believe. In beauty. In the impact of art.

Cornelia Hesse-Honegger

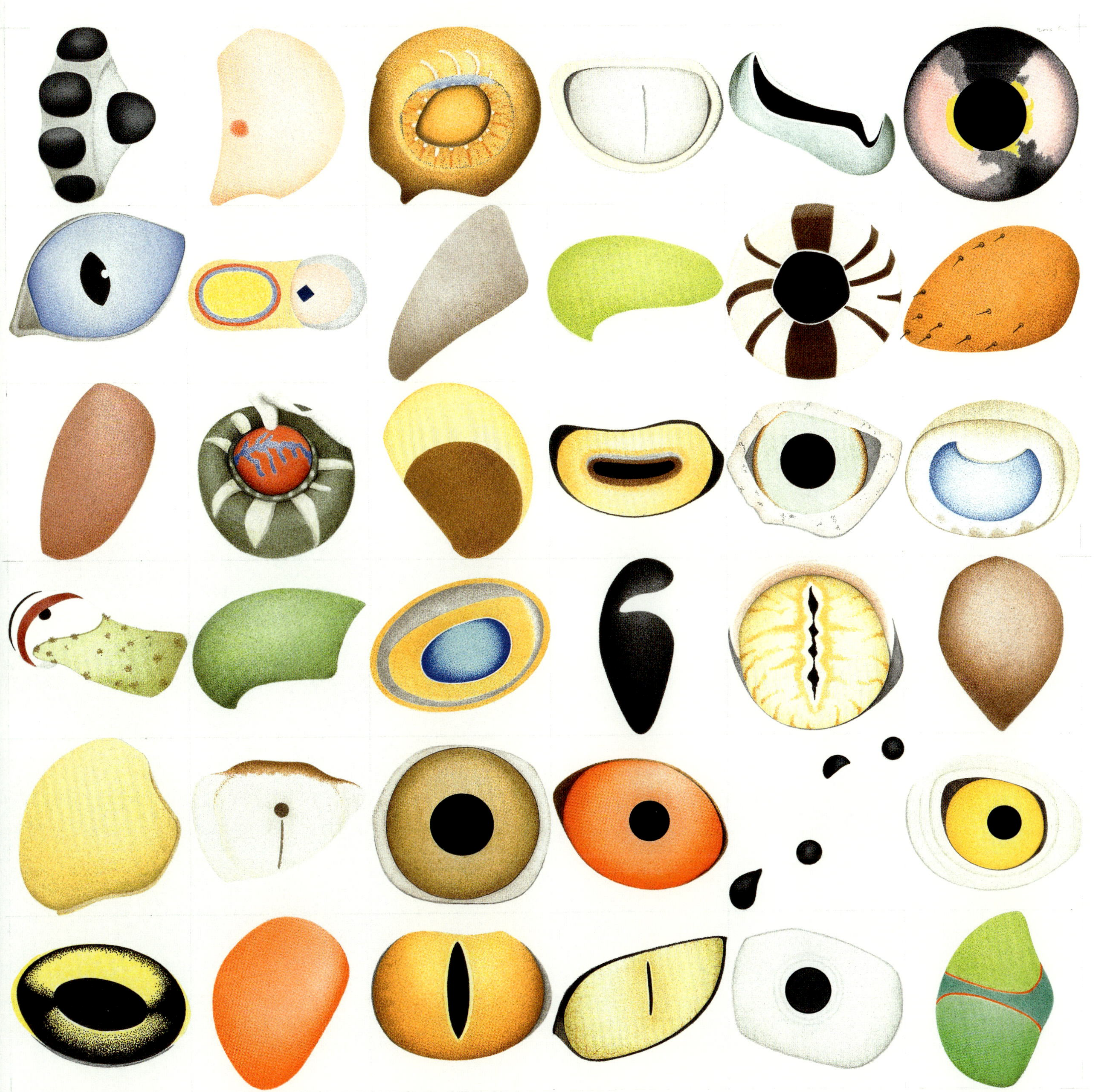

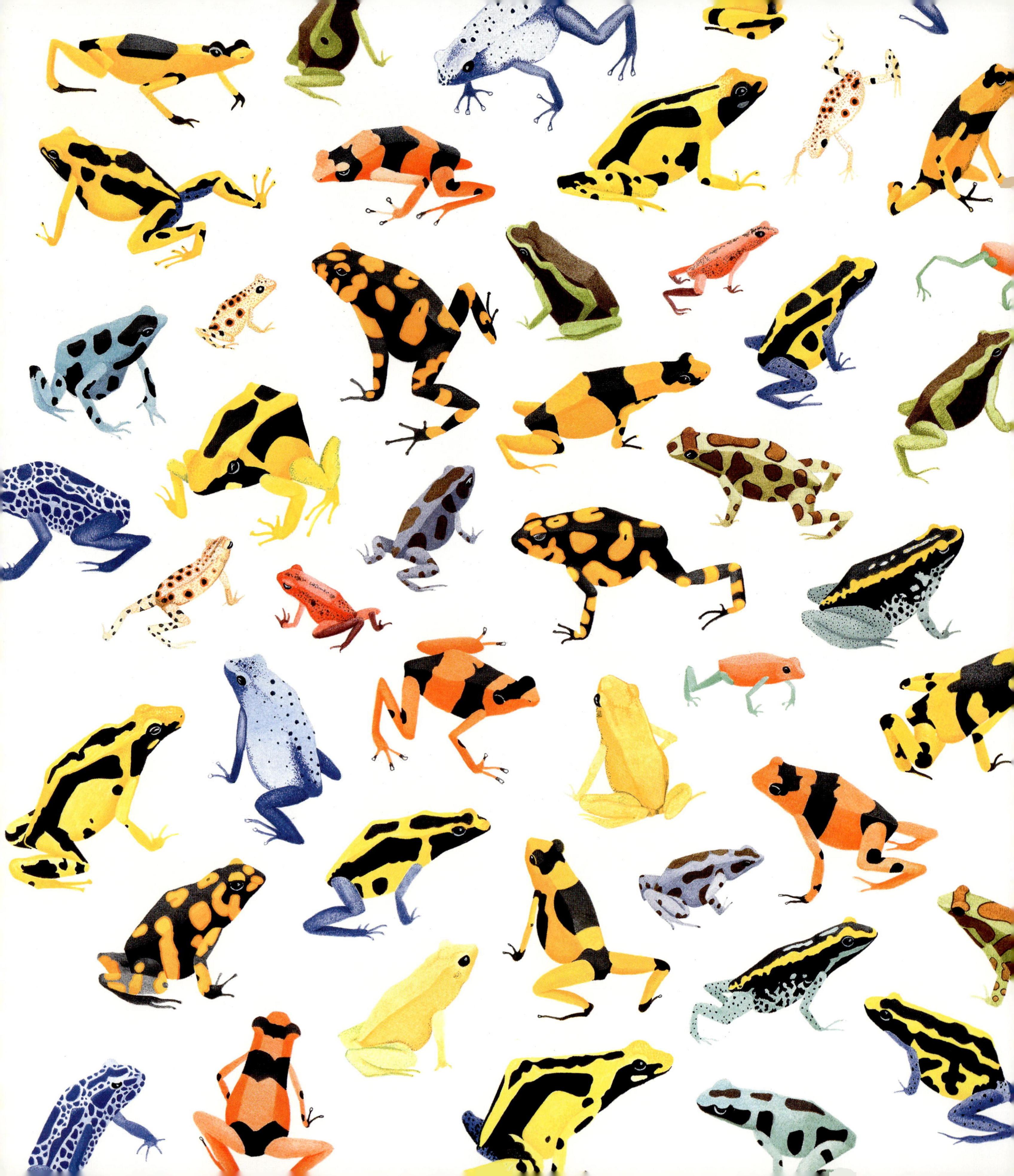

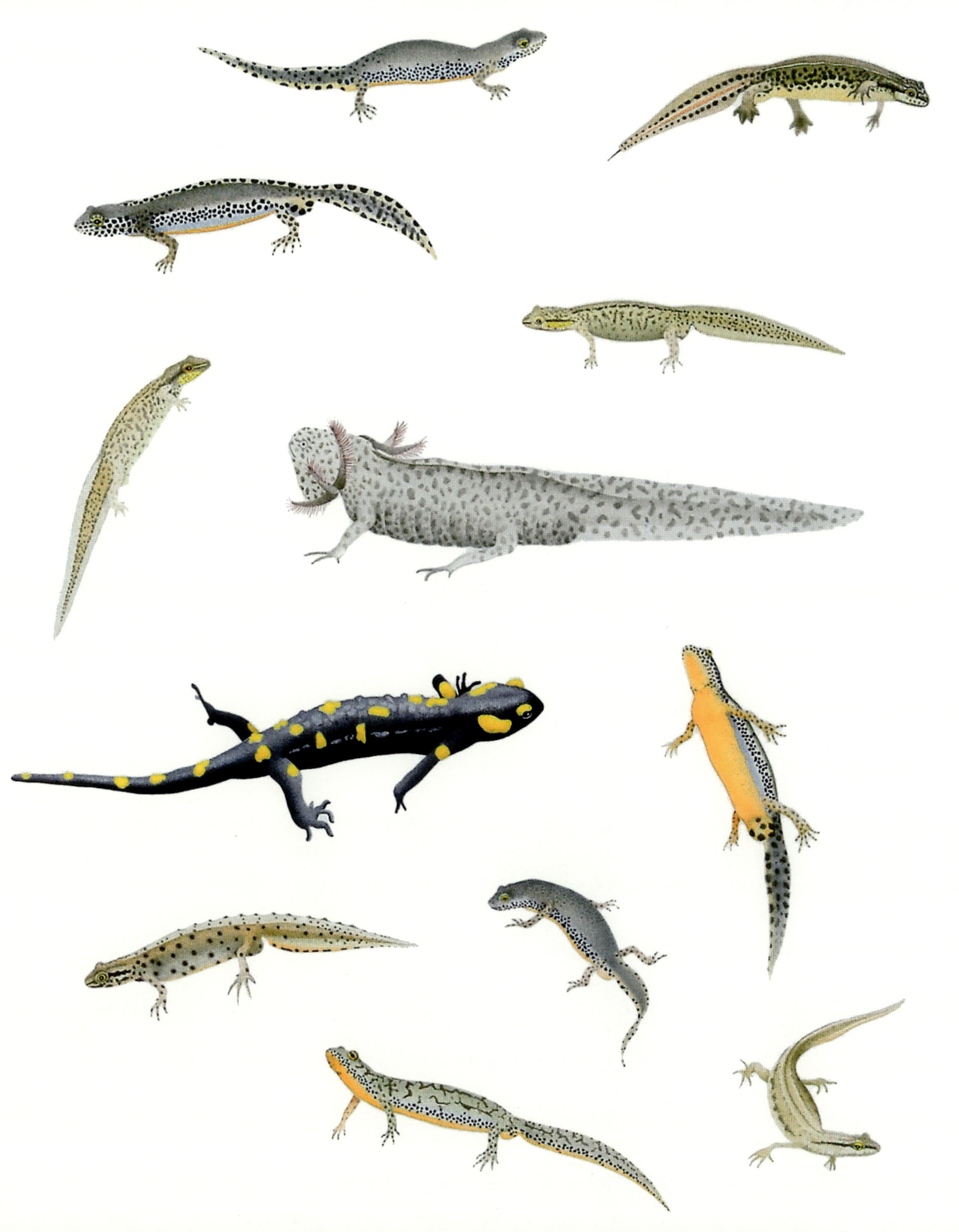

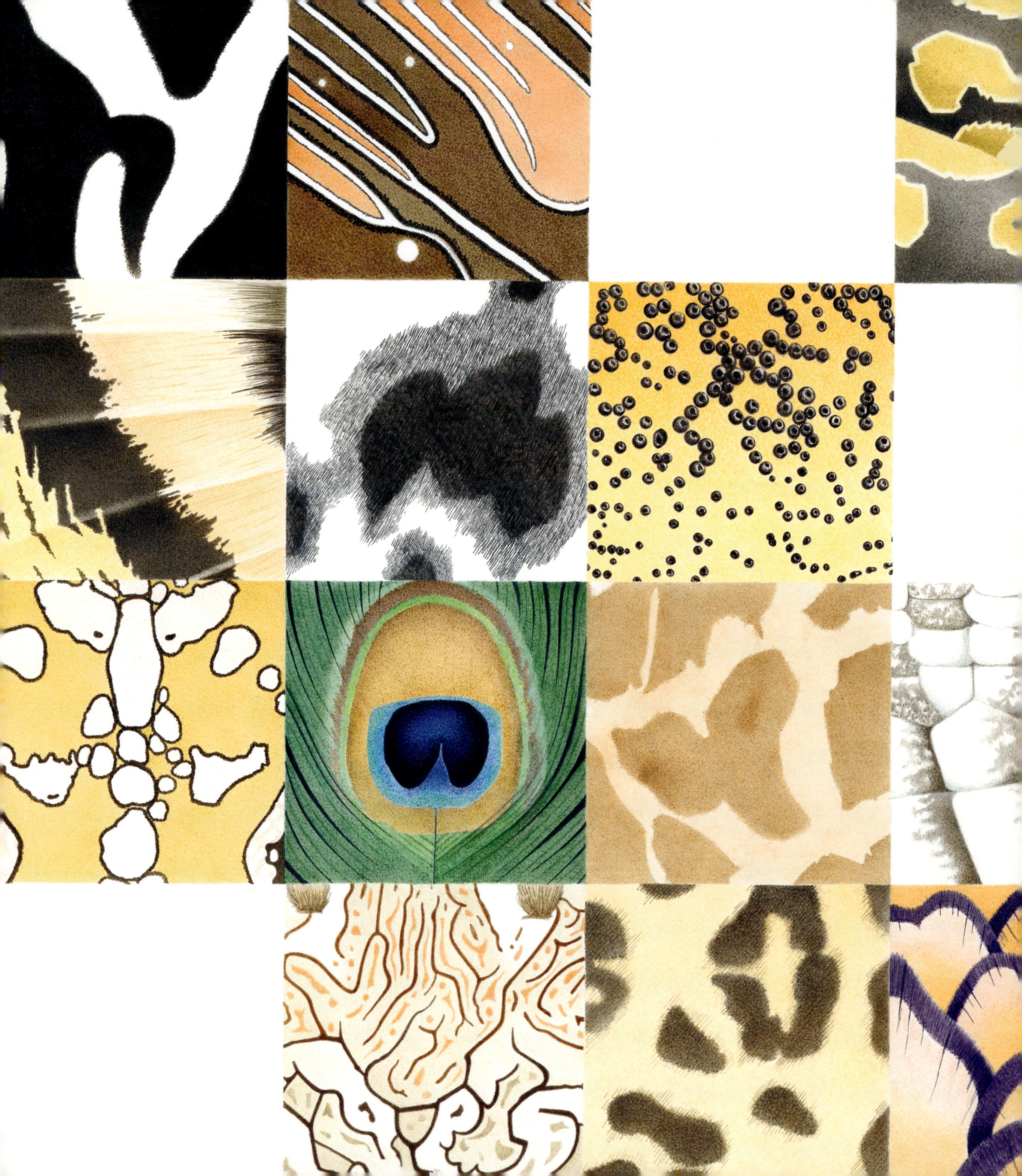

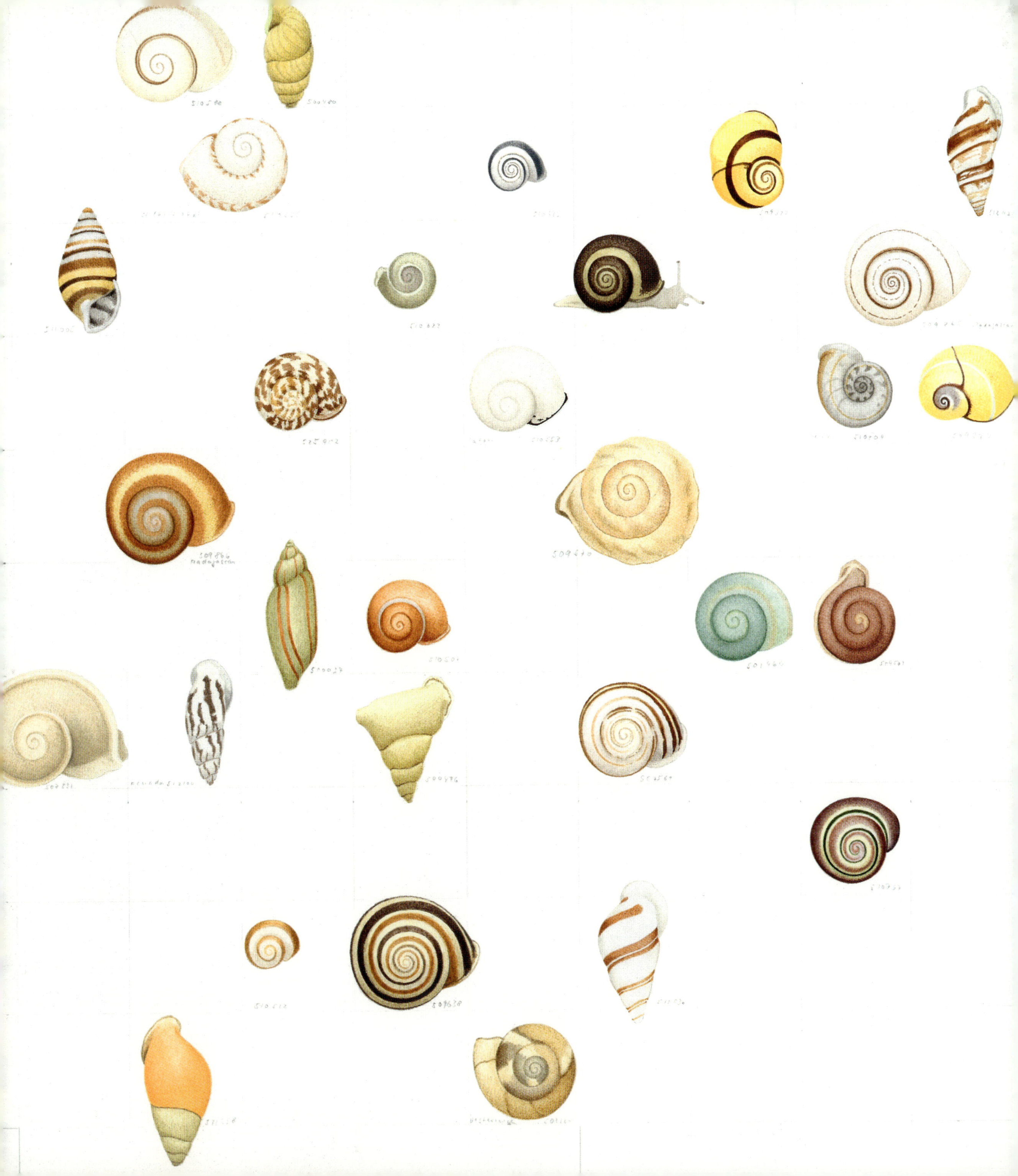

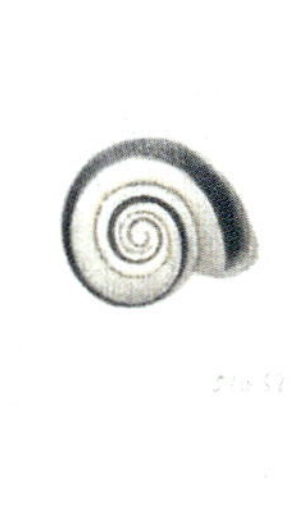
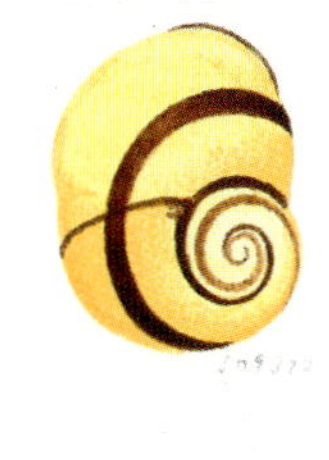
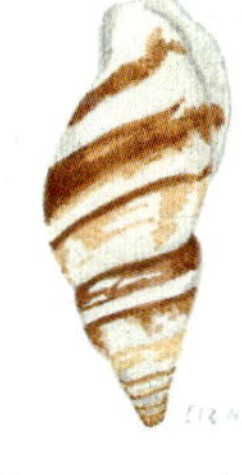
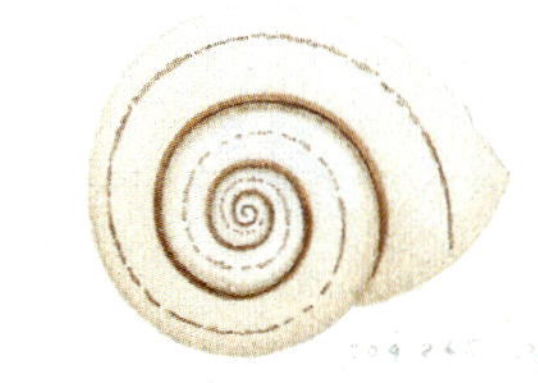
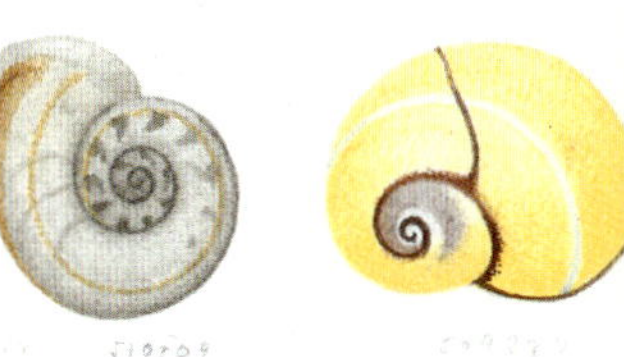
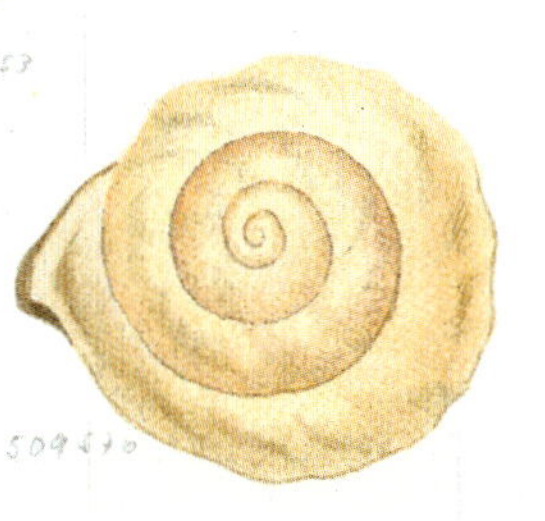
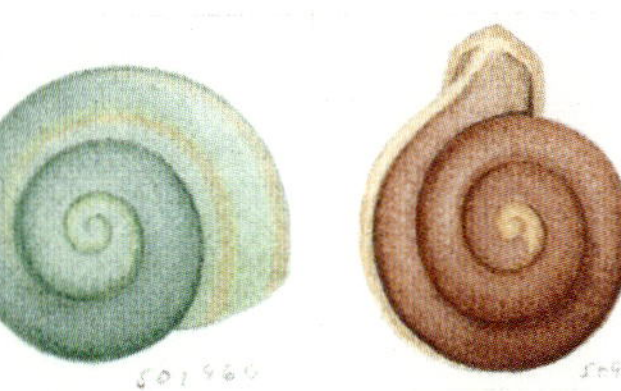
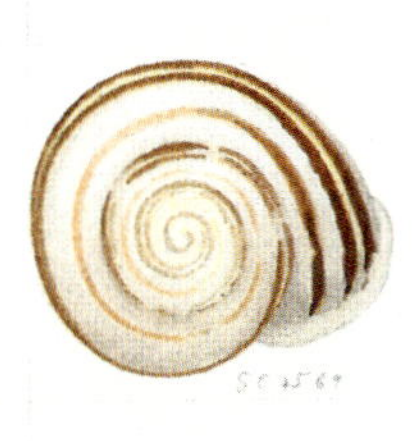
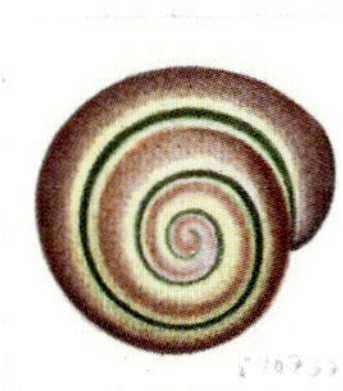
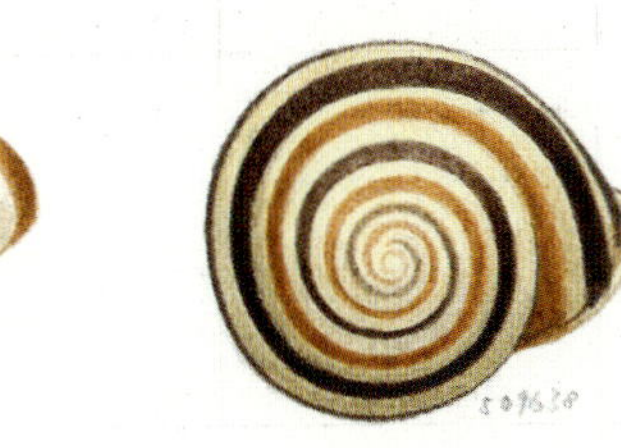
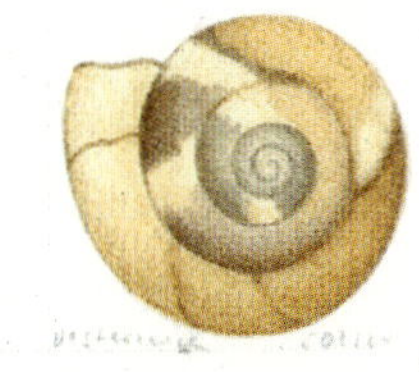
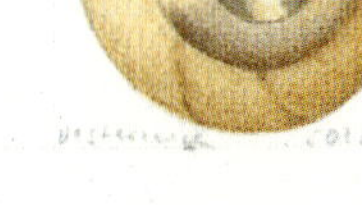

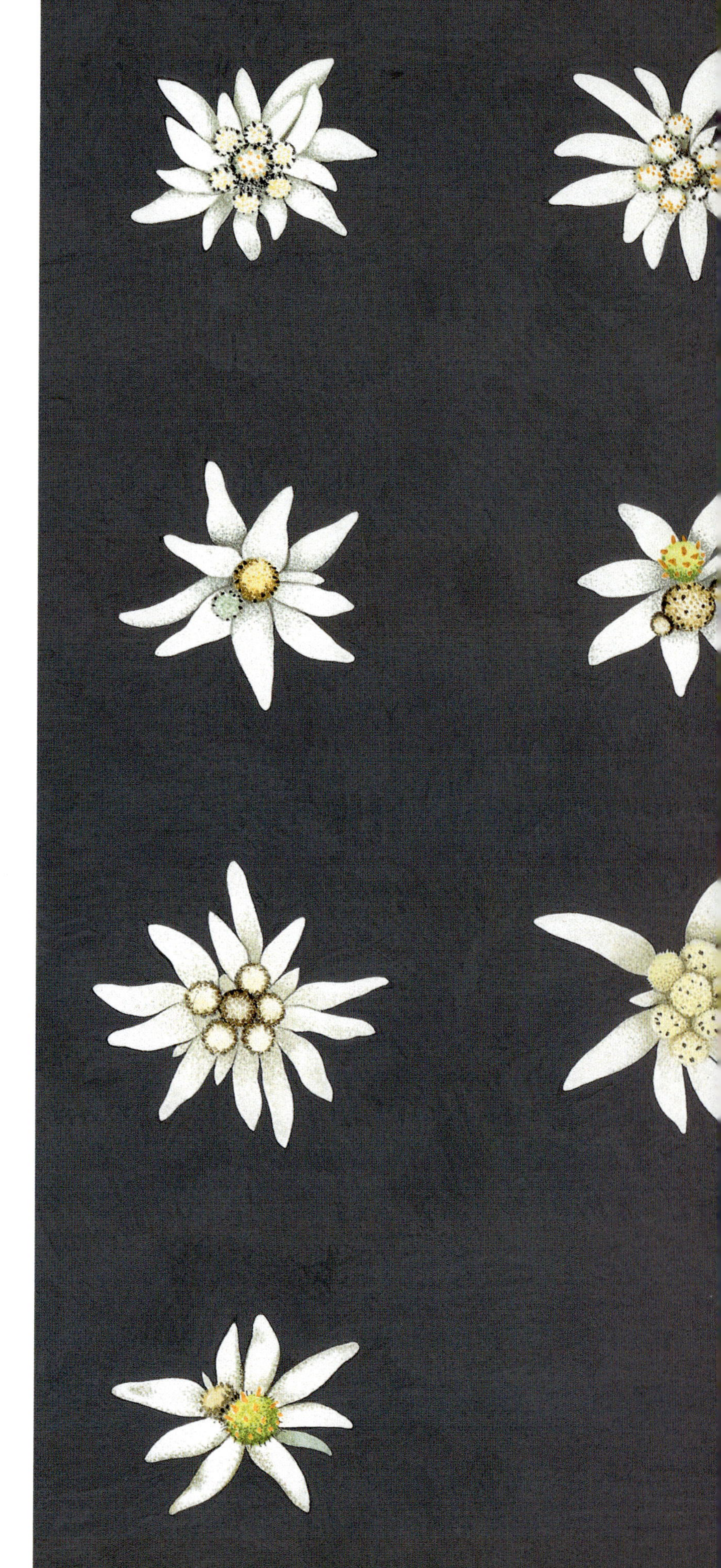

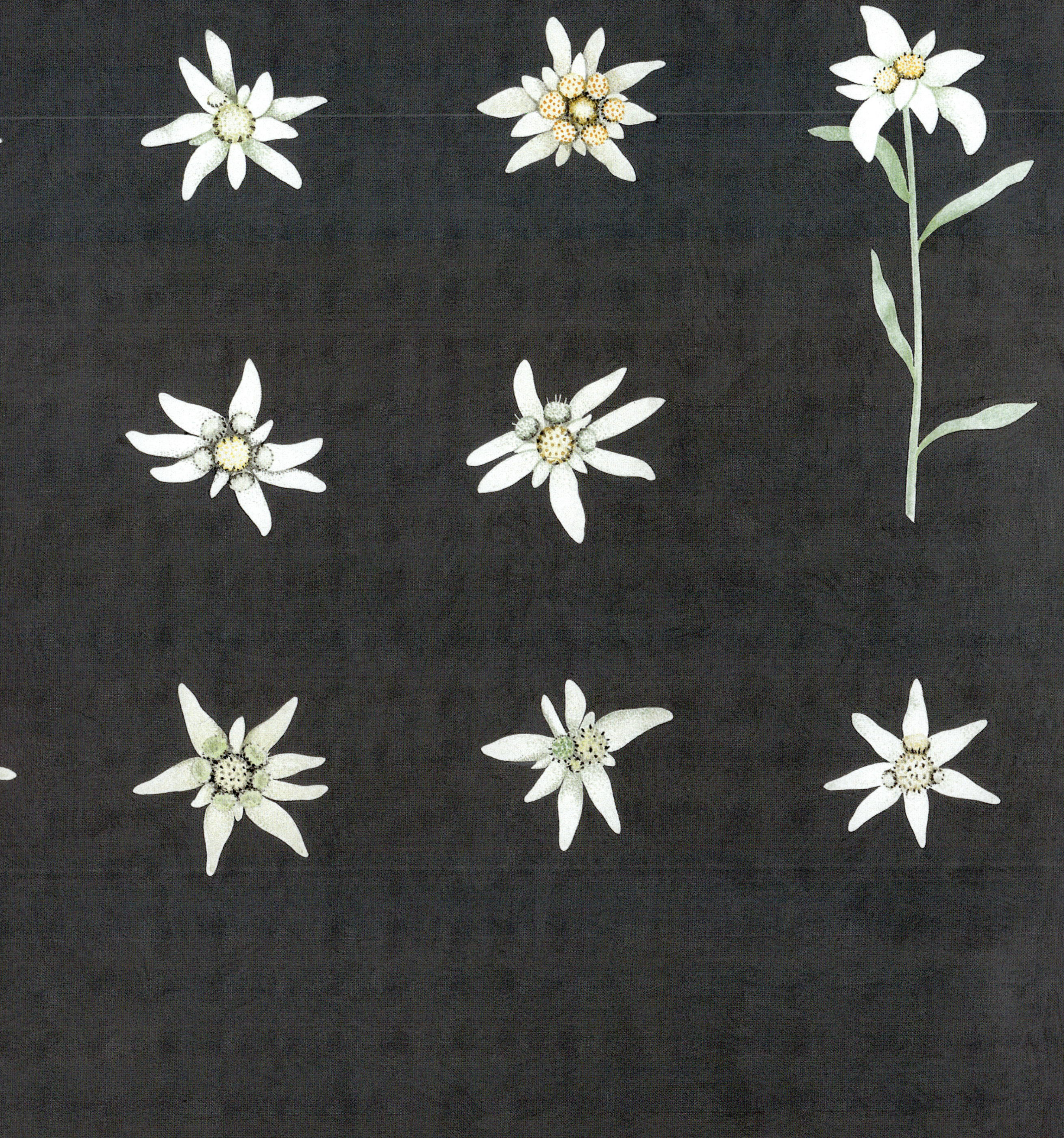

4/5 Nachtfalter, Aquarell, 1994
Moth, watercolor

6 Frühlingsblätter, Aquarell, 1990
New Leaves, watercolor

7 Tropenblumen, Aquarell, 1993
Tropical Flowers, watercolor

8/9 Mohnblumen, Aquarell, 1988
Poppies, watercolor

11 Pensées, Aquarell, 1989
Pensées, watercolor

12 Mineralien, Aquarell, 1989
Minerals, watercolor

13 Mineralien, Aquarell, 1989
Minerals, watercolor

15 Giftpilze, Aquarell, 1991
Poisonous Mushrooms, watercolor

16 Nüsse, Aquarell, 1989
Nuts, watercolor

17 Igel, Aquarell, 1996
Hedgehog, watercolor

20 Kamelie, Seide, 1989
Camellia, silk

21 Kamelie, Modell Akris, 1996
Camellia, model Akris

22 Christrosen, Seide, 1992
Hellebores, silk

23 Baumwolle, Seide, 1997
Cotton, silk

24 Klee, Seide, 1993
Clover, silk

25 Edelweiss, Seide, 1997
Edelweiss, silk

26 Schneeglöckchen, Seide, 1991
Snowdrops, silk

27 Gardenien, Seide, 1990
Gardenias, silk

28 Frühlingsblätter, Seide, 1991
New Leaves, silk

29 Mimose, Seide, 1996
Mimosa, silk

30 Giftpilze, Seide, 1992
Poisonous Mushrooms, silk

31 Giftpilz, Skizze, 1991
Poisonous Mushroom, sketch

32 Nüsse, Seide, 1990
Nuts, silk

33 Tannenzapfen, Seide, 1991
Fir Cones, silk

34 Pensées, Seide, 1990
Pensées, silk

35 Orchideen, Seide, 1993
Orchids, silk

36 Tropenblumen, Skizze, 1992
Tropical Flowers, sketch

37 Tropenblumen, Seide, 1994
Tropical Flowers, silk

38 Nelken, Seide, 1997
Carnations, silk

39 Narzissen, Seide, 1989
Narcissi, silk

40 Kapuziner, Seide, 1994
Nasturtiums, silk

41 Kapuziner, Skizze, 1993
Nasturtiums, sketch

42 «Bergmannli», Skizze, 1994
Alpine Pasque Flower, sketch

43 «Bergmannli», Seide, 1995
Alpine Pasque Flower, silk

44 Rosen, Seide, 1991
Roses, silk

45 Primeln, Seide, 1997
Primulas, silk

46 Mohn, Seide, 1989
Poppy, silk

47 Mohn, Skizze, 1988
Poppy, sketch

48/49 Mineralien, Seide, 1990
Minerals, silk

50 Schmetterlinge, Seide, 1989
Butterflies, silk

51 Schmetterlinge,
Modell Yves Saint Laurent, 1990
Butterflies, model Yves Saint
Laurent

52/53 Nachtfalter, Seide, 1995
Moths, silk

54 Giftfrösche, Skizze, 1989
Poisonous Frogs, sketch

55 Giftfrösche, Seide, 1990
Poisonous Frogs, silk

56 Salamander, Seide, 1994
Salamanders, silk

57 Salamander, Skizze, 1993
Salamanders, sketch

58 Schildkröten, Skizze, 1995
Tortoises, sketch

59 Schildkröten, Seide, 1996
Tortoises, silk

60 Neonfische, Seide, 1988
Neon Tetras, silk

61 Meerestiere, Seide, 1991
Marine Fauna, silk

62 Tropenfische, Skizze, 1991
Tropical Fish, sketch

63 Tropenfische, Seide, 1992
Tropical Fish, silk

64 Fetzenfische, Seide, 1996
Sea Dragons, silk

65 Fetzenfisch, Skizze, 1995
Sea Dragon, sketch

66 Katze, Skizze, 1995
Cat, sketch

67 Katzen, Seide, 1996
Cats, silk

68 Eichhörnchen, Skizze, 1994
Squirrels, sketch

69 Eichhörnchen, Seide, 1995
Squirrels, silk

71 Schnecken, Seide, 1992
Snails, silk

72 Wanzen dreieckig, Seide, 1992
Bug, triangular, silk

73 Marienkäfer, Seide, 1988
Ladybug, silk

74/75 Spinnen oval, Seide, 1993
Spiders, oval, silk

76 Vogelspinnen, Seide, 1996
Bird Spiders, silk

77 Igel, Seide, 1997
Hedgehog, silk

78/79 Augen, Seide, 1993
Eyes, silk

80 Exotische Vögel, Seide, 1996
Exotic Birds, silk

81 Exotischer Vogel, Skizze, 1995
Exotic Bird, sketch

82 Eulen, Seide, 1993
Owls, silk

83 Eulen, Skizze, 1992
Owls, sketch

85 Federn, Seide, 1993
Feathers, silk

86 Seidenäffchen, Skizze, 1997
Marmoset, sketch

87 Seidenäffchen, Seide, 1998
Marmosets, silk

88 Eisbären, Skizzen, 1989
Polar Bears, sketch

89 Eisbären, Seide, 1990
Polar Bears, silk

90 Ringelrobbenfell, Seide, 1996
Ringed Sealskin, silk

92/93 Königspinguine, Seide, 1996
King Penguins, silk

95 Kasuar, Seide, 1987
Cassowary, silk

96/97 Enten, Seide, 1996
Ducks, silk

99 Tierstrukturen, Seide, 1993
Animal Structures, silk

100 Feuer, Seide, 1996
Fire, silk

101 Feuer, Modell Vivenne Westwood,
1997
Fire, model Vivenne Westwood

102/103 Mezzanotte, Seide, 1999
Mezzanotte, silk

104 Expo.02-Tuch, Umriss ganze
Schweiz, Seide, 2001
Expo.02 scarf, Outline of Switzer-
land, silk

105 Expo.02-Tuch, Umrisse der
Schweizer Kantone, Seide, 2001
Expo.02 scarf, Outlines of the
Swiss Cantons, silk

106/107 Apokalypse, Seide, 1998
Apocalypse, silk

108 Scherenschnitte Stier,
Seide, 1988
Silhouette of a Bull, silk

109 Scherenschnitte Kamel,
Seide, 1988
Silhouette of a Camel, silk

110 Santi, Seide, 1998
Santi, silk

111 Höhlenmalerei, Seide, 1998
Cave Painting, silk

117 Augen, Aquarell, 1992
Eyes, watercolor

118 Giftfrösche, Aquarell, 1998
Tropical Frogs, watercolor

121 Salamander, Aquarell, 1993
Salamanders, watercolor

122 Tierstrukturen, Aquarell, 1992
Animal Structures, watercolor

123 Schnecken, Aquarell, 1991
Snails, watercolor

124/125 Edelweiss, Aquarell, 1994
Edelweiss, watercolor

Buchkonzept, Book concept
Cornelia Hesse-Honegger, Claudia Klein

Texte, Texts
Cornelia Hesse-Honegger, Gottfried Honegger

Fotografien, Photographs
Peter Schälchli, Zürich

Gestaltung, design
Claudia Klein, Zürich

Proofreading
Bronwen Saunders, Tradukas GbR

Druck und Bindung, Printed and bound by
DZA Druckerei zu Altenburg GmbH, Germany

Verlag Scheidegger & Spiess AG
Niederdorfstrasse 54
CH-8001 Zürich
Schweiz, Switzerland

Copyright für alle Werke von Cornelia Hesse-Honegger
© 2008 ProLitteris, Zürich
Copyright for all works by Cornelia Hesse-Honegger
© 2008 ProLitteris, Zurich

© 2008 Verlag Scheidegger & Spiess AG, Zürich

Alle Rechte vorbehalten; kein Teil dieses Werkes darf in irgendeiner Form ohne
vorherige schriftliche Genehmigung des Verlags reproduziert oder unter
Verwendung elektronischer Systeme verarbeitet, vervielfältigt oder verbreitet
werden.
All rights reserved; no part of this publication may be reproduced, stored in
a retrieval system or transmitted in any form or by any means, electronic,
mechanical, photocopying, recording or otherwise, without the prior written
consent of the publisher.

ISBN 978-3-85881-203-2

www.scheidegger-spiess.ch